Web Page

Scripting Techniques

Hayden
Books

Web Page Scripting Techniques

Library of Congress Catalog Number: 96-77067
ISBN: 1-56830-307-6

This book is sold as is, without warranty of any kind, either express or implied. While every precaution has been taken in the preparation of this book, the publisher and author assume no responsibility for errors or omissions. Neither is any liability assumed for damages resulting from the use of the information or instructions contained herein. It is further stated that the publisher and author are not responsible for any damage or loss to your data or your equipment that results directly or indirectly from your use of this book.

98　97　96　　　　4　3　2　1

Interpretation of the printing code: the rightmost double-digit number is the year of the book's printing; the rightmost single-digit number is the number of the book's printing. For example, a printing code of 96-1 shows that the first printing of the book occurred in 1996.

Trademark Acknowledgments

All products mentioned in this book are either trademarks of the companies referenced in this book, registered trademarks of the companies referenced in this book, or neither. We strongly advise that you investigate a particular product's name thoroughly before you use the name as your own.

Warning and Disclaimer

This book is sold as is, without warranty of any kind, either express or implied. Although every precaution has been taken in the preparation of this book, the authors and Hayden Books assume no responsibility for errors or omissions. Neither is any liability assumed for damages resulting from the use of this information or instructions contained herein. It is further stated that the publisher and authors are not responsible for damage or loss to your data or your equipment that results directly or indirectly from your use of this book.

Credits

Publisher
Lyn Blake

Publishing Manager
Laurie Petrycki

Managing Editor
Lisa Wilson

Development Editor
Kezia Endsley

Copy/Production Editors
Meshell Dinn
Kevin Laseau

Interior Designers
Gary Adair

Cover Designer
Aren Howell

Production
Heather Butler
Daniel Caparo
David Garratt
Jason Hand
Joe Millay
Beth Rago
Erich Richter
Pamela Volk
Christy Wagner

Indexer
Andrew McDaniel

About the Authors

Jason Bloomberg

Director of Advanced Technology, Lighthouse Systems

Jason Bloomberg grew up in Albuquerque, New Mexico. He has a Bachelor's degree in physics from Pomona College in California and Masters degrees in both mathematics and history & philosophy of science from the University of Pittsburgh. After grad school he taught mathematics and computer at the Winchester Thurston School in Pittsburgh. Next, Jason became a Macintosh consultant and reseller for three years.

Jason was Production Manager at Lighthouse Systems, a Pittsburgh-based Web development firm, for one year, and is now their Director of Advanced Technology. You can visit his home page at **http://www.lhouse.com/~jbloomberg**.

Jeff Kawski

Jeffrey Kawski is a Summa Cum Laude graduate in Physics from SUNY Fredonia. He has been an avid Internet and computer user for more than 10 years. Jeff's latest interests include Web design and JavaScript. He is now thoroughly addicted.

Paul Treffers

Paul Treffers has been a professional programmer since 1989. He lives in Leiden, The Netherlands. The last four years he has been developing Client/Server applications with Visual Basic for Windows. He is also actively involved (as a board member, responsible for all interactive technologies) in the Leiden Free-Net initiative. You can email him at **treffers@xs4all.nl**.

Contents at a Glance

Web Page Scripting Techniques

Web Page Scripting Techniques

Introduction

Web Page Scripting Techniques attempts to take the rather technical endeavor of creating scripts for your Web pages and make this process a little more creative by providing you with finished examples, as well as the basic code you need to get started. It takes a design-oriented approach to advanced Web page scripting; you can implement these techniques without having to master the scripting language.

Written in a learn-by-example approach, this book focuses on deconstructing the best uses of scripting methods on the Web. The format of the book consists of an image of each Web page and the full code behind the Web page. One focus is featured on each page. The highlighted feature is fully deconstructed. Through the use of each technique, the book highlights sites in which scripting ideas are well designed into the entire site.

The book always looks for the least complex way of getting the job done. This will save you time, which is saving money! In addition, the book includes detailed tutorials, tips, and tricks for adding scripting and advanced HTML to your pages.

Our goal is that you will be able to find the techniques you want to incorporate by sight and/or by topic area, and then easily integrate them into your Web pages by following the steps and using the CD.

About the Reader

This book is primarily for existing Web publishers. You should be familiar with basic HTML coding and be ready to take the next step in advancing the look and feel of your Web pages.

Because you are suddenly faced with a whole new set of challenges, from learning the new tags, keywords, and scripting structures to coming up with creative ways to spice up your site, this book makes it as easy as possible to learn the techniques you need.

Part I

HTML Techniques

Controlling Navigation Options with Frames

Using the Absence of the Target Attribute

Type: HTML 3.2

Used in: *<FRAME>* used in *<FRAMESET>*; target attribute used in *<A HREF>*

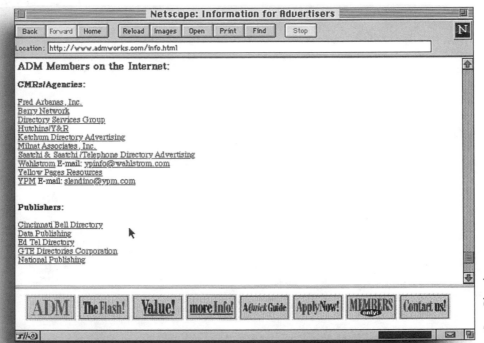

Jason Bloomberg

File: info.html

```
<HTML>
<HEAD>
 <TITLE>Information for Advertisers</TITLE>
</HEAD>
```

```
<frameset rows="*,60">
<frame src="info1.html" name="thetop" noresize>
<frame src="buttons.html" name="bottom" noresize>
</frameset>


<noframes>
<BODY BGCOLOR = "#FFFFFF" >

<CENTER>
<IMG SRC="images/info.gif"><BR>
</CENTER>

<P><h3>ADM Members on the Internet:</h3>
<p>
<P><A HREF="http://www.arbanas.com">Fred Arbanas, Inc.</A><BR>
<A HREF="http://www.bniyellowpages.com">Berry Network</A><BR>
</noframes>
</HTML>
```

File: info1.html

```
<HTML>
<HEAD>
<! Created on 04/24/96 at 21:32:52->
 <TITLE>Information for Advertisers</TITLE>
</HEAD>

<BODY>
<BODY BGCOLOR = "#FFFFFF" >

<CENTER>
<IMG SRC="images/info.gif"><BR>
</CENTER>

<P><h3>ADM Members on the Internet:</h3>
<p>
<P><A HREF="http://www.arbanas.com">Fred Arbanas, Inc.</A><BR>
<A HREF="http://www.bniyellowpages.com">Berry Network</A><BR>
</BODY>
</HTML>
```

Syntax Example

```
<frame src="info1.html" name="thetop" noresize>
```

Comments

Using frames to control where the user goes when leaving your site may be one of the most elegant uses of frames, as illustrated in this example.

Online Example

"Association of Directory Marketing Information for Advertisers," by Jason Bloomberg of Lighthouse Systems for ADM, Inc., email: **info@admworks.com**

URL: **http://www.admworks.com/info.html**

Description

ADM wanted to have a page full of links to associated sites. Nothing new there. The problem: do you really want to give users multiple opportunities to leave your site? How can you provide a list of links off your site without actually letting users leave? Here's the trick.

Step-by-Step

When you click a link that takes you to the "Information for Advertisers" page filled with links, you don't actually load that page. You load a frameset with two frames. The top frame contains the list of links, and the bottom frame contains the ADM site's button bar.

```
<A HREF="http://www.hutchinsyr.com">Hutchins/Y&R</A>
```

Make sure that the links in the list of links do *not* specify a target. Most people would specify "*_top*", but you want people to stay. By not specifying a target, users will load those other sites into the top frame. They will continue to navigate with the ADM button bar at the bottom, unless they back up (to the ADM site, naturally), or until they figure out how to load a URL at the top, which most casual users don't know how to do.

Notes

This technique works best when the button bar is relatively small. In this example, it takes up the bottom half inch of the screen. The buttons in the button bar *must* have appropriate targets.

Related Techniques

Displaying Frames in a Document

Using Frames to Create a Hierarchical Menu

Displaying Frames in a Document

Using Frames

Type: HTML

Used in: Browser documents

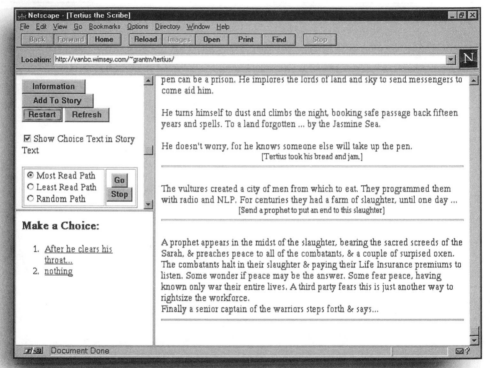

Grant McClure

```
<FRAMESET ROWS="1,*"  onload="top.TopInit(); " >
  <FRAME SRC="about:blank" NAME="frame_load" NORESIZE >
  <FRAMESET COLS="30%,70%">
    <FRAMESET ROWS="50%, *">
<FRAME SRC=control.html NAME="frame_control" NORESIZE>
     <FRAME SRC="about:blank" NAME="frame_choice" NORESIZE>
    </FRAMESET>
    <FRAME SRC="about:blank" NAME="frame_story">
  </FRAMESET>
</FRAMESET>
```

Syntax Example

```
<FRAMESET ROWS="150,*,150" >
```

Comments

Frames can be used to load multiple HTML documents into one browser window. This is accomplished using the *<FRAMESET>* tag. It can be used to separate sections of a Web site. It is often used to provide a table of contents for a site where one can select links on one frame while the files will be displayed on another.

Online Example

"Tertius the Scribe," by Grant McClure, email: **grantm@wimsey.com**

URL: **http://vanbc.wimsey.com/~grantm/tertius**

Description

This page creates an interactive story. You can choose the path that the story will take, and you can also add to the story. Frames are used to differentiate the various functions of the page. One frame is used to contain the story, whereas the other frames are used to change the paths of the story or other maintenance operations concerning the story.

Step-by-Step

A typical frame structure is in the form:

```
<FRAMESET ROWS="20%, *, 200">
<FRAME SRC="icons.htm" NAME="frame1">
<FRAME SRC="main.htm" NAME="frame2">
<FRAME SRC="ad.htm" NAME="frame3">
</FRAMESET>
```

In the *<FRAMESET>* tag the frames can be positioned in rows or columns using the *<ROWS>* or *<COLS>* parameter respectively. Following this parameter are values indicating how the frame should be positioned. The values can be in percentages, number of pixels, or represented by an asterisk. The asterisk is used to represent whatever space isn't accounted for. Thus, *COLS="60%, 40%"* and *COLS="60%, *"* represent the same thing. As in *<BODY>* tags, *<FRAMESET>* tags can also be given OnLoad and OnUnload event handers for use in JavaScript. Within the *<FRAMESET>* tags are *<FRAME>* tags. The *<FRAME>* tags are used to define the individual frames. The *<SRC>* parameter is assigned the URL or the filename of the page to be displayed in the frame. The optional *<NAME>* parameter gives the frame a name so it can be accessed in forms or scripting languages.

This page uses a series of nested frames to achieve its desired effect. Many of the frame sources in this page are initialized to "*about:blank.*" This source can be used to achieve a blank page. The reason this is done is because the frames will be written to later using JavaScript.

The outer frameset has the parameter *ROWS="1, *"*. The top frame is 1 pixel high, while the bottom frame encompasses the reset of the browser window. The top frame is barely visible. It is created for use with the JavaScript operations of this page. The bottom frame contains another frameset. This frameset has the parameter COLS="*30%,70%*". This splits the frame into a left frame taking up 30% of the window width, and a right frame taking up 70% of the window width. The right frame will be used to display the story. The left frame contains another frameset. This frameset splits the frame in half. The control file for the story is loaded to the top frame of this inside frameset. The bottom frame of this set will hold the story choices.

Related Techniques

Checking if All Frames Are Loaded

Controlling Navigation Options with Frames

Navigating Within a Frame

Using Frames to Create a Hierarchical Menu
Creative Use of Targets

Type: HTML scripting tip

Used in: Frames

The Silicon Surf team at Silicon Graphics, Inc.

File: index.html

```
<HTML>
<HEAD>
<TITLE>Silicon Graphics Silicon Surf: Global Sites</TITLE>
</HEAD>

<FRAMESET ROWS="125,*,85">
        <FRAME SRC="global_header.html" SCROLLING=NO>
```

continues

```
        <FRAMESET COLS="40%,60%">
                <FRAME SRC="global_toc.html"
NAME="global_toc">
                <FRAME SRC="global_main.html"
NAME="global_main">
        </FRAMESET>
        <FRAME SRC="global_footer.html" SCROLLING=NO>
</FRAMESET>


<NOFRAME>

<BODY BGCOLOR="#fcf0da" TEXT="#000000" LINK="0000ee" VLINK="#551a8b">

...
</BODY>

</NOFRAME>

</HTML>

global_toc.html:

<HTML VERSION="2.0">
<HEAD>

<TITLE>Global Sites: Index</TITLE>
</HEAD>
<BODY>


<P><A HREF="au_dir.html" TARGET="global_toc"><IMG SRC=
"images/australia_up.jpg" BORDER="0" WIDTH="186"
HEIGHT="21" ALT="Australia"></A>
<P><A HREF="ca_dir.html" TARGET="global_toc"><IMG SRC=
"images/canada_up.jpg" BORDER="0" WIDTH = "185"
HEIGHT = "21" ALT="Canada"></A>

</BODY>
</HTML>
```

Syntax Example

```
<A HREF="fr_dir.html" TARGET="global_toc"><IMG SRC=
"images/france_up.jpg" BORDER="0" WIDTH = "185"
HEIGHT = "21" ALT="France"></A>
```

Comments

It can be very challenging to use frames in such a way that you don't get lost. SGI uses a simple, yet elegant, technique to keep you oriented.

Online Example

"Silicon Graphics Silicon Surf: Global Sites," by the Silicon Surf team at SGI, email: **webmaster@www.sgi.com**

URL: **http://www.sgi.com/International/index.html**

Description

When you click a country name in the menu frame, a new page loads into the same frame, showing all the links for that country sandwiched between country names.

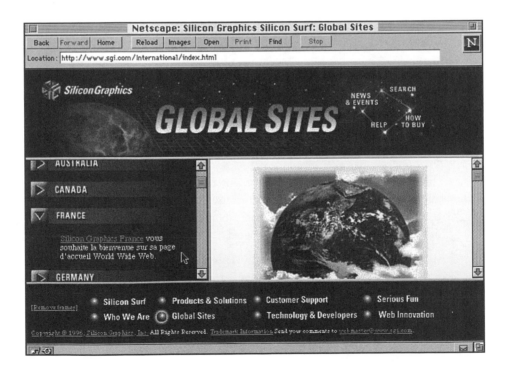

Note that when you click a country in the menu, an entirely new page loads into that frame. There is a different page for every country.

Step-by-Step

```
<A HREF="fr_dir.html" TARGET="global_toc"><IMG SRC=
"images/france_up.jpg" BORDER="0" WIDTH = "185"
HEIGHT = "21" ALT="France"></A>
```

The target for the anchor is *"global_toc,"* which is the name of the frame that has the menu that you just clicked. This name is defined in the *<FRAMESET>* of the enclosing page:

```
<FRAMESET ROWS="125,*,85">
        <FRAME SRC="global_header.html" SCROLLING=NO>

        <FRAMESET COLS="40%,60%">
                <FRAME SRC="global_toc.html" NAME="global_toc">
                <FRAME SRC="global_main.html" NAME="global_main">
        </FRAMESET>
        <FRAME SRC="global_footer.html" SCROLLING=NO>
</FRAMESET>
```

According to the *<FRAME>* tag, the file *global_toc.html* loads into this frame first. However, when you click the image *france_up.jpg*, the file *fr_dir.html* loads into the frame named *global_toc*.

Notes

The bulk of the file index.html is contained in the *<NOFRAME>* tag, which is only visible to non-frames-compatible browsers. Although this level of detail may seem redundant, it is essential for any professional quality page with frames that might be hit by a non-frames-compatible browser.

Another indication of a professionally designed page is the use of the *<ALT>* attribute in the *<IMG>* tags for all of the image buttons. If you choose not to load images, you will see this alternate text. You must use the *<ALT>* attribute with buttons in order to see where you are going.

Related Techniques

Displaying Frames in a Document

Creative Page Navigation Using Frames

Using Frames to Create Complex Navigation Schemes

Nested Framesets with Various Targets

Type: HTML (Netscape Navigator 2.0 and Microsoft Internet Explorer 3.0 specific)

Used in: *<FRAMESET>* in document; *<FRAME>* in FRAMESET

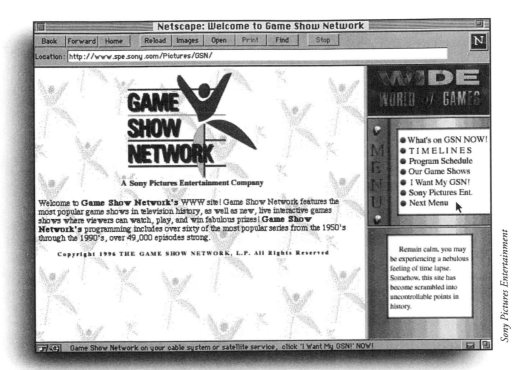

Sony Pictures Entertainment

File: index.html

```
<html><head><title>Welcome to Game Show Network</title></head>

<frameset cols="*,175">
    <frame name="timelines" NORESIZE src="homepage.html">
    <frame name="homepage_control" NORESIZE src=
"homepage_control.html">
</frameset>
```

continues

File: homepage_control.html

```
<html>
<head><title></title></head>

<frameset rows="73,152,*">
    <frame scrolling=no name="date" NORESIZE
src="continue.html">
    <frame scrolling=no name="menu" NORESIZE
src="menu2.html">
    <frame scrolling=no name="display" NORESIZE
src="text.html">
</frameset>
```

File: menu2.html

```
<html><head><title>Main Menu</title></head>
<body>

<MAP NAME="MAIN">
<AREA SHAPE=RECT COORDS="1,11,144,21"
HREF="whatsonnow/index.html" target="_top">
<AREA SHAPE=RECT COORDS="0,25,144,37"
HREF="http://www.mgmua.com/random/index.shtml"
target="_top">
<AREA SHAPE=RECT COORDS="1,39,144,51"
HREF="gsnschedule/index.html" target="_top">
<AREA SHAPE=RECT COORDS="1,53,144,66"
HREF="gameshows/index.html" target="display">
<AREA SHAPE=RECT COORDS="0,68,144,81"
HREF="http://www.spe.sony.com/g/gsn/forms/GSNrequestform.html"
target="timelines">
<AREA SHAPE=RECT COORDS="0,82,144,94"
HREF="http://www.spe.sony.com/Pictures/index.html"
target="_top">
<AREA SHAPE=RECT COORDS="0,97,143,108" HREF="menu_set2.html"
target="menu">
</MAP>

<img border=0 src="images/text_box2.gif" USEMAP="#MAIN" ISMAP ALT="Sony
➡Pictures"></a>

</body></html>
```

Syntax Example

```
<frameset rows="73,152,*">
     <frame scrolling=no name="date" NORESIZE src="continue.html">
     <frame scrolling=no name="menu" NORESIZE src="menu2.html">
     <frame scrolling=no name="display" NORESIZE src="text.html">
</frameset>
```

Comments

The Game Show Network appears in four frames, which is usually a recipe for confusion. However, because of well-established navigation and clear graphics, this site is only slightly disorienting.

Online Example

"The Game Show Network," by Sony Pictures Entertainment, email:
callback@mis20.msmail.spe.sony.com

URL: **http://www.spe.sony.com/Pictures/GSN/**

Description

When you encounter this site, you see four frames. The first, called "timelines," takes up the left two-thirds of the screen. The other three are in a column on the right.

The top-right frame ("date") contains a graphic displaying the title of the area that you are in; the middle-right frame ("menu") has a menu with seven options; and the lower-right frame ("display") contains an animated graphic that appears as scrolling text, serving as a background to the site.

When you click one of the menu items in the frame menu, several things might happen. In many cases, an entirely new page fills the window; in other cases, a new page loads into the frame "timelines" or into the frame "menu."

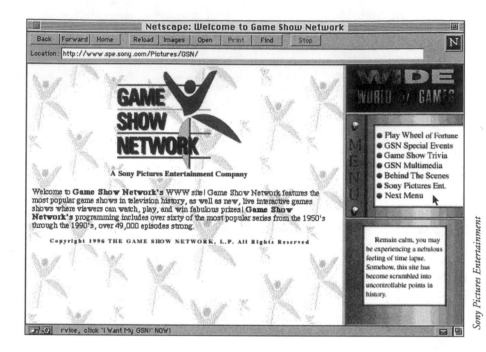

Step-by-Step

```
<frameset cols="*,175">
    <frame name="timelines" NORESIZE src="homepage.html">
        frame name="homepage_control" NORESIZE
    src="homepage_control.html">
    </frameset>
```

Even though four frames appear onscreen, the outermost page, index.html, actually has two frames, "timelines" and "homepage_control." However, the homepage_control.html page loads into the frame homepage_control, and this page itself has three frames:

```
frameset rows="73,152,*">
    <frame scrolling=no name="date" NORESIZE
    src="continue.html">
    <frame scrolling=no name="menu" NORESIZE
    src="menu2.html">
    <frame scrolling=no name="display" NORESIZE
    src="text.html">
</frameset>
```

As a result, you see four frames.

If you look more closely at the page menu.html, you see that the menu consists of a client-side imagemap that provides for the seven links.

```
<MAP NAME="MAIN">
<AREA SHAPE=RECT COORDS="1,11,144,21"
HREF="whatsonnow/index.html" target="_top">
<AREA SHAPE=RECT COORDS="0,25,144,37"
HREF="http://www.mgmua.com/random/index.shtml" target="_top">
<AREA SHAPE=RECT COORDS="1,39,144,51"
HREF="gsnschedule/index.html" target="_top">
<AREA SHAPE=RECT COORDS="1,53,144,66"
HREF="gameshows/index.html" target="display">
<AREA SHAPE=RECT COORDS="0,68,144,81"
HREF="http://www.spe.sony.com/g/gsn/forms/GSNrequestform.html"
target="timelines">
<AREA SHAPE=RECT COORDS="0,82,144,94"
HREF="http://www.spe.sony.com/Pictures/index.html" target="_top">
<AREA SHAPE=RECT COORDS="0,97,143,108" HREF="menu_set2.html" target="menu">
</MAP>
```

The *<SHAPE>* and *<COORDS>* attributes specify the clickable areas (more about this in the section on client-side imagemaps), and the *<HREF>* attribute specifies the destination of the link. The key attribute here is the *target* because it designates what frame the specified file will load into.

There are some predefined targets in HTML, which all begin with the underscore character; one of these is *"_top"*. When the target is *_top*, the specified file will fill the entire window. Four of the links in this example load at the top. However, the three other links load into three of the frames appearing onscreen: timelines, display, and menu.

Notes

The last link loads into the frame "menu," which causes a file to load over the file that you are clicking. In fact, this action is the default; if you do not specify the target, then the new file will load over the current frame.

Also note that it is irrelevant that "timelines" is on a different level from the other frames. After a frame is named, a page can be loaded into it, as long as the frame is in the current window.

Related Techniques

Creating Client-Side Imagemaps

Using Frames to Create a Hierarchical Menu

Controlling the Appearance and Speed of Tables

Using the <COLSPEC> Attribute of the <TABLE> Tag

Type: HTML 3.0

Used in: Body text

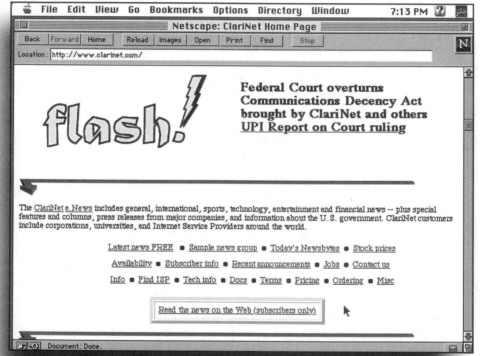

ClariNet Communications Corp.

```
<HTML>
<HEAD><BASE HREF="http://www.clari.net/">
<TITLE>ClariNet Home Page</TITLE>
</HEAD>
<BODY BGCOLOR="#FFFFFF">

<CENTER>
<UL>
```

```
<TABLE COLSPEC="L20 L20 L20 L20">
<TR><TD><a href="/index.html#tearsheets">
Latest news FREE</a></TD>
<TD><LI><a href="/index.html#sample news group">
Sample news group</a></TD>
<TD><LI><a href="/index.html#nbbrief">
Today's Newsbytes</a></TD>
<TD><LI><a href="/index.html#stocks">
Stock prices</a></TD></TR>
</TABLE>

<p>This page and all supporting pages copyright
ClariNet Communications Corp. 1996.</body>

</html>
```

Syntax Example

```
<TABLE COLSPEC="L20 C20 R20">
```

Comments

The seldom-used *<COLSPEC>* attribute of the *<TABLE>* tag provides you with the ultimate table control and speed.

Online Example

"ClariNet Home Page," by ClariNet Communications Corp., email: **webmaster@clari.net**

URL: **http://www.clarinet.com**

Description

There is nothing unusual about the appearance of the ClariNet home page. Below the masthead and introductory text lie three rows of links, which are separated by bullets. Lower on the page you will find large icons on the left and bulleted links on the right.

The browser does not have to wait for the contents of the cells to load in order to calculate the sizes of the tables because the *<COLSPEC>* attribute causes the tables to load onto the screen very quickly.

Step-by-Step

Here is the HTML which creates the first table (the one with the three rows of bulleted links):

```
<TABLE COLSPEC="L20 L20 L20 L20 L20 L20 L20 L20">
<TR><TD><a href="/index.html#availability">
Availability</a></TD>
<TD><LI><a href="/index.html#subscriber info">
Subscriber info</a></TD>
<TD><LI><a href="/index.html#recent">
Recent announcements</a></TD>
<TD><LI><a href="/index.html#jobs">Jobs</a></TD>
<TD><LI><a href="/index.html#contact">
Contact us</a> </TD></TR>
</TABLE>
```

The value of the *<COLSPEC>* attribute contains one term for each column in the table. The terms consist of one capital letter (L, C, or R), followed immediately by a number. The letters stand for left, center, and right, respectively; they align the contents of all the cells in the specified column.

Notes

It is important to note that Netscape Navigator and Internet Explorer do not yet support the *<COLSPEC>* attribute, so it is best used sparingly!

ClariNet used the *<LI>* tag within the table cells to generate a bullet, even though there are no *<UL>* tags. This usually works, although the bullets will not be indented. Note that in the Mosaic browser, the *<LI>* tag forces a line break, which causes the table to fall apart.

Related Techniques

Using Tables for Page Formatting

Using Nested Tables as a Graphical Element

Using Tables to Format Pages

Using Tables

Type: HTML

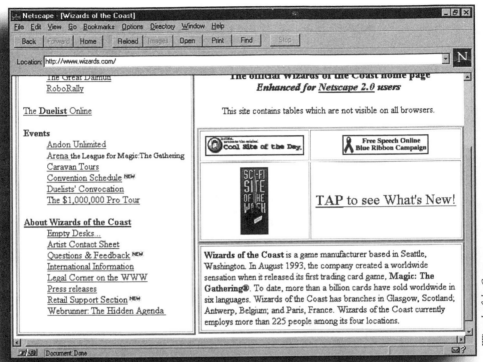

```
<center>
<table border=0 width=500>
<tr>
<td nowrap valign=top>
<table border=3 cellpadding=8>
<tr>
<td><dl>
<dt><B>Deckmaster</B>
<dd><a href="Magic/Welcome.html">Magic: The Gathering</a>

        .
        .
        .
```

continues

```
<dd><a href="Netrunner/Webrunner/Welcome.html">
Webrunner: The Hidden Agenda </a>
</dl></td></tr>
</table></td>
<td valign=top ALIGN=center>
<table border=3>
<tr><td><IMG  SRC="images/WotC-1.50in.gif" WIDTH=272 HEIGHT=113
 ALT="Wizards of the Coast, Inc."></td>
</tr>
</table>
<center><H3> The official <B>Wizards of the Coast</B> home page<br>
<i>Enhanced for
<a href="http://home.netscape.com/comprod/mirror/index.html">
 Netscape 2.0</a> users</i> </H3>
<p>
This site contains tables which are not visible on all browsers.
<p>

<table cellpadding=8 border=3>
<tr>
<td align=center><a href="http://www.infi.net"><IMG WIDTH=168
HEIGHT=30  SRC="images/coolsitelogo.gif"></a></td>
<TD ALIGN=Center><a href="http://www.eff.org/"><IMG WIDTH=143
HEIGHT=30  SRC="images/rib_bar_wh.gif"></a></td>
</tr>
<tr>
<td align=center><a href="http://www.scifiweekly.com">
<IMG SRC="images/sfsite.gif" WIDTH=45 HEIGHT=111 ALT="Sci-Fi Weekly">
</a></td>
<td nowrap><font size=5><a href="Whats_New.html">
<b>TAP</b> to see What's New!</a></font></td>

</tr></table>

<a name="About">
<table border=3 cellpadding=5>
<tr>
<td><B>Wizards of the Coast</B> is a game manufacturer based in
Seattle, Washington.  In August 1993, the company created a
worldwide sensation when it released its first trading card game,
<B> Magic: The Gathering&reg;</B>.  To date, more than a billion
cards have sold worldwide in six languages.  Wizards of the Coast
has branches in Glasgow, Scotland; Antwerp, Belgium; and Paris,
France.  Wizards of the Coast currently employs more than 225
people among its four locations.</td>
</tr>
</table></a>
</td></tr>
</table>
</center>
```

Syntax Example

```
<table border=0 width=500>
```

Comments

Occasionally, the text formatting and image alignment tags do not place everything where you might want it. You can use an "invisible" table to format the page. The table is "invisible" because it is given no table borders.

Online Example

"Wizards of the Coast," by Wizards of the Coast, email: **webmaster@wizards.com**

URL: **http://www.wizards.com/**

Description

Because the one main table on this page has no borders, it causes the elements to appear in a two-column format. The first column is put in the left cell of the table, while the second column is put in the right cell. Using tables in this manner enables you to position text and pictures in a more readable and eye-pleasing format.

Step-by-Step

The main table in this page is defined by the tag *<table border=0 width=500>*. The table borders will not be displayed if you use the option *border=0*. The cells of this table contain the two columns of the page. This is the form of the main table in this page:

```
<table border=0 width=500>
<tr>
<td nowrap valign=top>

        [left column cell]
```

```
</td>
<td valign=top ALIGN=center>

        [right column cell]

</td></tr>
</table>
```

To make three or more columns, you simply need to include more cells in *<td>* tags.

You can also align the cell contents with respect to the cells. Within the *<td>* tag you can include two parameters for alignment. The *<align>* parameter can be given the options *<LEFT>*, *<RIGHT>*, and *<CENTER>*. This aligns the text according to the horizontal axis. The *<valign>* parameter can be given the options *<TOP>*, *<MIDDLE>*, and *<BOTTOM>*. This aligns the text according to the vertical axis.

Notes

The cells within the main table can contain any HTML format. This page displays pictures, text, and nested tables in the cells.

Related Techniques

Using Nested Tables as a Graphical Element

Creating Page Layouts Using Floating Images in Tables

Using <IMG ALIGN> and Tables

Type: HTML 3.0

Used in: <IMG> tag

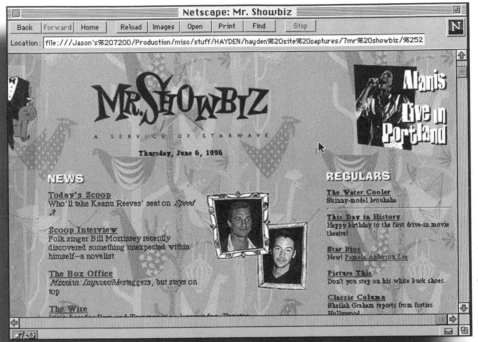

Starwave Corporation

```
<html><head><title>Mr. Showbiz</title></head>
<body background= "/showbiz/img/home/tile32.jpg">

<center>

<table border="0" cellspacing=0 cellpadding="0" width=730>

<tr>
```

continues

```
<td WIDTH=182 HEIGHT=158 valign=bottom><a
href="http://www.mrshowbiz.com/cgi/custom/"><img
src="/showbiz/custom/img/custom1.jpg" border=0></a></td>

<td valign=center align=center WIDTH=405 HEIGHT=100>

<img src="/showbiz/img/showbiz.gif" alt="Mr. Showbiz"
width=246 height=100 border=0>
</td>

<td align=left  valign=center width=200>

<a href="/showbiz/musicreviews/music/morissetteconcert.html">
<img src="/showbiz/img/alanishpg.gif" border=0 align=right
width=130 height=122></a>
</td>
</tr>
</table>

<table border="0" cellspacing=0 cellpadding="0" width=730>
<tr>
<td width=165 height=640 valign=top align=left>
<a href="/showbiz/img/home/mainmenuvert.map">
<img src="/showbiz/img/home/mainmenuvert.jpg" border="0"
width=165 height=670 ISMAP USEMAP="#mainmenuvert"></a>
</td>
</tr></table>
</body>
</html>
```

Syntax Example

```
<td align=left  valign=center width=200>

<a href="/showbiz/musicreviews/music/morissetteconcert.html">
    <img src="/showbiz/img/alanishpg.gif"
    border=0 align=right width=130 height=122></a>

</td>
```

Comments

The *<ALIGN=left>* and *<ALIGN=right>* attributes for the *<IMG>* tag enable text to wrap properly around images, making them "floating" images. The *<td>* tag for table cells also enables *<ALIGN=left>* and *<ALIGN=right>*, as well as *<VALIGN=top>* and

<VALIGN=bottom>, which enable you to place the contents of a cell along any edge or corner of a cell. Using these attributes in combination results in extensive formatting options.

Online Example

"Mr. Showbiz," by Starwave Corporation, email: **info@starwave.com**

URL: **http://www.mrshowbiz.com**

Description

The Mr. Showbiz page is laid out in three columns. The first column contains a graphic and an imagemap; the second column contains the masthead and the News, Features, and Reviews sections; and the third column contains the Regulars section. Each of the sections has a graphic associated with it; in many cases, this graphic is on the right side of the column and has the text wrapped around it.

Step-by-Step

Even though the page appears as three columns, the tables actually run all the way across the page. The first table contains the graphics at the top of the page, and the second table contains the imagemap on the left, along with the bulk of the text.

Let's take a closer look at the cell that contains the News section:

```
<td align=left  valign=top width=400 height=467>
<p>
<!--NEWS-->
<img src="/showbiz/img/home/newstype.gif" border="0" vspace=5>
<br>
<a href="/showbiz/scoop/scoop.html"><img src=
"/showbiz/img/partygirlhpg.gif" align=right width=130
height=140 border=0 vspace=00 hspace=6></a>
<b><a href="/showbiz/scoop/scoop.html">Today's Scoop</a></b>
<br>
<i>Party Girl</i>'s Parker Posey picked a peck of promising
projects
<p>
<b><a href="/showbiz/scoop/week/">Week in Review</a></b>
<br>
<i>Speed</i>less Keanu . . . Sex-Crazed Sigourney . . .
Mama Pam . . . and more news from June 1 to June 7<p>
...
</td>
```

First, the cell itself is fixed in size. With two alignment attributes set, the cell's content will appear in the upper left of the cell. In fact, *<align=left>* is the default, so that attribute is not necessary, but the *<valign=top>* is necessary.

The first item in the cell is the masthead "newstype.gif," which appears to the left of the cell. Its border is set to 0 (which is not necessary), and *vspace=5* is also set, which specifies a margin of five pixels of blank space above and below the graphic.

The next item in the cell is the image "partygirlhpg.gif," which is a clickable image (because it is surrounded by an *<A HREF>* tag). This image contains *<align=right>*, which places it at the right side of the cell, and allows the text to wrap around it on the left. However, *<hspace=6 >*is also set, which provides a margin of six pixels on the left and right of the image. This keeps the text from pressing up against the image. The *<vspace=0>* attribute is unnecessary, but setting *<border=0>* is necessary in this case because the image is clickable. If the border wasn't set to 0, you would see a blue or purple border around the image, indicating whether you had followed the link.

Following the right-aligned image is plenty of text, which wraps nicely around the image.

Notes

The greatest danger in using left- or right-aligned images is that it is often difficult to control just how much content will actually wrap around the image. Because you typically have no control over the width of the window or the size of the text, too much or too little content may actually wrap around your image for some users. Also, images may wrap around other images, leaving undesirable effects.

By placing the right-aligned graphics into table cells with fixed dimensions, The Mr. Showbiz site has avoided the lack of control of the window's width. If you can't use this solution on your page, there is a more general answer.

Netscape has expanded the *
* (line break) tag to handle just this problem. Place a *<BR clear=right>* below a right-aligned image, and the next object will always appear below that image. *<BR clear=left>* works the same way; *<BR clear=all>* moves the rest of your content below all floating images.

Related Techniques

Using Nested Tables as a Graphical Element

Using Nested Tables as a Graphical Element

Using the <TABLE> Command

Type: HTML+ and HTML 3.0

Used in: Body

DreamMedia

```
<HTML>
<HEAD><TITLE>Gloria Estefan.info</TITLE></HEAD>
<BODY BGCOLOR="FFFFFF">

<CENTER>
<TABLE BORDER=0 CELLSPACING=0 CELLPADDING=0 WIDTH=524
ALIGN=CENTER>
<TR>
<TD COLSPAN=3 WIDTH=446 ALIGN=CENTER >
```

continues

```
<IMG SRC="/Epic/gifs/headers/56.GIF" ALIGN=TOP WIDTH="396"
HEIGHT="100" BORDER="0" ALT="Estefan header graphic pending">
<TD ROWSPAN=5 WIDTH=75 VALIGN=TOP>
<IMG SRC="/Epic/gifs/artistinfo.GIF" ALIGN=TOP WIDTH="75"
HEIGHT="593" BORDER="0">

<TD ROWSPAN=2 WIDTH=224 VALIGN=TOP>
<TABLE WIDTH=224 HEIGHT=276 VALIGN=CENTER BORDER=1
CELLPADDING=1>
<TR VALIGN=TOP><TD><CENTER><b><FONT COLOR="#FF0000">Gloria
Estefan Update</b></FONT></CENTER><p>
<P>The "Reach" single is out now and blasting up the charts!
</TD></TR>
</TABLE>

<TD WIDTH=111  VALIGN=TOP HEIGHT="116">
<A HREF="/Epic/artistpress.qry?artistid=56"><IMG SRC=
"/Epic/gifs/press.GIF" ALIGN=TOP WIDTH="108" HEIGHT="116"
BORDER="0"></a>
</FORM>

</TABLE>
</BODY>
</HTML>
```

Syntax Example

```
<table>
<tr><td>
<table border><tr><td>Bordered text</td></tr></table>
</td></tr>
<tr><td>another cell in outer table</td></tr></table>
```

Comments

It is possible to place an entire table into a cell of another table. In fact, you can repeat this process, with tables inside of tables. In practice, however, nesting tables is best done in moderation.

Online Example

"Gloria Estefan info," 550 Music Magazine at Epic Records, by DreamMedia

URL: **http://www.sony.dreammedia.com/Epic/artistdetail.qry?artistid=56**

Description

The artist detail pages at 550 Music Magazine feature a well designed, yet graphics heavy page. It consists of large buttons in two columns, alternating with an album cover and descriptive text (in a border), along with a large vertical banner on the right.

Step-by-Step

The graphics are laid out on the page using a strictly defined table format:

```
<TABLE BORDER=0 CELLSPACING=0 CELLPADDING=0 WIDTH=524
ALIGN=CENTER>
<TR>
<TD COLSPAN=3 WIDTH=446 ALIGN=CENTER >
<IMG SRC="/Epic/gifs/headers/56.GIF" ALIGN=TOP WIDTH="396"
HEIGHT="100" BORDER="0" ALT="Estefan header graphic pending">
```

The widths and positions of the table, its cells, and the images in the cells are very carefully calculated to achieve the desired look.

Within one of the cells of the larger table lies another table:

```
<TABLE WIDTH=224 HEIGHT=276 VALIGN=CENTER BORDER=1
CELLPADDING=1>

<TR VALIGN=TOP><TD><CENTER><b><FONT COLOR="#FF0000">
Gloria Estefan Update</b></FONT></CENTER><p>
<P>The "Reach" single is out now and blasting up the
charts!</TD></TR>
</TABLE>
```

This table has a border and one cell, which creates the effect of a single rectangular border around the text. It is important to note that Netscape does not support the *<HEIGHT>* or *<VALIGN>* attributes of the *<TABLE>* tag; in fact, these two attributes appear to be in error.

The border is set to 1, which is the default value for a border. It would be sufficient for the tag to read *<TABLE BORDER>*.

<CELLPADDING=1> keeps the text away from the border by a small amount. It is best to experiment with this attribute to *achieve* the effect you desire.

Notes

Notice the use of the *<FONT COLOR>* tag, as well as the generous use of *<P>* tags within one cell of a table. It is important to remember that just about anything can go into the cells of a table.

Related Techniques

Using Tables to Format Pages

Creating Page Layouts Using Floating Images in Tables

Using Font Sizes and Background Colors

Using <FONT SIZE> and <BODY> Color Attributes

Type: HTML 3.2

Used in: <BODY> used in the document; <FONT> used in the body

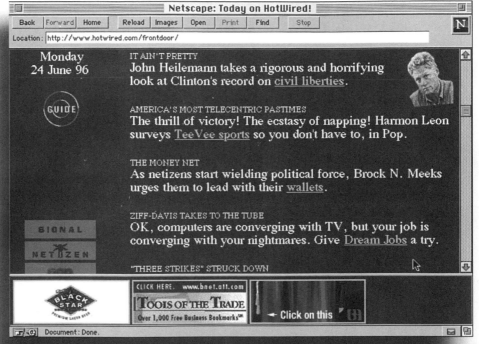

```
<html><head><title>HotWired: Front Door - Text Page</title>
</head>
<body  bgcolor= "#ffff00" link= "#ff0000"  alink="#ffff00"
vlink="#ff00ff">
<table width=%100>
<tr><td>
```

continues

```
<IMG    WIDTH=4 HEIGHT=1 SRC="/frontdoor/images/spacer.gif"
alt="[spacer]"></td>
<td valign=top nowrap width=110>
<br>
<p align=center><a href="/staff/" target="_top"><IMG
WIDTH=100 HEIGHT=96 SRC="/frontdoor/images/logo.yellow.gif" border=0
alt="[logo]"></a>
<p align=center>

<font size=5>Weekend</font><br>
<font size=5>7-9 June 96

<p align=center>

<a href="/piazza/" target="_top"><IMG    WIDTH=60
HEIGHT=50 SRC="/frontdoor/images/talk.yellow.gif"
border=0 alt="[Talk]"></a><p>

<p align=center>




<font size=3>LIVE FROM SAN FRANCISCO</font>

<br><font size=5><a href="/popfeatures/96/23/index4a.html"
target="_top">Netcast</a> from the Imagination <a href="/popfeatures/96/23/
↪index4a.html" target="_top"><IMG
align=right  WIDTH=95 HEIGHT=73 SRC="/frontdoor/96/23/stuff/
one4a.gif" border=0 alt="[Laurie Anderson]"></a> Conference
- Brian Eno, Laurie Anderson, and Spike Lee.</font>

<p>
<br>

</td>
</tr>
</table>
</body>
</html>
```

Syntax Example

```
<body  bgcolor= "#ffff00" link= "#ff0000"
    alink="#ffff00" vlink="#ff00ff">
<font size=3>OBEY AUTHORITY</font><br>
<font size=5><cite>Washington Post</cite>
    writer John Schwartz says ...
</font>
```

Comments

HotWired is *Wired* magazine's online cousin. *Wired* is known for its cutting edge (read: garish) use of color and text effects so it's only natural that HotWired wanted to convey the same effect on their Web site.

Online Example

"HotWired," by HotWired, Inc., email: **consent@hotwired.com**

URL: **http://www.hotwired.com/frontdoor**

Description

The front door screen of HotWired consists of two frames. The bottom frame contains the ads; the copy goes into the top. The backgrounds are bright yellow; unfollowed links are bright red; and followed links are magenta. Most text appears in large type—18 point or so. Images appear here and there.

Step-by-Step

```
<body  bgcolor= "#ffff00" link= "#ff0000"  alink="#ffff00"
vlink="#ff00ff">
```

Let's look at the *<BODY>* tag first. The background color is set to "ffff00." Can you tell what color that is? Don't worry, HotWired made it easy for us. The six digit hexadecimal number that browsers use to describe colors consists of two digits that stand for red, two that stand for green, and two that stand for blue, in that order.

"00" turns the color all the way off, while "ff" turns it all the way on. So "ffff00" means red and green are all the way on, which for colored light, makes pure yellow.

You can easily tell that the link color, "ff0000," is pure red, and visited links are "ff00ff," which is red plus blue, or magenta.

```
<font size=3>VICTORY DRINK</font><br>
<font size=5>Cocktail samples the Ward Eight, a
turn-of-the-century <a href="/cocktail/96/23/index4a.html"
target="_top">twist</a> on the whiskey sour.</font>
```

The next feature that HotWired uses is the *<FONT SIZE>* tag. This tag is either absolute or relative. There are seven different font sizes ranging from 1 to 7, where 3 is the default. These numbers do not correspond to point sizes; just remember that 3 stands for whatever size is chosen as the browser's default.

By setting *<FONT SIZE=5>*, HotWired increases the font size to 5, which may take it from 12 to 18 point. This is an example of absolute font sizes. *<FONT SIZE=+2>* would have increased the font size two notches, for the same effect. Likewise, *<FONT SIZE=-1>* is also an example of relative font sizes.

Notes

You could nest *<FONT>* tags, but there is rarely, if ever, a need to do so. You might find occasions to nest *<FONT>* and *<SUP>* (for superscript) tags. However, there is a trick to this: for some reason, you can't put the *<FONT>* tags inside the *<SUP>* tags, or the *<FONT>* tags won't work. They must go the other way!

```
Trademark<font size=-1><sup>TM</sup></font>
```

Related Techniques

Flashing Color Over Frames

Creating Special Graphical Effects

Making Your Page Easily Searchable

Using the <META> Tag

Type: HTML 2.0

Used in: Headings

Greer Consulting Services

```
<html>
<head><Title> GORP - Great Outdoor Recreation Pages</title>

<meta name="description" content="GORP features outdoor
recreation activities, attractions, gear and active travel
opportunities around the world! Attractions - national parks,
forests, wilderness, wildlife refuges, archaeology, and more!">

<meta name="keywords" content="hiking, biking, cycling,
walking, trekking, birding, fishing, climbing, wildlife,
```

continues

```
ecology, backpacking, flyfishing, paddling, canoeing,
kayaking, rafting, whitewater, skiing, rvs, scenic driving">

</head>

<body>

...

<! -- hiking, biking, cycling, walking, trekking, birding,
fishing, climbing, wildlife, ecology, backpacking, hunting,
flyfishing, fly fishing, paddle, paddling, canoeing, kayaking,
 rafting, whitewater, floating, boating, skiing >

</body>
</html>
```

Syntax Example

```
<meta name="keywords" content="hiking, biking, cycling">
```

Comments

The creators of this example clearly realize the Web is no "Field of Dreams"—and they are relying on search engines to make them come. They try two tricks to get the pages to come up more often. However, it doesn't seem to help much!

Online Example

"GORP—Great Outdoor Recreation Pages," by Greer Consulting Services, Inc., email: **Diane.Greer@www.gorp.com**

URL: **http://www.gorp.com**

Description

When you view the page, you have no idea that the *<META>* tag is being used; all you see is an attractively designed page. When a search engine encounters the page, however, it is supposed to catch the "description" and "keywords" values of the *<META>* tags, and include them in the results.

Step-by-Step

```
<meta name="description" content="GORP features outdoor
recreation activities, ...">

<meta name="keywords" content="hiking, biking, cycling,  ...">
```

The idea behind the *<META>* tag is that it is a place to convey special instructions to the HTTP (Web) server (that it may read, if it can). The name attribute can be whatever you expect the server to understand; other common names are "Expires," "Reply-to," and the like. The *<META>* tag is always optional, and in practice, very rarely used.

```
<! -- hiking, biking, cycling, walking, ... >
```

Just in case, the keywords here are included in an HTML comment so that search engines have one more place to look for hits.

Notes

A Lycos search for "horsebacking," one of the more obscure keywords in the *<META>* list, did not bring up this example. After a search on Excite, these pages took nine of the top ten hits! However, most of the pages do not use the *<META>* tag, and the home page was not the highest scoring hit.

A search on Excite for "Antarctica" brought up the GORP Antarctica page, but not the home page.

Related Techniques

Grouping Variables Together

Client-Side Searching

Creating Client-Side Imagemaps with HTML

Using <MAP> and <AREA> to Define Imagemaps

Type: HTML 3.2

Used in: Body text

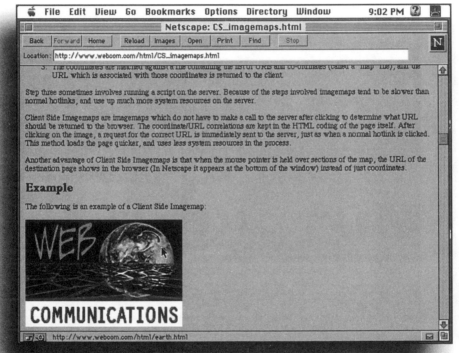

Jason Bloomberg

```
<html>
<head>
   <title></title>
</head>
<body>
<h1>Client Side Imagemaps</h1>
```

```
<p>The following is an example of a Client Side Imagemap: </p>

<p><map NAME="MyMap">
<area SHAPE="rect" COORDS="1,114, 224,150"
HREF="communications.html">
<area SHAPE="polygon" COORDS="10,15,99,4,105,24,77,57,23,54" HREF="web.html">
<area SHAPE="circle" COORDS="162,55,50" HREF="earth.html">
<area SHAPE=default HREF="none.html">
</map>

<img usemap="#MyMap" src="/graphics/webcomi.gif" border=0 USEMAP="#MyMap" ></p>

</body>
</html>
```

Syntax Example

```
<area SHAPE="rect" COORDS="1,114, 224,150" HREF="communications.html">
```

Comments

There are two different ways to program imagemaps: on the server ("server-side") and within the HTML ("client-side"). Server-side imagemaps have the advantage that they are browser-independent. Client-side imagemaps, on the other hand, have several advantages. They reduce server load; the URLs of the linked areas appear in the status bar; and they're much easier to program.

Online Example

"Client Side Imagemaps," by Web Communications, email: **support@webcom.com**

URL: **http://www.webcom.com/html/CS_imagemaps.html**

Description

This sample page explains client-side imagemaps. Its imagemap features each of the different *<AREA>* types: polygons, circles, rectangles, and the default type.

Step-by-Step

Client-side imagemaps come in two pieces: the *<MAP>* tag, and the *<IMG USEMAP>* tag.

The *<MAP>* tag is defined as follows:

```
<map NAME="MyMap">
<area SHAPE="rect" COORDS="1,114, 224,150"
HREF="communications.html">
<area SHAPE="polygon" COORDS="10,15,99,4,105,24,77,57,23,54"
     HREF="web.html">
<area SHAPE="circle" COORDS="162,55,50" HREF="earth.html">
<area SHAPE=default HREF="none.html">
</map>
```

Maps must have names and at least one *<AREA>*. Each *<AREA>* has a *<SHAPE>*. The "rect," or rectangle shape, has exactly four coordinates corresponding to the x and y coordinates of the upper-left and lower-right corners of the rectangle. (And don't forget, the 0,0 point is in the upper-left corner; x goes up as you go across, and y goes up as you go down.)

The "poly," or polygon shape, has any number of coordinate pairs that correspond to the x and y coordinates of the vertices (corners) of the polygon.

The "circle" shape has three coordinates, corresponding to the coordinates of the center, followed by the radius.

And last, but not least, is the default shape, which is the "none of the above" shape.

Each of the different *<AREA>* tags also has an *<HREF>* attribute, which is the URL that loads if you click in the specified region of the image.

The next piece of the imagemap is the *<IMG>* tag itself:

```
<img src="/graphics/webcomi.gif" border=0 USEMAP="#MyMap" >
```

If an image has a *<USEMAP>* attribute, it will be a client-side imagemap. The map name must be preceded by a #. The border is usually set to zero because the border indicating that the image is clickable is on by default.

If you want an image to be a server-side imagemap, the *<IMG>* tag must have the *<ISMAP>* attribute. If both *<USEMAP>* and *<ISMAP>* are present, the *<USEMAP>* takes precedence for those browsers that can understand it. Therefore, all professional sites with *<USEMAP>*s should also have *<ISMAP>*s.

Notes

When the user moves the cursor over a client-side imagemap, the destination URL appears in the status window. When the user moves the cursor over a server-side imagemap, the coordinates of the cursor's location appear in the status window.

Herein lies a very important trick for developing quick, easy client-side imagemaps. The big question: How do you calculate the coordinates? The answer: Take the *<USEMAP>* attribute out of the *<IMG>* tag temporarily and make sure an *<ISMAP>* tag is in there. Now, load the page, and move the cursor over your image to show you the coordinates of the regions you want to program. Jot them down. Now, put the *<USEMAP>* back in and use the numbers you wrote down to create your shapes. Simple!

Related Techniques

Creating Client-Side Imagemaps in VBScript

Creating Client-Side Imagemaps in JavaScript

Using Alternate Graphics

Using the LOWSRC Attribute to the IMG Tag

Type: Netscape 2.0 specific

Used in: IMG tag

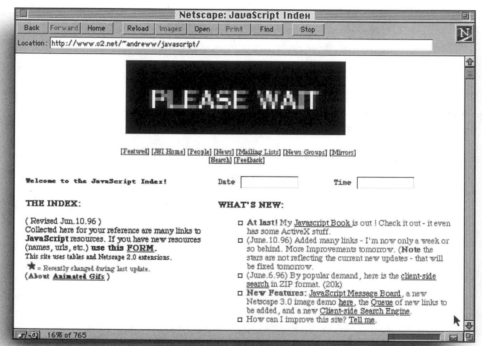

Andrew Wooldridge

```
<HTML>
<HEAD>
<TITLE>JavaScript Index</TITLE>
</HEAD>
```

```
<BODY bgcolor="#ffffff" text="#000000" link="#0000ff"
alink="#008000" vlink="800080" onLoad="startclock()">
<H1 ALIGN=CENTER><a href="http://www.c2.org/~andreww/
javascript/javascript.map"><img src="javascript.gif"
alt="JavaScript" ISMAP
height=100 width=300 border=0 lowsrc=low.gif></a> </H1>
<b>HotSpots - <a href="http://www.freqgrafx.com/411">
<img src="faq.gif"
lowsrc="low.gif" height="15" width="60" border=0
align=absmiddle></a>
</BODY>
</HTML>
```

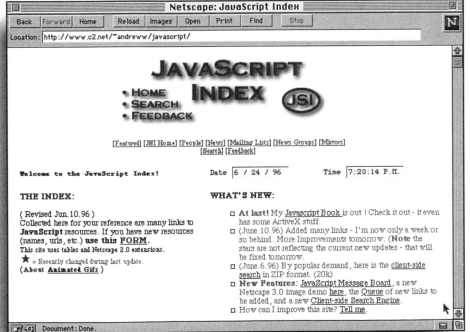

Syntax Example

```
<img src="newdot.gif" lowsrc="low.gif" height=14 width=14>
```

Comments

You should definitely check out the JavaScript Index. It is one of the best JavaScript resources available on the Web. Naturally, the JSI home page is set up with some of the more popular gimmicks, such as the time and the date.

This page is frequently updated. Many features, such as animated gifs and the scrolling status bar, have come and gone. One gimmick worth noticing is the use of the *<LOWSRC>* attribute of the *<IMG>* tag.

Online Example

"The JavaScript Index," by Andrew Wooldridge, email: **andreww@c2.org**

URL: **http://www.c2.org/~andreww/javascript/**

Description

The JSI is a straightforward menu of sites, with occasional gimmicks, such as the clock. As the page first loads, a blocky black-and-white image that reads "please wait" appears. As soon as the browser can, it loads the actual image over the low-res "please wait" images.

Step-by-Step

There is really very little to this technique:

```
<img src="newdot.gif" lowsrc="low.gif" height=14 width=14>
```

In addition to its regular *<SRC>* attribute, the *<IMG>* tag has a *<LOWSRC>* attribute that indicates the graphic that will load when the browser first encounters the page. The image indicated in the *<SRC>* loads after all the text has loaded.

It is very important to use the *<HEIGHT>* and *<WIDTH>* attributes when using *<LOWSRC>*, unless the low- and high-resolution images happen to be the same size. The idea is to speed up loading, and if the browser must recalculate the position of the text, then the purpose of the *<LOWSRC>* attribute is defeated.

Notes

Keep in mind that the browser only loads the low-res image if the high-res image is not in the cache. Therefore, when you reload a page with the *<LOWSRC>* attribute, you typically will not see the low-res image again.

It is possible to use the *<LOWSRC>* attribute for some basic two-frame animation. However, the limitation mentioned above makes this much less appealing than an animated gif.

The creator of this script uses the same image *low.gif* for all his low-res images. You might want to try reducing your high-res images in size to create your low-res images. If you remember to use the *<HEIGHT>* and *<WIDTH>* attributes, what you will see load first is a blurry version of your final image.

Related Techniques

Creating Page Layouts Using Floating Images in Tables

Creating Special Graphical Effects

Creating Page Layouts Using Floating Images in Tables

Using <IMG ALIGN> in Tables

Type: HTML 3.0

Used in: <IMG>

Starwave Corporation

```
<html><head><title>Mr. Showbiz</title></head>
<body background= "/showbiz/img/home/tile32.jpg">

<center>

<table border="0" cellspacing=0 cellpadding="0" width=730>

<tr>
```

```
<td WIDTH=182 HEIGHT=158 valign=bottom><a
href="http://www.mrshowbiz.com/cgi/custom/"><img
src="/showbiz/custom/img/custom1.jpg" border=0></a></td>

<td valign=center align=center WIDTH=405 HEIGHT=100>

<img src="/showbiz/img/showbiz.gif" alt="Mr. Showbiz"
width=246 height=100 border=0>
</td>

<td align=left  valign=center width=200>

<a href="/showbiz/musicreviews/music/morissetteconcert.html">
<img src="/showbiz/img/alanishpg.gif" border=0 align=right
width=130 height=122></a>
</td>
</tr>
</table>

<table border="0" cellspacing=0 cellpadding="0" width=730>
<tr>
<td width=165 height=640 valign=top align=left>
<a href="/showbiz/img/home/mainmenuvert.map">
<img src="/showbiz/img/home/mainmenuvert.jpg" border="0"
width=165 height=670 ISMAP USEMAP="#mainmenuvert"></a>
</td>
</tr></table>
</body>
</html>
```

Syntax Example

```
<td align=left  valign=center width=200>
<a href="/showbiz/musicreviews/music/morissetteconcert.html"><img
src="/showbiz/img/alanishpg.gif" border=0 align=right width=130
height=122></a>

</td>
```

Comments

The *<ALIGN=left>* and *<ALIGN=right>* attributes for the *<IMG>* tag enable text to wrap properly around images, making them "floating" images. The *<TD>* tag for table cells also enables *<ALIGN=left>* and *<ALIGN=right>*, as well as *<VALIGN=top>* and *<VALIGN=bottom>*, which enable you to place the contents of a cell along any edge or corner of a cell. Using these attributes in combination results in extensive formatting options.

Creating a Pull-Down Menu

Using the <SELECT SIZE=1> Tag to Create a Pull-Down Menu

Type: HTML 2.0

Used in: Forms

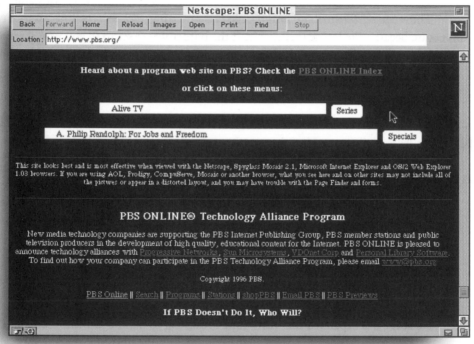

```
<HTML>
<HEAD>
<TITLE>PBS ONLINE</TITLE>
</HEAD>
<BODY>

<FORM METHOD="POST"
ACTION="http://www.pbs.org/cgi-bin/pagefinder.pl">
```

```
<SELECT NAME="Series">
  <OPTION Value="http://www2.pbs.org/ktca/alive/">Alive TV
  <OPTION Value="http://www.boston.com/wgbh/americanexp">
American Experience, The
  <OPTION Value="http://www.klru.org/ACL.html">
Austin City Limits
</SELECT>

<INPUT TYPE="submit" name="submit" VALUE="Series">
</FORM>
<FONT SIZE="-1">Copyright 1996 PBS.</FONT>
</BODY>
</HTML>
```

Syntax Example

```
<FORM METHOD="POST"
ACTION="http://www.pbs.org/cgi-bin/pagefinder.pl">
<SELECT NAME="Series">
  <OPTION Value="http://www2.pbs.org/ktca/alive/">Alive TV
...
</select>
```

Comments

The pagefinder CGI script is one of the simplest; it takes the value of the *<SELECT>* object, which is a URL, and it loads that page.

Online Example

"PBS Online," by PBS, email: **www@pbs.org**

URL: **http://www.pbs.org/**

Description

There are two pop-up lists on the PBS home page: one lists series and the other lists specials. Choose a show, click the button, and the desired page loads.

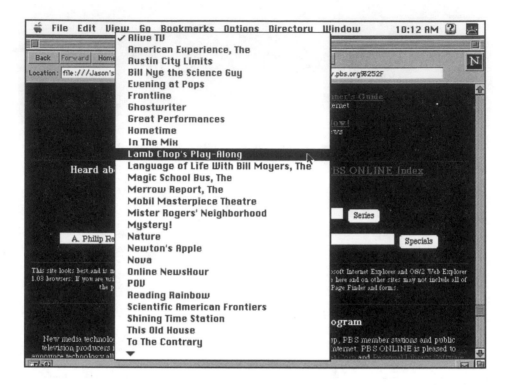

Step-by-Step

Here is the entire form, with some of the options removed:

```
<FORM METHOD="POST"
ACTION="http://www.pbs.org/cgi-bin/pagefinder.pl">
<SELECT NAME="Series">
<OPTION Value="http://www2.pbs.org/ktca/alive/">Alive TV
<OPTION Value="http://www.boston.com/wgbh/americanexp">
American Experience, The
<OPTION Value="http://www.klru.org/ACL.html">
Austin City Limits
...
</SELECT>

<INPUT TYPE="submit" name="submit" VALUE="Series">
</FORM>
```

The *<METHOD="POST">* attribute indicates that submitting the form will pass information to the CGI script indicated in the *<ACTION>*. The value passed to the script is nothing more than a URL. Clicking the Submit button executes the script. That's all there is to it!

Notes

The *<SELECT>* tag has no *<SIZE>* attribute; therefore, the size defaults to 1. A size 1 *<SELECT>* object is a pull-down menu; a size larger than 1 creates a scrolling menu.

Also notice that the submit button has the attributes *<NAME="submit">*, which is unnecessary, and *<VALUE="Series">*, which is the text that will appear in the button. Remember that you can put any text you want on a button; your buttons don't all have to be *<SUBMIT>* and *<RESET>*.

Related Techniques

Using Frames to Create a Hierarchical Menu

Navigating Within a Frame

Calling Java Applets

Using the <APPLET> Tag and the Associated <PARAM> Tag

Type: HTML 3.2

Used in: <APPLET> used in body; <PARAM> used in APPLET

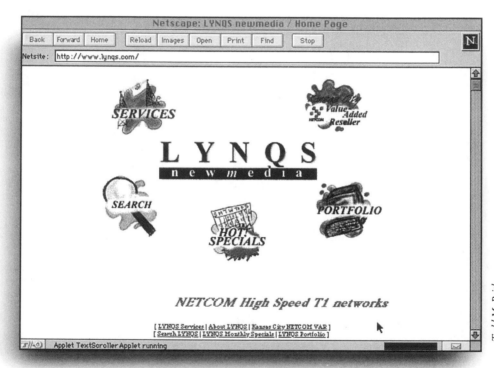

Todd M. Reith

```
<HTML>
<HEAD>
<TITLE>LYNQS newmedia / Home Page</TITLE>
</HEAD>


<BODY>
<IMG BORDER="0" SRC="lynqs_index.gif" ALT="LYNQS newmedia Logo"
     USEMAP="#lynqs_index">
```

```
<APPLET CODE="TextScrollerApplet.class"
WIDTH=400 HEIGHT=30>
   <PARAM NAME=text VALUE="Welcome to LYNQS newmedia">
   <PARAM NAME=remoteText VALUE="LYNQSjava.txt">
   <PARAM NAME=speed VALUE="10">
   <PARAM NAME=dist VALUE="5">
   <PARAM NAME=font VALUE="Arial">
   <PARAM NAME=size VALUE="18">
   <PARAM NAME=style VALUE="Bold Italic">
   <PARAM NAME=alignment VALUE="Center">
   <PARAM NAME=textColor VALUE="255.0.0">
   <PARAM NAME=backgroundColor VALUE="255.255.255">
</APPLET>
</BODY>
</HTML>
```

Syntax Example

```
<APPLET CODE="TextScrollerApplet.class"
WIDTH=400 HEIGHT=30>
   <PARAM NAME=text VALUE="Welcome to LYNQS newmedia">
</APPLET>
```

Online Example

"LYNQS newmedia Home Page," by Todd M. Reith, email: **treith@lynqs.com**

URL: **http://www.lynqs.com/**

Description

The Lynqs home page is attractive and understated; its main feature is a bright red scrolling banner written in Java.

Step-by-Step

The scrolling banner applet is becoming very popular, so focusing on it makes sense:

```
<APPLET CODE="TextScrollerApplet.class"
WIDTH=400 HEIGHT=30>
    <PARAM NAME=text VALUE="Welcome to LYNQS newmedia">
    <PARAM NAME=remoteText VALUE="LYNQSjava.txt">
    <PARAM NAME=speed VALUE="10">
    <PARAM NAME=dist VALUE="5">
    <PARAM NAME=font VALUE="Arial">
    <PARAM NAME=size VALUE="18">
    <PARAM NAME=style VALUE="Bold Italic">
    <PARAM NAME=alignment VALUE="Center">
    <PARAM NAME=textColor VALUE="255.0.0">
    <PARAM NAME=backgroundColor VALUE="255.255.255">
</APPLET>
```

The *<APPLET>* tag appears in the HTML wherever you want the applet to appear. *<CODE>* works much like *<HREF>*; it points to the applet itself. You also need the *<WIDTH>* and *<HEIGHT>* attributes.

Many applets will take parameters, which are passed to the applet by a *<PARAM>* tag. The name and value of each parameter depends on the applet, and yes, you could script the parameters in JavaScript. In the case of the text scroller, there are ten parameters, indicating that this applet is very versatile.

Notes

The *<APPLET>* tag also takes attributes such as *<ALT>*, *<ALIGN>*, *<HSPACE>*, and *<VSPACE>*; in fact, as far as the HTML is concerned, it works much like an image.

Related Techniques

Encrypting Text in a Page

Using Scrolling Option Lists

Using the <SELECT> Tag with the SIZE Attribute Set to More Than One

Type: HTML 2.0

Used in: Forms

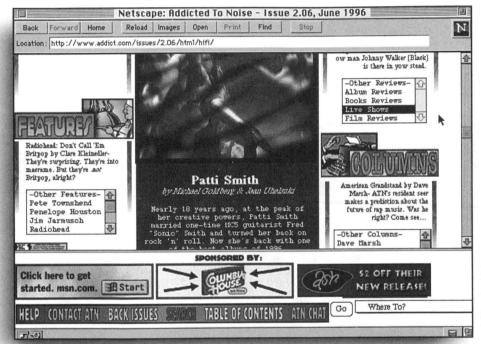

```
<HTML><HEAD>
<TITLE>Addicted To Noise - Issue 2.06, June 1996</TITLE>
</HEAD>
<BODY BGCOLOR="#FFFFFF" BACKGROUND="/images/bgs/hp-bg.jpg">

<TABLE BORDER=0 CELLPADDING=0 CELLSPACING=0 WIDTH=585>
```

continues

```
<TR>
<TD WIDTH=130 ALIGN=left>
<FONT SIZE=2>
Radiohead: Don't Call 'Em Britpop by Clare Kleinedler-
They're surprising. They're into macrame. But they're
<I>not</I> Britpop,
alright?
        <FORM>
        <SELECT SIZE=5>
        <OPTION>-Other Features-
            <OPTION>Pete Townshend
            <OPTION>Penelope Houston
            <OPTION>Jim Jarmusch
            <OPTION>Radiohead
            <OPTION>Magnapop
            <OPTION>Stereolab
        </SELECT>
            </FORM>
</FONT>
</TD>

<TD WIDTH=130 ALIGN=left>
<FONT SIZE=2>
Is your fear of leaving your house outweighed only by your
terror of being without new music?
        <FORM>
        <SELECT SIZE=5>
        <OPTION>-Other Hype-
            <OPTION>User Feedback
            <OPTION>Staff
            <OPTION>Tshirts
            <OPTION>Order CDs
            <OPTION>Contact ATN
            <OPTION>Support Sponsors
        </SELECT>
            </FORM>
</FONT>
</TD>
</TR>
</TABLE>
</BODY>
</HTML>
```

Syntax Example

```
<FORM>
      <SELECT SIZE=5>
              <OPTION>-Other Features-
              <OPTION>Pete Townshend
              <OPTION>Penelope Houston
              <OPTION>Jim Jarmusch
              <OPTION>Radiohead
      </SELECT>
</FORM>
```

Comments

Option lists are usually used for selection or navigational purposes. This example, however, uses them as a way to list items in an interactive fashion. You must scroll down each list, which draws you in and makes you pay attention.

Online Example

"Addicted to Noise," by Addicted to Noise, email: **atn-support@addict.com**

URL: **http://www.addict.com/issues/2.06/html/hifi/**

Description

Addicted to Noise is, logically, a noisy site. Loud graphics, animated ads, and links to music clips abound. This is essentially the table of contents for an entire magazine; the goal is to cram as much information onto the page as they can without losing you in the rush. Scrolling option lists are used in the main frame to display the magazine contents; and while they're at it, a pop-up list of pages appears on the lower, advertising frame.

Step-by-Step

```
<FORM>
<SELECT SIZE=5>
<OPTION>-Other Columns-
  <OPTION>Dave Marsh
  <OPTION>England's Dreaming
  <OPTION>Fuzzyland
  <OPTION>Editorial Rant
  <OPTION>Greil Marcus
  <OPTION>Hitsville
  <OPTION>Film
  <OPTION>Richard Meltzer
  <OPTION>Sunshine Country
  <OPTION>TV Eye
</SELECT>
  </FORM>
```

The *<FORM>* tag encloses the *<SELECT>* tag, which in turn encloses *<OPTION>* tags. The *<SELECT>* tag requires a *</SELECT>*, while the *<OPTION>* tag does not.

You control the appearance of the *<SELECT>* tag with its size. *<SIZE=1>* creates a pull-down menu, while a larger size creates a scrolling box. However, the scrollbar only appears if there are more options than the size, like in the above example.

Related Techniques

Loading a Page via a Selection List

Navigating Tricks and Pitfalls Using Scrolling Lists

Creative Indenting for Attractive Pages

Using the <DL>, <DT>, <DD>, and <UL> Tags for Indenting Text

Type: HTML 1.0 tags

Used in: Body text

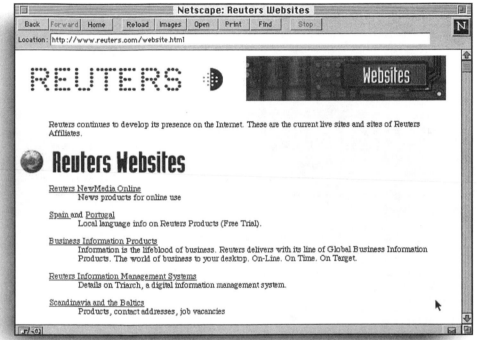

James O'Reilly

```
<HTML>
<HEAD><TITLE>Reuters Websites</TITLE></HEAD>

<BODY bgcolor="#ffffff">

<UL>
<DL>
<dt><a href="http://www.online.reuters.com/">
Reuters NewMedia Online</a><br>
<dd>News products for online use<br><br>
```

continues

```
<dt><a href="http://www.es.reuters.com/">Spain </a> and
<a href="http://www.es.reuters.com/pt/index.html">
Portugal</a><br>
<dd>Local language info on Reuters Products (Free Trial).
<br><br>
<dt><a href="http://www.bizinfo.reuters.com/">Business
Information Products</a><br>
<dd>Information is the lifeblood of business.  Reuters
</DL>
</UL>
</BODY>

</HTML>
```

Syntax Example

```
<DL>
<DT>Term<DD>This is the definition of the first term.
<DT>Term<DD>This is the definition of the second term.
</DL>
```

Comments

The *<DL>*, *<DT>*, and *<DD>* tags constitute what is called a definition list. It was originally intended for creating glossaries; now, however, it is used for creative formatting of text in a wide variety of applications.

Online Example

"Reuters Websites," by James O'Reilly, email: **webmaster@reuters.com**

URL: **http://www.reuters.com/website.html**

Description

The list of Reuters Web sites was constructed using banner graphics, indented links, and descriptions of the links that are indented even further.

Step-by-Step

```
<IMG SRC="images/headers/earth.jpg"><IMG SRC="images/headers/
    header8.gif"><BR>
<UL>
<DL>
<dt><a href="http://www.online.reuters.com/">Reuters NewMedia
Online</a><br>
<dd>News products for online use<br><br>
</DL>
</UL>
```

The *<UL>* tag is used to set off the text from the banners. It indents and adds some vertical white space below the banner. The *<UL>* tag is usually used with the *<LI>* tag to create a bulleted list; however, the *<UL>* tag can be useful on its own simply for indenting purposes.

Next, the text is enclosed within the *<DL> </DL>* tags, which designate the text as a definition list. The *<DT>* tag sets off the "term," which in this case is the link, and the *<DD>* tag sets off the "definition," which is the descriptive text.

Notes

The *<DL>* tag requires a closing *</DL>* tag, but the *<DT>* and *<DD>* tags, like *<LI>*, do not have closing tags.

<COMPACT>, a seldom-used attribute of the <DL> tag, reduces the amount of indenting and white space that appears in the browser. Its syntax is *<DL COMPACT>*.

Related Techniques

Creating Special Text Effects

Streaming Text into Documents

Creating Special Text Effects

Using the <TT>, <BLINK>, <FONT>, and <BLOCKQUOTE> Tags

Type: HTML 1.0, HTML 3.0

Used in: Body text

W3-design, Inc.

```
<HTML>
<HEAD><TITLE>MISSION IMPOSSIBLE</TITLE></HEAD>

<BODY BGCOLOR=#000000
TEXT=#00FF00 LINK=#FF0000 VLINK=#00FFFF>
```

```
<TT>
<CENTER>
<FONT SIZE=+2>
<B>"MISSION: IMPOSSIBLE"</B></FONT><P>
<FONT COLOR=#00FF00 SIZE=+1>
<B>NOW PLAYING ALL OVER NORTH AMERICA</B></FONT>
</CENTER>
<P>

<FONT COLOR=#FF0000 SIZE=+1>
<BLOCKQUOTE><B>DIRECTIVE FROM IMF HEADQUARTERS:
</B></BLOCKQUOTE>
Declassification begins on selected merchandise
direct from IMF supplies and requisition, order
now to ensure necessary covert attire for future
classified missions.

</FONT>
<BLINK><B>Be advised to avoid high-security files
without proper authorization.</B></BLINK>
</BODY>
</HTML>
```

Syntax Example

```
<TT>
<FONT SIZE=+2>
<B>"MISSION: IMPOSSIBLE"</B></FONT><P>
<FONT COLOR=#00FF00 SIZE=+1><B>
NOW PLAYING ALL OVER NORTH AMERICA</B></FONT>
</TT>
```

Comments

<TT>, which causes the browser to display in a "typewriter" font (usually Courier), and *<BLINK>*, a Netscape tag that causes the text to blink, are widely regarded as the lamest tags in HTML. The Mission Impossible site, however, uses these tags to give the impression of a top secret "impossible mission" type document. They never would have achieved this result, though, if the text weren't green and red!

71

Online Example

"Mission: Impossible," by w-3 Design, Inc., for Paramount Pictures, Inc., email:
pde@paramount.com

URL: **http://www.missionimpossible.com/**

Description

The Mission Impossible screen features three frames: the top contains the masthead,
the middle contains the body copy, and the bottom contains the main navigation
buttons. Let's take a closer look at the middle frame.

All of the text on the site is green or red, and it appears in various sizes of the Courier
font (on most computers, anyway). The text reads like a C.I.A. classified document,
and the style supports this feeling. Occasionally, text such as "*NOW DECLASSIFIED*"
blinks.

Step-by-Step

The tags themselves are very easy to work with; the only catch is to close the tags in
the reverse order that you open them. The key is to assemble tags so that your text
conveys the desired impression:

```
<TT>
<CENTER>
<FONT SIZE=+2>
<B>"MISSION: IMPOSSIBLE"</B></FONT><P>
<FONT COLOR=#00FF00 SIZE=+1><B>
NOW PLAYING ALL OVER NORTH AMERICA</B></FONT>
</CENTER>
...
<BLOCKQUOTE><B>DIRECTIVE FROM IMF HEADQUARTERS:
</B></BLOCKQUOTE>
...
<B><BLINK>NOW DECLASSIFIED</BLINK></B>
</TT>
```

The *<TT>* tag encloses this entire example, changing the font throughout. The first sentence is increased by two font sizes, whereas the next sentence is only one font size larger than the default. Notice that the one *<FONT>* tag has both its *<SIZE>* and *<COLOR>* attributes set, and yet needs only one *</FONT>*.

The *<BLOCKQUOTE>* tag indents the text with a twist by moving the right margin in, as well. And, yes, there is an example of the dreaded *<BLINK>* tag.

Notes

When nesting tags, it is essential that you close them in reverse order. For example, the correct way is:

```
<TT><FONT SIZE=+1><B>This is correct!</B></FONT></TT>
```

whereas this next example is wrong:

```
<TT><FONT SIZE=+1><B>This is incorrect!</FONT></B></TT>
```

because the <FONT> and <B> tags overlap. Many browsers will interpret this mistake correctly, but some will not, and even if the text appears on-screen, there can be negative side effects (such as a form that doesn't work, and so on).

Related Techniques

Creative Indenting for Attractive Pages

Streaming Text into Documents

Part II

JavaScript
Techniques

Using JavaScript with Frames

Using the *document.write* Method

Type: JavaScript

Used in: Method of the document object

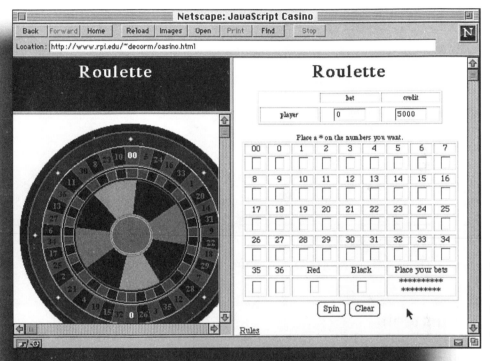

Greer Consulting Services

```
<html>
<head><title>Roulette Game</title></head>
<SCRIPT LANGUAGE="JavaScript">

function startwheel() {
    parent.frames[0].document.open();
    parent.frames[0].document.write('<body bgcolor="black" text="white">');
```

continues

```
   if ((eval(credit)) <= 0) {
       parent.frames[0].document.write('<center>
<h1>You are out of money!');
       parent.frames[0].document.write('</h1></center>');
       parent.frames[0].document.write('Click reload
to play again.');
       parent.frames[0].document.close();
       return; }
   if ((eval(bet)) > (eval(credit))) {
       parent.frames[0].document.write('<center><h1>Nice Try Wiseguy!</h1>');
       parent.frames[0].document.write('</center>');
       parent.frames[0].document.write('You can\'t bet
more than you have.');
       parent.frames[0].document.close();
       return; }
   parent.frames[0].document.close();
   return; }
}
</SCRIPT>
```

Syntax Example

```
parent.frames[1].document.write('roulette.gif"></center>')
```

Comments

Using the *document.write* method, it is possible to generate any or all of the HTML in a page on the fly. You essentially have ultimate control of all your pages from within JavaScript.

Online Example

"JavaScript Casino," by Michael DeCorpo and Arjun Menon, email: **decorm@rpi.edu**

URL: **http://www.rpi.edu/~decorm/casino.html**

Description

A roulette wheel is set up in the left frame. You enter your bet by typing asterisks in text fields in the right frame. Click the Spin button; watch the wheel turn; and lose your money!

Step-by-Step

The interesting part of this game takes place in the upper-left frame. This frame displays text that reflects the status of the game, like whether you won or lost, how much the bet paid, and whether you attempted to make an illegal bet.

Here is how the text is placed into the frame:

```
parent.frames[0].document.open();

if ((eval(bet)) > (eval(credit))) {
        parent.frames[0].document.write('<center><h1>Nice Try Wiseguy!</
h1>');
        parent.frames[0].document.write('</center>');
        parent.frames[0].document.write('You can\'t bet
more than you have.');
        parent.frames[0].document.close();
        return; }

parent.frames[0].document.close();
```

First, the *document.open* function is used to prepare the frame for text. While this statement does not seem to be necessary (the *document.write* statements work regardless), it is still recommended.

Next, the *document.write* method is used to write HTML to the page. In the above example, there are four write statements; they could have combined these into one, but they probably chose four to make the code more readable.

The most important thing to remember about this process is that you must still write valid HTML to the page. Begin a page with
document.write ("<html><head><title>This is the title</title></head>"), and continue to follow HTML rules, such as closing your tags.

Remember that you are actually writing strings to the page—so all the rules about strings apply. For example, it is valid to write:

```
document.write("<a href='thelink.html'>" + thetext + "</a>")
```

In this statement, the text will become a string whether it was one before or not. Notice that double quotes are used to set off the strings, so single quotes had to be used within the string to indicate quotes in the HTML. The rule here is that you must alternate what type of quote you use. This example's use of single quotes in the statement is just as good as using double quotes:

```
parent.frames[0].document.write('You can\'t bet more than you have.');
```

Now, you should be asking yourself what that word *"can\'t"* is for? What if they had written this statement without the backslash?:

```
parent.frames[0].document.write('You can't bet
more than you have.');
```

What would happen if you tried to load this page? You would have gotten a JavaScript error that talked about *'t bet more...'* JavaScript thought you were trying to print the string *'You can'*; when it got to the *'t bet,'* it couldn't make sense out of the statement.

The trick is to use the backslash to indicate that you want to print the single quote. The backslash won't print, but the quote will.

The following statement could have been used to create the same result:

```
parent.frames[0].document.write("You can't bet
more than you have.");
```

Notes

The backslash (\) can be used to indicate a set of special non-printing characters as well: \b is backspace; \f is form feed; \n is new line; \r is return; and \t is tab.

Related Techniques

Loading Pages into Frames

Manipulating Information in Multiple Frames

Controlling Frames in VBScript

Loading Pages into Frames

Using the onChange Event Handler

Type: JavaScript

Used in: Event handler, text field, text area, or select objects

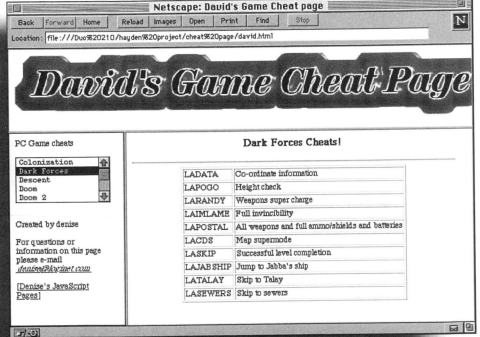

Denise K Wynn

```
<HTML><HEAD>
<TITLE>David's Game Cheat page</TITLE>

<script language="Javascript">
<!--
```

continues

```
function pc_cheats(){
var cheatInteger, cheatString
cheatInteger=document.pcform.pcselect.selectedIndex
cheatString=document.pcform.pcselect.options[cheatInteger].value
parent.cheats.location=cheatString + ".html"
}
//-->
</script>
</head>

<body bgcolor=#ffffff>
PC Game cheats<p>
<form name="pcform">
<select name="pcselect" onChange="pc_cheats()" multiple size="5">
<option value="Colonization">Colonization
<option value="Dark_Forces">Dark Forces
<option value="Descent">Descent
</select><p>
</form>
</body></html>
```

Syntax Example

```
<select name="pcSelect" onChange="pcFunction()" size="5">
```

Comments

Because a text field or a text area changes whenever you type any characters in the object, the *onChange EventHandler* is often too awkward to use. It is best used in a select object.

Online Example

"David's Game Cheat Page," by Denise K Wynn, email: **denise@loginet.com**

URL: **http://www.loginet.com/users/d/denise/cheats/david.html**

Description

The result is a frameset consisting of three frames: the header, the menu (called cheats.html), and the display frame. The select object appears as a scrolling list. Whenever an item in the scrolling list is clicked, a new page is loaded into the display frame.

Step-by-Step

```
<select name="pcselect" onChange="pc_cheats()"
multiple size="5">
```

Whenever the select object changes, the *onChange EventHandler* executes the script *pc_cheats()*. This function assigns the *selectedIndex* value for the select object to the variable *cheatInteger*. This value corresponds to the options you have selected.

```
function pc_cheats(){
var cheatInteger, cheatString
cheatInteger=document.pcform.pcselect.selectedIndex
cheatString=document.pcform.pcselect.options[cheatInteger]
.value
parent.cheats.location=cheatString + ".html"
}
```

Next, the function assigns the value of your selected option to the variable *cheatString*. Finally, the string *".html"* is attached to *cheatString*, making the string a URL. The location of the display window frame is assigned to this URL.

Notes

The display frame created in the frameset is named "cheats." To load a different page into the display frame, set the value of parent.cheats.location to the new URL. Here, the parent is the frameset (david.html), and cheats is the name of the frame.

Related Techniques

Using JavaScript with Frames

Manipulating Information in Multiple Frames

Flashing Color Over Frames

Using Document Object (BgColor Property)

Type: JavaScript object

Used in: Frames

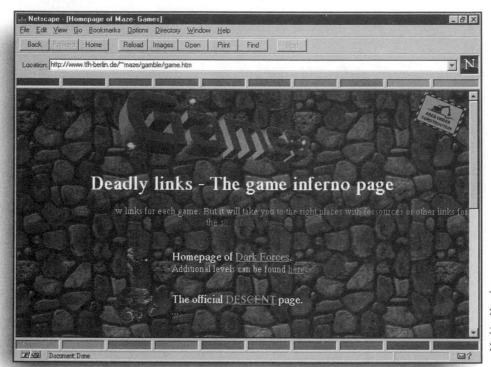

File: Col_Row.htm

This file sets up 10 small frames within the top and bottom frames of the page. These small frames use the file *color.htm*, which contains no data and is only controlled by the script in *game.htm* to change its color.

```
<FRAMESET COLS="10%,10%,10%,10%,10%,10%,10%,10%,10%,10%">
    <FRAME SRC="COLOR.HTM" SCROLLING=no NORESIZE>
    <FRAME SRC="COLOR.HTM" SCROLLING=no NORESIZE>
    <FRAME SRC="COLOR.HTM" SCROLLING=no NORESIZE>
    <FRAME SRC="COLOR.HTM" SCROLLING=no NORESIZE>
    <FRAME SRC="COLOR.HTM" SCROLLING=no NORESIZE>
    <FRAME SRC="COLOR.HTM" SCROLLING=no NORESIZE>
    <FRAME SRC="COLOR.HTM" SCROLLING=no NORESIZE>
    <FRAME SRC="COLOR.HTM" SCROLLING=no NORESIZE>
    <FRAME SRC="COLOR.HTM" SCROLLING=no NORESIZE>
    <FRAME SRC="COLOR.HTM" SCROLLING=no NORESIZE>
</FRAMESET>
```

File: Game.htm

This file is the index file of the page. It contains all the JavaScript code and sets up the three row frameset of the page.

```
<SCRIPT LANGUAGE="JavaScript"><!--

// Feel free to modify or copy this Script
//or parts of it for non-commercial use, but please leave
//the comment in the code.
//
// written and (c) by Mathias Hoeschen, Tel./FAX:
//+49 30 6283675, maze@tfh-berlin.de,
//Home: http://www.tfh-berlin.de/~maze/

var r=0.0, g=0.0, b=0.0;
var id=0, high=0, low=0;
var s="F", left="F", right="F", string="FF",
var color_hr="FF", color_hg="FF", color_hb="FF";

function MakeArray(n){
this.length=n;
for(var i=1; i<=n; i++) this[i]=i-1;
return this
}
hex=new MakeArray(16);
hex[11]="A"; hex[12]="B"; hex[13]="C";
hex[14]="D"; hex[15]="E"; hex[16]="F";

function MakeStringArray(n){
this.length=n;
for(var i=1; i<=n; i++) this[i]="#";
return this
}
color=new MakeStringArray(10);
```

continues

```
function ToHex(x){
// Converts a int to hex (in the range 0...255)
high=x/16;
s=high+"";          //1.
s=s.substring(0,2);
//2. These three lines do the same as a 'trunc'-function
//(because there is no trunc, unfortunately!)
high=parseInt(s,10);    //3.
left=hex[high+1];       // left part of the hex-value
low=x-high*16;          // calculate the rest
s=low+"";               //1.
s=s.substring(0,2);     //2. see above
low=parseInt(s,10);     //3.
right=hex[low+1];       // right part of the hex-value
string=left+""+right;   // put the high and low together
return string;
}
function Fader(){
if(r>=Math.PI) r=0.0;
// let the smooth fading never end
if(g>=Math.PI) g=0.0;
if(b>=Math.PI) b=0.0;
color_hr=ToHex(255*Math.sin(r));
// to change the colors, edit the formula
(dont't let the value get greater than 255!)
color_hg=ToHex(255-255*Math.sin(g));
color_hb=ToHex(255*Math.sin(b));
r+=0.05;
// the greater the values=the faster the colors change
g+=0.04;
b+=0.033;
for(i=0; i<10; i++) color[10-i]=color[9-i];
color[1]="#"+color_hr+color_hg+color_hb;
for(i=0; i<10; i++){
frames[0].frames[i].document.bgColor=color[i+1];
frames[2].frames[i].document.bgColor=color[10-i];
}
id=setTimeout("Fader()",50);
}


//--></SCRIPT></HEAD>

<FRAMESET ROWS="20,*,20" onLoad="Fader();"
 onUnload="clearTimeout(id);">
<FRAME SRC="COL_ROW.HTM" SCROLLING=no NORESIZE>
<FRAME SRC="game_m.htm" MARGINWIDTH=0 MARGINHEIGHT=0 NORESIZE>
<FRAME SRC="COL_ROW.HTM" SCROLLING=no NORESIZE>
</FRAMESET>
```

Syntax Example

```
document.bgcolor='#67CD23'
```

Comments

JavaScript can be used to change some of the color properties of a page. The background color, text color, and link colors can all be accessed through the document object in JavaScript. In this script the background colors of the frames of this page are changed to create interesting effects.

Online Example

"Homepage of Maze-Games," by Mathias Hoeschen, email: **maze@tfh-berlin.de**

URL: **http://www.tfh-berlin.de/~maze/gamble/game.html**

Description

This page creates a series of 10 small frames at the top and bottom of the page. The colors are changed in these frames in a rotating fashion to create a flashing light effect. This is purely a cosmetic effect. It can be used to grab the user's attention.

Step-by-Step

1. There are multiple color properties in the document object. Normally these properties are declared once in the <BODY> tags of the document. To change them after the page is displayed, use JavaScript.

   Here are the color properties of the document object:

   alinkColor is the color of a link when it is selected.

   vlinkColor is the color of a visited link.

   bgColor is the background color.

   fgColor is the text color.

   linkColor is the color of an unselected link.

2. In this page, after the page is loaded and the frames are created, the *onLoad* event handler executes the *Fader()* function. This function is used to change the colors of all the small frames in a cyclical fashion. It is a recursive function that uses the *setTimeout* function to call itself after every 50 milliseconds. Three variables (*r*, *g*, and *b*) are incremented by a small number each time this function is called unless they are greater than pi.

3.
```
color_hr=ToHex(255*Math.sin(r));
color_hg=ToHex(255-255*Math.sin(g));
color_hb=ToHex(255*Math.sin(b));
```

The *Math.sin* method is used on the variables *r*, *g*, and *b* to get a number from 0 to 1 and this is multiplied by 255 to get a number from 0 to 255. The number obtained from *g* is subtracted from 255 to obtain a slightly different effect. This is then converted to the hex values using the *ToHex()* function and saved in variables *color_hr*, *color_hg* and *color_hb*. The use of the *Math.sin* method creates the cyclical pattern to the colors. Actually, any kind of method or formula giving a number from 0 to 255 is valid. You could change this formula to produce random numbers, if you desired the colors to be random.

4. *color[i]* is an array to store the colors for the 10 different frames. Using a *for* loop, the values are moved up one element in the array. The new color values are put in *color[1]*. Using another *for* loop, the values are stored to the *document.bgColor* properties of all the frames. This causes the colors to seem as if they are moving across the frames, almost in an animated fashion.

Related Techniques

Displaying Frames in a Document

Accessing Multiple Frames for a Cosmetic Effect

Checking if All Frames Are Loaded

Navigating Within a Frame

History Object

Type: JavaScript object

Used in: Document objects

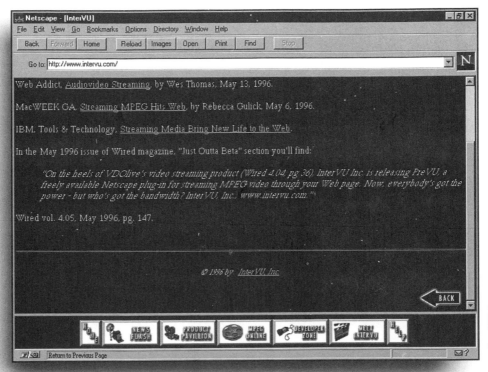

```
<A HREF="javascript:history.back()"
  onMouseOver="window.status='Return to Previous Page';
  return true"><IMG ALT="Back Button"
  ALIGN=RIGHT SRC="images/backarrow.gif" BORDER=0>
</A>
```

Syntax Example

```
history.go(-3)
```

Comments

The browser maintains lists of URLs that the user has visited. There is a list for the main page, which you can usually see as a menu choice in the browser. There are also lists for every frame in a page that are usually hard to access directly in the browser. The history object can jump to the URLs in any of these lists.

Online Example

"InterVU," by InterVU, Inc., email: **info@intervu.com**

URL: **http://www.intervu.com/**

Description

It is often difficult to navigate in a framed page. One typical scenario is that the user wants to go to the previous document in a frame. The user will press the BACK button on the browser and the browser will take the user to the previous page in the main window (the one before the framed page was loaded). This is not the user's desired effect. This page uses the history object to put JavaScript navigational buttons within the framed pages.

Step-by-Step

The history object has the following methods:

back()	Loads the previous URL in the history list.
forward()	Loads the next URL in the history list.
go(integer)	Loads a URL *integer* number positions away from the current URL.
history.length	Obtains the number of URLs in the history list.

This page implements a back button inside a frame. It does this by creating a link object that links to *javascript:history.back()*. Thus, when the button is clicked, the previous page will be loaded into the frame and not to the main window.

Related Techniques

Creative Page Navigation Using Frames

Page Navigation via Frames

Using Frames to Create Complex Navigation Schemes

Manipulating Information in Multiple Frames

Window Object (Parent Property)

Type: JavaScript object

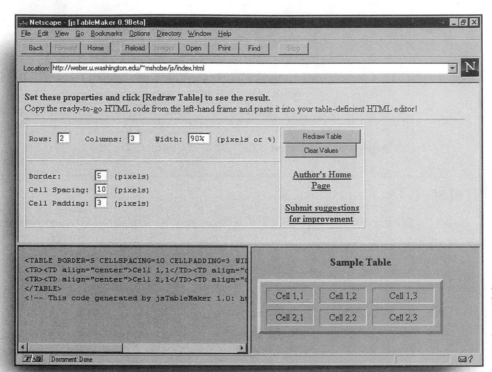

Matthew N. Shobe

File: index.html

```
<TITLE>jsTableMaker 0.9Beta</TITLE
</HEAD>
<FRAMESET ROWS="60%,*">
 <FRAME SRC="control.html" name="ctrl">
<FRAMESET COLS="50%,*">
 <FRAME SRC="preview.html" name="preview">
 <FRAME SRC="text.html" name="text">
</FRAMESET>
</FRAMESET>
```

File: control.html

```
<HTML>
<HEAD>
<SCRIPT LANGUAGE="JavaScript">
<!-- hide script from old browsers

function draw () { //a method for the table object

//loop through the two document frames;
// print an HTML table in the first, plain text in the second
for (var frameCount = 1; frameCount<=2; frameCount++) {

 parent.frames[frameCount].document.clear()
 parent.frames[frameCount].document.close()

 if (frameCount==2) {
parent.frames[frameCount].document.open("text/html")
  parent.frames[frameCount].document.writeln("
<H3 align=\"center\">Sample Table</H3>")

} else parent.frames[frameCount].document.open("text/plain")

parent.frames[frameCount].document.writeln ("
<TABLE BORDER="+this.border+" CELLSPACING="+this.cellSp
+" CELLPADDING="+this.cellPad+" WIDTH="+this.width+">")
 for (var rowCount = 1; rowCount<= (this.rows); rowCount++) {
        //outer row loop
  parent.frames[frameCount].document.write ("<TR>")
for (var colCount= 1; colCount <= (this.cols); colCount++) {
          //inner column loop
   parent.frames[frameCount].document.write ("
<TD align=\"center\">Cell "+(rowCount)+","+(colCount)+"</TD>")
  }
  parent.frames[frameCount].document.writeln ("</TR>")
 }
 parent.frames[frameCount].document.writeln ("</TABLE>")
parent.frames[frameCount].document.writeln ("<!-- This
code generated by jsTableMaker 1.0:
http://weber.u.washington.edu/~mshobe/js-->")

} //main loop bracket

} //draw close bracket

function table (rows,cols,width,border,cellSp,cellPad) {
//define table's properties
```

continues

91

```
 this.rows=rows
 this.cols=cols
 this.width=width
 this.border=border
 this.cellSp=cellSp
 this.cellPad=cellPad
//now define methods for table object
 this.draw=draw
}
//create the table object when the form is first loaded
//(a default table)
table1=new table(2,2,"100%",1,2,2)

//set values of controls equal to settings of 1st sample table
setCtrls()

//draw it
table1.draw()

// end script hiding -->
</SCRIPT>

<BODY BGCOLOR="beige">
<FORM name="tblControls">
<STRONG>Set these properties and click [Redraw Table] to see the
 result.</STRONG><BR>
Copy the ready-to-go HTML code from the left-hand frame and paste
it into your table-deficient HTML editor!

<HR NOSHADE>

<TABLE BORDER=1 CELLSPACING=1 CELLPADDING=4 WIDTH=75%>

<TR>
<TD><PRE>Rows: <INPUT TYPE="text" NAME="rows" SIZE=2
 onChange="table1.rows=this.value">
Columns: <INPUT TYPE="text" NAME="cols" SIZE=2
 onChange="table1.cols=this.value">
Width: <INPUT TYPE="text" NAME="tblWidth" SIZE=4
 onChange="table1.width=this.value"> (pixels or %)</PRE>
</TD>

<TD ROWSPAN="2" align="CENTER" valign="top">
<INPUT TYPE="button" NAME="btnDraw" VALUE="Redraw Table"
onClick="table1.draw()"><br>
<INPUT TYPE="reset" NAME="btnClear" VALUE="Clear Values">
<P><A TARGET="_top" HREF="../index.html">
<STRONG>Author's Home Page</STRONG></A>
```

```
<P><STRONG><A HREF="mailto:mshobe@u.washington.edu">
Submit suggestions for improvement</A></STRONG>
</TD>

</TR>

<TR>
<TD>
<PRE>Border:        <INPUT TYPE="text" NAME="tblBorder" SIZE=2
 onChange="table1.border=this.value"> (pixels)
Cell Spacing: <INPUT TYPE="text" NAME="tblCellSp" SIZE=2
 onChange="table1.cellSp=this.value"> (pixels)
Cell Padding: <INPUT TYPE="text" NAME="tblCellPad" SIZE=2
 onChange="table1.cellPad=this.value"> (pixels)</PRE>
</TD>
</TR>
</TABLE>
</BODY>

</HTML>
```

Syntax Example

```
parent.frames[1].document.clear()
```

Comments

In this framed page, you enter information in one frame of the page. Using this information, the *window.parent* property changes the display on the other frames. This demonstrates how you can display information from one frame to another.

Online Example

"jsTableMaker 0.9Beta," by Matthew N. Shobe, email: **Matthew_N._Shobe@ac.com**

URL: **http://weber.u.washington.edu/~mshobe/js/index.html**

Description

This page uses frames to generate a generic table and the HTML code used to create it from user supplied data. You can enter data in one frame specifying the size, dimensions, and formatting of a table. The JavaScript function will take that data to create your specified table and display it in another frame.

93

Step-by-Step

In the *index.html* file, three frames are created. All the JavaScript code is contained in the frame *control.html*. What is contained in the frames, *preview.html* and *text.html* do not matter. The JavaScript functions in *control.html* write a 2×2 frame and corresponding code to these frames as soon as the page fully loads.

In *control.html*, a new object is formed by using the *table()* function, created with six parameters. The statement *table1=new table* creates a custom object *(table1)*, six properties *(rows, cols, width, border, cellSp, cellPad)*, and one method *(date)*. Using the *onChange* event handler in the text objects allows the properties of *table1* to be modified. For example:

```
Cell Padding: <INPUT TYPE="text" NAME="tblCellPad" SIZE=2
onChange="table1.cellPad=this.value"> (pixels)</PRE>
```

With values attributed on *table1*, when the *"Redraw Table"* button is pushed, the *onClick* event handler calls the *table1.draw()* method.

In this method, the *window.parent* property is used to manipulate the other frames. *parent* refers to the previous frame *(index.html)*. *parent.frames[x]* will refer to the *x* numbered frame. In this case, *parent.frames[0]* would be *control.html*, *parent.frames[1]* would be *preview.html*, and *parent.frames[2]* would be *text.html*. The frames could also be accessed by names (if given). For example, *text.html* could be accessed by *parent.text*. By accessing the other frames, the function initializes the frames and displays the desired information specified by the user.

Notes

Note in the code that the *window.parent* property is simply referenced as *parent*. Because *window* is the top-level object, it never needs to be referenced in any command.

Related Techniques

Creating a Remote in a Separate Window

Accessing Multiple Frames for a Cosmetic Effect

Checking if All Frames Are Loaded

Accessing Multiple Frames for a Cosmetic Effect

Using the Frame Object

Type: JavaScript

Used in: Document object

João Aires de Sousa

File: index.html

Index.html is the main file that is loaded. It sets up all of the frames:

```
<FRAMESET ROWS="5%,90%,5%">
<FRAMESET COLS="33%,33%,33%">
<FRAME NAME="a1" SRC="a1.html" scrolling=no>
<FRAME NAME="a2"  SRC="a1.html" scrolling=no >
```

continues

```
<FRAME NAME="a3"  SRC="a1.html" scrolling=no>
</FRAMESET>
<FRAMESET COLS="5%,90%,5%">
<FRAME NAME="b1" SRC="a1.html" scrolling=no>
<FRAME NAME="b2"  SRC="b2.html" >
<FRAME NAME="b3"  SRC="a1.html" scrolling=no>
</FRAMESET>
<FRAMESET COLS="33%,33%,33%">
<FRAME NAME="c1"  SRC="a1.html" scrolling=no>
<FRAME NAME="c2"  SRC="a1.html" scrolling=no>
<FRAME NAME="c3"  SRC="a1.html" scrolling=no>
</FRAMESET>
</FRAMESET>
```

File: b2.html

This is the center frame that contains all the JavaScript code.

```
<head>
<! *********  Copyright (C) 1996 Joao Aires de Sousa  ************
All Rights Reserved
This code can be used provided that the origin is mentioned
and I am informed. email: jas@mail.fct.unl.pt
******************************************************************>
<script>


function MakeArray(n){
     this.length = n;
             for (var i= 1; i<=n; i++){
                     this[i] = 0}
                     return this
                     }

var p=0;
colors = new MakeArray(10);
     colors [1]='brown';
     colors [2]='yellow';
     colors [3]='orange';
     colors [4]='red';
     colors [5]='violet';
     colors [6]='purple';
     colors [7]='bordeaux';
     colors [8]='blue';
     colors [9]='green';
     colors [10]='white';
```

```
function surprise1 (){

parent.a2.document.bgColor='yellow' ;
parent.b1.document.bgColor='teal';


     .
     .
     .

parent.b1.document.bgColor='teal';
parent.a1.document.bgColor='teal';
timerID=setTimeout("surprise1()",50);
}


function surprise2(){
var m=0;
parent.a1.document.bgColor='teal';
parent.a2.document.bgColor='yellow' ;
for (var n= 1; n<150; n++){m++;m=0};
parent.c3.document.bgColor='teal';
parent.b3.document.bgColor='red' ;
for (var n= 1; n<150; n++){m++;m=0};


     .
     .
     .

for (var n= 1; n<150; n++){m++;m=0};
parent.c2.document.bgColor='teal';
parent.c3.document.bgColor='red';
for (var n= 1; n<150; n++){m++;m=0}
parent.a1.document.bgColor='teal';
parent.c3.document.bgColor='teal';
timerID=setTimeout("surprise2()",5);
}


function surprise3(){

parent.a1.document.bgColor=colors [Math.abs(p-1)] ;
parent.a2.document.bgColor=colors [Math.abs(p-2)] ;
parent.a3.document.bgColor=colors [Math.abs(p-3)] ;
parent.b3.document.bgColor=colors [Math.abs(p-4)] ;
parent.c3.document.bgColor=colors [Math.abs(p-5)] ;
parent.c2.document.bgColor=colors [Math.abs(p-6)] ;
parent.c1.document.bgColor=colors [Math.abs(p-7)] ;
parent.b1.document.bgColor=colors [Math.abs(p-8)] ;
```

continues

```
++p;if (p==9){p=0};
timerID=setTimeout("surprise3()",10);
}

function surprise4(){

var m=0;
parent.a1.document.bgColor='teal';
parent.a2.document.bgColor='yellow';
for (var n= 1; n<150; n++){m++;m=0};
parent.a2.document.bgColor='teal';
parent.a3.document.bgColor='yellow';
for (var n= 1; n<150; n++){m++;m=0};

        .
        .
        .

for (var n= 1; n<150; n++){m++;m=0};
parent.b1.document.bgColor='teal';
parent.a1.document.bgColor='yellow';
for (var n= 1; n<150; n++){m++;m=0}
parent.a1.document.bgColor='teal';
timerID=setTimeout("surprise4()",10);
}

</script>

</head>

<body bgcolor="teal"  onLoad="surprise3()">
<center>
<pre>

</pre>
<FONT COLOR="white"><h2 ><b><i>Welcome to Java Flash !
</b></i></h2></FONT>
<p>
<h3> Please try the outstanding JavaScript flashes:</h3>

<form>
<INPUT TYPE="button" VALUE="Flash 1" OnClick="surprise2()">

<INPUT TYPE="button" VALUE="Flash 2" OnClick="surprise1()">

<INPUT TYPE="button" VALUE="Flash 3" OnClick="p=0;surprise3()">

<INPUT TYPE="button" VALUE="Flash 4" OnClick="p=0;surprise4()">
</form>


<form>
<INPUT TYPE="button" VALUE="STOP" OnClick="clearTimeout(timerID)">
</form>
```

File: a1.html; this is a blank page.

Syntax Example

```
<FRAME NAME="c3"  SRC="a1.html" scrolling=no>
```

Comments

Using small frames around a document with JavaScript can create some interesting cosmetic effects. You can change the background colors or add text to the frames. This can be used to signal users when they perform an action.

Online Example

"JAVA Flash," by João Aires de Sousa, email: **jas@mail.fct.unl.pt**

URL: **http://www.dq.fct.unl.pt/qoa/java**

Description

This page contains eight small frames on the border of the window. JavaScript is used to change the background color of these frames in various patterns. Buttons on the middle frame are used to control the functions that change the colors.

Step-by-Step

The frames are created in the *index.html* file. The framesets are nested to achieve the desired effect. The outer frame splits the window into a 5% top, a 5% bottom, and a 90% middle. The top and bottom frames are divided into columns by thirds and are named a1, a2, a3 and c1, c2, c3 respectively. The middle frame is also split into columns but in a 5%, 90%, 5% format. These frames are named b1, b2, and b3. The large center frame is loaded with the file *b2.html*, which contains all the JavaScript and buttons controlling the JavaScript. The rest of the frames are loaded with the file *a1.html*, which is a blank file.

With all the frames given names, their properties can be accessed in JavaScript. For example, to change the background color in the upper-left frame, you can use the command:

```
parent.a1.document.bgColor='yellow';
```

The four functions in this page manipulate the background color of the frames in various ways. All of the functions are recursive. That is, they use the *setTimeout* method to call their functions again after a specified delay. The user can stop the functions using a button on the center frame. The *onClick* event hander of this button executes the command:

```
clearTimeout(timerID)
```

timerID is the variable created from the *setTimeout* methods in the recursive functions. The *clearTimeout* method uses this variable to cancel the *setTimeout* operations. This stops the recursive process of the functions. Delays are also inserted in some of the functions by using *for* loops that don't do anything. For example:

```
for (var n= 1; n<150; n++){m++;m=0};
```

These statements serve no actual purpose. The amount of time that it takes to execute these statments inserts a small delay into the JavaScript.

Related Techniques

Manipulating Information in Multiple Frames

Navigating Within a Frame

Page Navigation via Frames

User-Customized Links in a Frame

Using JavaScript Cookies

Type: JavaScript

Used in: Document object

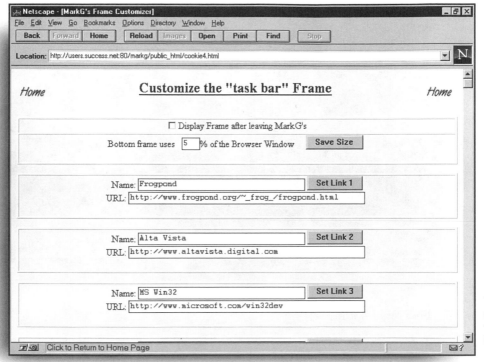

Mark Gamber

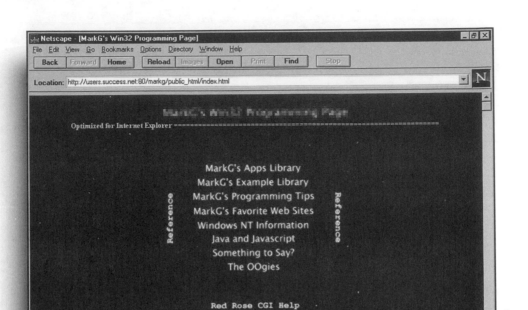

Mark Gamber

File: cookie4.html

This page enables you to customize the links in the qlink.html frame in the main page:

```
<script Language="JavaScript">

function getCookieVal( offset )
{
var endstr = document.cookie.indexOf( ";", offset );
if( endstr == -1 )
endstr = document.cookie.length;
return unescape( document.cookie.substring( offset, endstr ) );
}
```

```
function GetCookie( name )
{
var arg = name + "=";
var alen = arg.length;
var clen = document.cookie.length;
var i = 0;
while( i < clen )
{
var j = i + alen;
if( document.cookie.substring( i, j ) == arg )
return getCookieVal( j );

i = document.cookie.indexOf( " ", i ) + 1;
if( i == 0 ) break;
}
return null;
}


function SetCookie( name, value )
{
var exp = new Date();
var argv = SetCookie.arguments;
var argc = SetCookie.arguments.length;
exp.setTime( exp.getTime() + ( 1000 * ( 24 * 60 * 60 * 1000 ) ) );

var expires = ( argc > 2 ) ? argv[ 2 ] : exp;
var path = ( argc > 3 ) ? argv[ 3 ] : null;
var domain = ( argc > 4 ) ? argv[ 4 ] : null;
var secure = ( argc > 5 ) ? argv[ 5 ] : false;
document.cookie = name + "=" + escape( value ) +
( (expires == null ) ? "" : ( "; expires=" + expires.toGMTString()))+
( (path == null ) ? "" : ( "; path=" + path ) ) +
( (domain == null ) ? "" : ( "; domain=" + domain ) ) +
( (secure == true ) ? "; secure" : "" );
}


function DeleteCookie( name )
{
var exp = new Date();
exp.setTime( exp.getTime() - 1001 * ( 24 * 60 * 60 * 1000 ) );
var cval = GetCookie( name );
SetCookie( name, cval, exp )
}
```

continues

```
function DeleteAllCookies()
{
DeleteCookie( "TagName1" );
DeleteCookie( "TagURL1" );
DeleteCookie( "TagName2" );
DeleteCookie( "TagURL2" );
DeleteCookie( "TagName3" );
DeleteCookie( "TagURL3" );
DeleteCookie( "TagName4" );
DeleteCookie( "TagURL4" );
DeleteCookie( "TagName5" );
DeleteCookie( "TagURL5" );
DeleteCookie( "TagName6" );
DeleteCookie( "TagURL6" );

DeleteCookie( "KeepFrame" );

document.geturl1.nametext.value = "Frogpond";
document.geturl1.urltext.value =
 "http://www.frogpond.org/~_frog_/frogpond.html";
document.geturl2.nametext.value = "Alta Vista";
document.geturl2.urltext.value = "http://www.altavista.digital.com";
document.geturl3.nametext.value = "MS Win32";
document.geturl3.urltext.value = "http://www.microsoft.com/win32dev";
document.geturl4.nametext.value = "Lancaster Weather";
document.geturl4.urltext.value =
 "http://www.intellicast.com/weather/lns";
document.geturl5.nametext.value = "MS KBase";
document.geturl5.urltext.value = "http://www.microsoft.com/KB";
document.geturl6.nametext.value = "IDenticard";
document.geturl6.urltext.value = "http://www.identicard.com";
}

</script>


<table border=1 width="100%">
<td align="center">
<FORM NAME="geturl1">
Name: <INPUT NAME="nametext" SIZE=35>
<INPUT TYPE="BUTTON" NAME="button1" VALUE="Set Link 1"
 onClick="SetCookie( 'TagName1', geturl1.nametext.value );
 SetCookie( 'TagURL1', geturl1.urltext.value );"><BR>
URL: <INPUT NAME="urltext" SIZE=50 VALUE="http://">
</FORM>
</td></table>

<BR>
```

```
<table border=1 width="100%">
<td align="center">
<FORM NAME="geturl2">
Name: <INPUT NAME="nametext" SIZE=35>
<INPUT TYPE="BUTTON" NAME="button1" VALUE="Set Link 2"
 onClick="SetCookie( 'TagName2', geturl2.nametext.value );
 SetCookie( 'TagURL2', geturl2.urltext.value );"><BR>
URL: <INPUT NAME="urltext" SIZE=50 VALUE="http://">
</FORM>
</td></table>
```

File: qlink.html

A frame in the main page loads this file. This file displays your customized links (if given):

```
<script Language="JavaScript">
<!--
function getCookieVal( offset )
{
var endstr = document.cookie.indexOf( ";", offset );
if( endstr == -1 )
endstr = document.cookie.length;
return unescape( document.cookie.substring( offset, endstr ) );
}


function GetCookie( name )
{
var arg = name + "=";
var alen = arg.length;
var clen = document.cookie.length;
var i = 0;
while( i < clen )
{
var j = i + alen;
if( document.cookie.substring( i, j ) == arg )
return getCookieVal( j );

i = document.cookie.indexOf( " ", i ) + 1;
if( i == 0 ) break;
}
return null;
}
```

continues

```
//-->
</script>
</HEAD>

<BODY BGCOLOR="FFFFC0" LINK="000000" VLINK="000000" ALINK="000000">
<FONT SIZE=2 COLOR="000000">

<CENTER>

<script language="JavaScript">
<!--
var i = 0;
var newItem = "";
var newURL = "";

var KeepBox = GetCookie( "KeepFrame" );

for( i = 1; i < 7; i++ )
{
newItem = GetCookie( "TagName" + i );
if( newItem != "" )
{
newURL = GetCookie( "TagURL" + i );
if( newURL != "" && newURL != null )
{
document.write( "<A HREF=" );
document.write( newURL );
if( KeepBox == "true" )
document.write( " target='title'>" + newItem + "</A>    " );
else
document.write( " target='_top'>" + newItem + "</A>    " );
}
}
if( newItem == "" || newItem == null )
{
if( i == 1 )
{
if( KeepBox == "true" )
document.write( "<A HREF='http://www.frogpond.org/~_frog_/
frogpond.html' target='title'>Frogpond</A>    " );
else
document.write( "<A HREF='http://www.frogpond.org/~_frog_/
frogpond.html' target='_top'>Frogpond</A>    " );
}
if( i == 2 )
{
```

```
if( KeepBox == "true" )
document.write( "<A HREF='http://www.altavista.digital.com'
 target='title'>Alta Vista</A>    " );
else
document.write( "<A HREF='http://www.altavista.digital.com'
 target='_top'>Alta Vista</A>    " );
}
```

Syntax Example

```
SetCookie( 'TagURL1', geturl1.urltext.value );
```

Comments

Cookies allow JavaScript to store and recall information. This page uses cookies to create a personal bookmark list within a frame on a page. If your page is updated frequently and the user visits often, the user can use the script to customize how she navigates through your page.

Online Example

"MarkG's Frame Customizer," by Mark Gamber, email: **markg@users.success.net**

URL: **http://users.success.net:80/markg/public_html/cookie4.html**

Description

A small frame on the bottom of this main page contains a variety of links. You can access a separate page to change the current links to other links that you may want to view. Within the separate page are text objects listing the current names and URLs of the links. You can change the values in the text objects and press a button to save the values to a cookie. The frame on the main page checks for this cookie file, and if found, uses the links from the cookie.

Step-by-Step

The file *cookie4.html* enables you to manipulate the links. Previously written cookie functions such as *SetCookie( )* do all the work needed to use cookies. Within this page are 14 text objects for the name and URL of seven links. Every link has a button that will set the link. An *OnClick* event handler calls the *setCookie( )* function twice. If X is the number of the link to be stored, the name of the link is stored in a cookie called *TagNameX*, while the URL is stored in a cookie called *TagURLX*.

Given the stored cookies of the new links, the file *qlink.html* will display those links. A *for* loop is used to count from 1 to 7 (representing the number of links). For each number in the loop, it verifies that there is a cookie stored for that link. If there is a cookie, then that link is displayed. Otherwise, a series of if statements are used to determine the default link to be displayed.

Related Techniques

Loading Pages into Frames

Navigating Within a Frame

Controlling Navigation Options with Frames

Page Navigation via Frames

Frame Object

Type: JavaScript object

Used in: Window objects

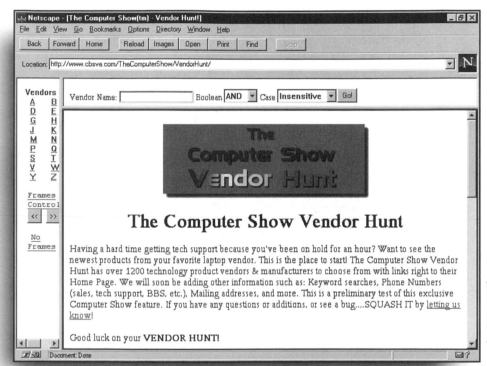

File: index.htm

```
<FRAMESET COLS="80,*">
<FRAME SRC="side.htm" NAME="sidemenu" SCROLLING="auto"
MARGINWIDTH="1" MARGINHEIGHT="1">

<FRAMESET ROWS="45,*">
<FRAME SRC="topmenu.htm" NAME="topmenu" SCROLLING="no"
MARGINWIDTH="1" MARGINHEIGHT="1">
<FRAME SRC="mainmenu.htm" NAME="mainmenu" SCROLLING="auto"


MARGINWIDTH="10" MARGINHEIGHT="10">
```

File: side.htm

```
function goback ()
{
parent.mainmenu.history.go(-1);
}
function goforward ()
{
parent.mainmenu.history.go(1);
}
function home ()
{
parent.mainmenu.location.href
="http://www.cbsva.com/TheComputerShow/VendorHunt/mainmenu.htm";
}


<A HREF="http://www.cbsva.com/TheComputerShow/VendorHunt/a.htm"
 TARGET="mainmenu">A</A>
<A HREF="http://www.cbsva.com/TheComputerShow/VendorHunt/b.htm"
 TARGET="mainmenu">B</A>
<A HREF="http://www.cbsva.com/TheComputerShow/VendorHunt/c.htm"
TARGET="mainmenu">C</A>
<A HREF="http://www.cbsva.com/TheComputerShow/VendorHunt/
framehlp.htm" TARGET="mainmenu">Frames</A>
<A HREF="http://www.cbsva.com/TheComputerShow/VendorHunt/
framehlp.htm" TARGET="mainmenu">Control</A>
<INPUT TYPE="button" VALUE="<<" onClick="goback()">
<INPUT TYPE="button" VALUE=">>" onClick="goforward()">
```

File: topmenu.htm

```
<BODY BGCOLOR="#FFFFFF" LINK="#FF0000" VLINK="#FF0000"
ALINK="#FF0000"> <BASE TARGET="mainmenu">
<FONT  SIZE=-1><form method=POST action="http://
www.cbsva.com/cbsva/cgi-bin/vendor-search.pl">
Vendor Name: <input type=text name="terms" size=15> Boolean
<select name="boolean"><option>AND<option>OR</select>
Case <select name="case"><option>Insensitive<option>Sensitive
</select><input type=submit value="Go!">
</form></FONT>
</BODY>
```

Syntax Example

```
<A HREF="http://www.xyz.com/a.htm" TARGET="frame1">
```

Comments

A good use for frames in a page is to use some small frames to give navigation tools to a large frame. This way a user can click a link in one of the small frames and the page will load into the large frame. The small frame will still be there so you can easily access it. Check out some of the pages in the "Related Techniques" section for some other ideas on page navigation in frames.

Online Example

"The Computer Show—Vendor Hunt!," by The Computer Guys

URL: **http://www.cbsva.com/TheComputerShow/VendorHunt/**

Description

This page has three frames, one main frame, and two small frames. One small frame is on the top of the page, whereas the other small frame is on the left side of the page. The top frame has a form that accesses a CGI search engine to navigate within the main frame. The left frame has navigational links and JavaScript forward and backward buttons for the main frame.

Step-by-Step

1. In the *topmenu* frame, use a form with a text object and two select objects to access a CGI script. To display the resulting page to the *mainmenu* frame instead of the whole page, use the command *<BASE TARGET="mainmenu">*.

2. In the *sidemenu* frame, create various links for each letter of the alphabet. Each link goes to a specific section of the index.

3. Use the *TARGET="mainmenu"* command in the anchor tag to indicate that this page should be loaded into the *mainmenu* frame. Otherwise, the page would be loaded in the current frame.

Also include buttons that can be used to go backward and forward in the *mainmenu* frame. These buttons are different from the backward and forward buttons on the browser, because they control the whole window, not just the frame. These buttons have *onClick* event handlers that execute functions which use the history object to navigate within the frame.

Notes

Within an anchor tag for a link, you can use a *TARGET="_top"* command to erase the frames and load the next page into the full browser window. For example, all the links that exit your group of pages like:

```
<A HREF="http://www.yahoo.com/" TARGET="_top"> Yahoo! </A>
```

should use this so the frames will be removed. Because the frames probably don't have much use outside your domain they would not be wanted by the user.

Related Techniques

Flashing Color Over Frames

Navigating Within a Frame

Loading a Page via a Selection List

Creative Page Navigation Using Frames

Checking if All Frames Are Loaded

Frame Object

Type: JavaScript object

Used in: Window objects

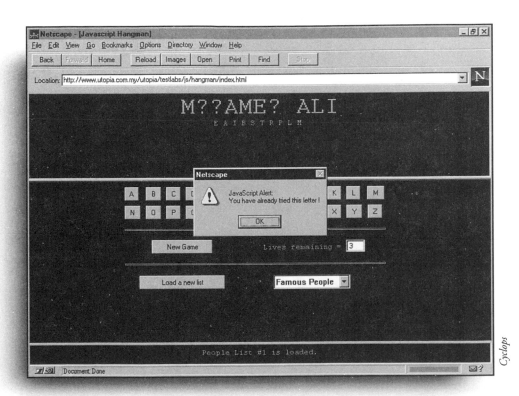

File: index.html

```
var floaded0 = false;
var floaded1 = false;
var floaded2 = false;

// each subframe makes these yes when they load.
```

continues

```
<FRAMESET ROWS = "150,*,40">
  <FRAME SRC = "main.html" NAME = "main" MARGINHEIGHT = 1 NORESIZE
 SCROLLING = NO>
<FRAME SRC = "control.html" NAME = "control" MARGINHEIGHT = 1 >
  <FRAME SRC = "movies.html" NAME = "words" MARGINHEIGHT = 1
 NORESIZE SCROLLING = NO>
</FRAMESET>
```

File: movies.html

```
function comeondown() {
    window.parent.floaded2 = true;
}


<BODY BGCOLOR="#000000"
  TEXT="#AAAACC"
  VLINK = "#A0A0A0"
  LINK = "#D0D0D0"  onLoad = "comeondown()">
```

File: control.html

```
function junk() {}

function init() {
  var chkbadg = document.alphabet.selectlists.selectedIndex + 1;
    badguesses = easelevel[chkbadg];
    presenturl = wlarray[chkbadg];

    rembad = badguesses;
    while (window.parent.floaded2 == false) {
        timerID = setTimeout ('junk()',1000);
        }
    update();
}
<BODY BGCOLOR = "#000000" TEXT="#AAAACC" onLoad = "init()">
```

Syntax Example

```
window.parent.flag1 = true
```

114

Comments

Sometimes in pages with multiple frames, an event handler on one frame will access an object on another frame. If this event handler is executed before the other frame is loaded, an error might occur, stopping the JavaScript. This script prevents such an error from occurring.

Online Example

"Javascript Hangman," by Cyclops, email: **cyclops@utopia.com.my**

URL: **http://www.utopia.com.my/utopia/testlabs/js/hangman/index.html**

Description

This page implements the game of hangman using JavaScript. One frame contains a variable word list. If the new game button is pressed on the main window before this frame is loaded, an error occurs. Therefore, the main frame script will not execute until the word list frame is loaded.

Step-by-Step

1. The three frames of this page are created in the file *index.html*.

2. Three Boolean variables initialized to false are declared representing whether each frame has loaded.

   In the file *movies.html*, there is an *onLoad* event handler in the body tags. This event handler executes a function that sets the Boolean variable in *index.html* to true. This lets the other frames know that the *movies.html* frame is loaded.

   In the frame *control.html*, the *onLoad* event handler executes an initialization function called *init()*. Within this function is a *while* loop that loops until the Boolean variable associated with *movies.html* is true. After the loop exits the JavaScript continues and the buttons can then be accessed.

Related Techniques

Manipulating Information in Multiple Frames

User-Customized Links in a Frame

Loading Pages into Frames

115

Creative Page Navigation Using Frames

Frame Object

Type: JavaScript object

Used in: Window objects

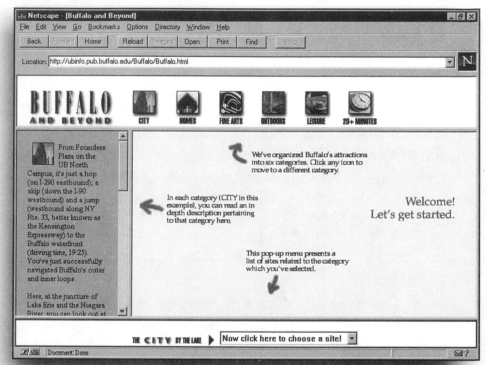

SUNY Buffalo

File: Buffalo.html

```
<FRAMESET ROWS="96, *">
  <FRAME SRC="Navigation.html" NORESIZE SCROLLING=no NAME="Navigation">
  <FRAME SRC="City/Intro.html" NORESIZE SCROLLING=auto NAME="Display">
</FRAMESET>
```

File: Navigation.html

```
<TABLE WIDTH=635 HEIGHT=100%>
<TR>
<TD ALIGN=middle VALIGN=middle>
<IMG WIDTH=154 HEIGHT=68 SRC="Standard/Logo.gif">
</TD>
<TD>
<A HREF="City/City.html" TARGET="Display" onMouseOver="self.status=
'Click here for exciting places within the City of Buffalo.'; return
true"><IMG WIDTH=70 HEIGHT=68 BORDER=0 SRC="Standard/Button1.gif">
</A>
<A HREF="Homes/Homes.html" TARGET="Display" onMouseOver="self.status=
'Click here for popular residential areas around Buffalo.';  return
true"><IMG WIDTH=70 HEIGHT=68 BORDER=0 SRC="Standard/Button2.gif">
</A>
<A HREF="FineArts/FineArts.html" TARGET="Display" onMouseOver=
"self.status='Click here for offerings of art and music.';  return
true"><IMG WIDTH=70 HEIGHT=68 BORDER=0 SRC="Standard/Button3.gif">
</A>
<A HREF="Outdoors/Outdoors.html" TARGET="Display" onMouseOver=
"self.status='Click here for popular outdoor destinations.';  return
 true"><IMG WIDTH=70 HEIGHT=68 BORDER=0 SRC="Standard/Button4.gif">
</A>
<A HREF="Leisure/Leisure.html" TARGET="Display" onMouseOver=
"self.status='Click here for a large collection of shops,
restaurants, and other places to visit on a weekend.';  return
true"><IMG WIDTH=70 HEIGHT=68 BORDER=0 SRC="Standard/Button5.gif">
</A>
<A HREF="20Plus/20Plus.html" TARGET="Display" onMouseOver=
"self.status='Click here for destinations beyond 20 minutes away.';
  return true"><IMG WIDTH=70 HEIGHT=68 BORDER=0
SRC="Standard/Button6.gif"></A>
</TD>
</TR>
</TABLE>
```

File: City/Intro.html

```
<FRAMESET ROWS="*,39">

    <FRAMESET COLS="200, *">
    <FRAME SRC="Text.html" SCROLLING=auto NAME="DisplayLeft">
    <FRAME SRC="Info.html" SCROLLING=auto NAME="DisplayRight">
    </FRAMESET>

    <FRAME SRC="BarNew.html" SCROLLING=no NAME="DisplayBottom">

</FRAMESET>
```

File: City/BarNew.html

```
<SCRIPT LANGUAGE="JavaScript">


<!-- Hide JavaScript code from older browsers
function update(form){
if(form.select1[0].selected){
  parent.DisplayRight.location.assign('Info.html')}
if(form.select1[1].selected){
  parent.DisplayRight.location.assign('1.html')
  parent.DisplayBottom.location.assign('Bar.html')}
if(form.select1[2].selected){
  parent.DisplayRight.location.assign('2.html')
  parent.DisplayBottom.location.assign('Bar.html')}
if(form.select1[3].selected){
  parent.DisplayRight.location.assign('3.html')
  parent.DisplayBottom.location.assign('Bar.html')}
if(form.select1[4].selected){
  parent.DisplayRight.location.assign('4.html')
  parent.DisplayBottom.location.assign('Bar.html')}
if(form.select1[5].selected){
  parent.DisplayRight.location.assign('5.html')
  parent.DisplayBottom.location.assign('Bar.html')}
if(form.select1[6].selected){
  parent.DisplayRight.location.assign('6.html')
  parent.DisplayBottom.location.assign('Bar.html')}
if(form.select1[7].selected){
  parent.DisplayRight.location.assign('7.html')
  parent.DisplayBottom.location.assign('Bar.html')}
if(form.select1[8].selected){
  parent.DisplayRight.location.assign('8.html')
  parent.DisplayBottom.location.assign('Bar.html')}
}<!-- Done hiding JavaScript -->


</SCRIPT>

<BODY>
<BODY BGCOLOR="ffffff">

<CENTER>
<FORM>
<IMG WIDTH=148 HEIGHT=25 ALIGN=middle SRC="Graphics/Arrow.gif">
<SELECT NAME="select1" onChange="update(this.form )">
<OPTION SELECTED>Now click here to choose a site!
<OPTION>Darwin Martin House
<OPTION>The Guaranty Building
```

```
<OPTION>The Cargill Grain Elevator
<OPTION>The Museum of Science
<OPTION>Buffalo Zoo
<OPTION>The Historical Society
<OPTION>NorthAmeriCare Park
<OPTION>Marine Midland Arena
</SELECT>
</FORM>
</CENTER>
```

Syntax Example

```
parent.DisplayBottom.location.assign('Bar.html')
```

Comments

Sometimes a Web site with excellent content is avoided if not presented in a pleasing manner or easy to navigate. This example is organized in such a way to be enjoyable to browse through. It is presented in an organized manner where each section is clearly defined. Each section is navigated in the same manner but the content is different and doesn't overlap.

It is frustrating to go to a page and not know how to find the information you want. It is also considered poor design if a user can encounter the same information through several links within the same page. This can be confusing to the user.

See the "Related Techniques" section for other methods of page navigation with frames.

Online Example

"Buffalo and Beyond," by SUNY Buffalo, email: **eUB@pub.buffalo.edu**

URL: **http://ubinfo.pub.buffalo.edu/Buffalo/Buffalo.html**

Description

This page presents a virtual tour of the city of Buffalo. On the top-most frame are six buttons corresponding to six sections of the site. For each section of the site a new page is loaded into the bottom most frame, which then contains a section list to navigate within that section.

Step-by-Step

1. The main file *Buffalo.html* creates two frames. The top frame *Navigation.html* named *Navigation* contains six navigational images for each section of the page. This frame does not change throughout the tour. The bottom frame, named *Display*, changes for each section. The bottom frame starts out with an introductory frame in the City section called *City/Intro.html.*

2. Within the *Navigation* frame are six image links. Each link refers to a different section of the site. The files for each section are contained in a different directory. Within each link is a *TARGET="Display"* parameter so that the new section will be displayed in the lower frame. Also a *OnMouseOver* event handler executes a statement in the anchor tags. The statement assigns a string to the *self.status* window property to display a meaningful message on the status bar.

3. The *Display* frame is always of the same form for each section of the page. It has three frames. The initial frameset is defined in the file *City/Intro.html.* The left frame named *DisplayLeft* contains text about that section. The right frame named *DisplayRight* contains pictures and text to be viewed in that section. The bottom frame named *DisplayBottom* allows the users to navigate through that section.

4. The *DisplayBottom* frame initially is loaded with the file *City/BarNew.html.* This frame contains a select object where various places within the section can be explored. An *OnChange* event handler within the select object executes the *update()* function passing *this.form.* This function contains a series of *if* statements for each selection in the select object. Each *if* statement uses the *location.assign* method to load new files in the *DisplayRight* and *DisplayBottom* frames. Note that the file *Bar.html* is loaded into the *DisplayBottom* frame. This file is similar to the *BarNew.html* file except the *"Now click here to choose a site!"* selection is not given.

Notes

All the images on this page are given *WIDTH* and *HEIGHT* parameters. For example,

```
<IMG WIDTH=70 HEIGHT=68 BORDER=0 SRC="Standard/Button2.gif">
```

This is a good idea for all types of pages so that the browser can create space for the image and the text around the image can be displayed while the image loads. Including these parameters when using JavaScript is important because sometimes the image will not appear if these parameters are not given. This is just a bug in the current versions of JavaScript.

Related Techniques

Page Navigation via Frames

Flashing Color Over Frames

Navigating Within a Frame

Displaying an HTML Practice Window

Document Object

Type: JavaScript object

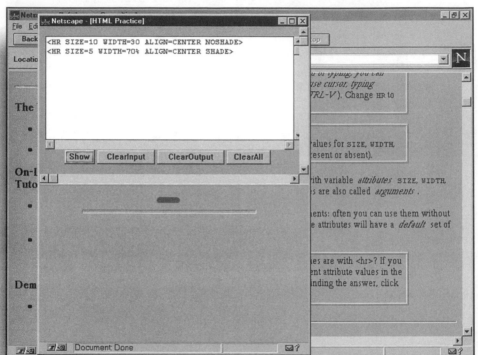

InfoAccess

File: htmlintr.htm

```
function PracticeWindow() {
window.open("try.htm","MainWindow","status,resizable,
height=538,width=460")
}
```

File: try.htm

```
<frameset rows="50%, 50%">
   <frame src="input.htm" name="frame1">
   <frame src="output.htm" name="frame2">
</frameset>
```

File: input.htm

```
<script>

parent.frame2.document.open()

function DoHTML() {
parent.frame2.document.write (document.frm_try.txt_try.value + "<P>")
}

function ClearAll () {
parent.frame1.document.frm_try.txt_try.value=""
ClearOutput()
}

function ClearInput () {
parent.frame1.document.frm_try.txt_try.value=""
}

function ClearOutput () {
parent.frame2.document.close()
parent.frame2.document.open()
parent.frame2.document.write ("<P>")
parent.frame2.document.close()
//parent.frame2.document.bgColor="CBCBCB"
}
</script>
<BODY BGCOLOR="8AC4C0" TEXT="000000" LINK="000000" VLINK="000000"
ALINK="000000">

<form name="frm_try">
<TEXTAREA NAME="txt_try" align=center ROWS="10" COLS="52"></TEXTAREA>
<center>
<INPUT TYPE="button" NAME="do" VALUE="Show" SIZE="50"
ONCLICK="DoHTML()">
<INPUT TYPE="button" NAME="clear" VALUE="ClearInput"
SIZE="50" ONCLICK="ClearInput()">
<INPUT TYPE="button" NAME="clear" VALUE="ClearOutput"
SIZE="50" ONCLICK="ClearOutput()">
```

continues

123

```
<INPUT TYPE="button" NAME="clear" VALUE="ClearAll"
SIZE="50" ONCLICK="ClearAll()">
</center>
</form>
</BODY>
```

File: output.htm

```
<BODY BGCOLOR="CBCBCB" TEXT="000000" LINK="000000" VLINK="000000"
ALINK="000000">
</BODY>
```

Syntax Example

```
parent.frame2.document.write (document.frm_try.txt_try.value + "<P>")
```

Comments

The document object can be accessed from various frames to display data from one frame to another. This allows the JavaScript functions in one frame not to be restricted to that frame. The functions can access the objects and property in any of the frames.

Online Example

"An Introductory HTML Tutorial," by InfoAccess, email: **infoxs@ozemail.com.au**

URL: **http://www.ozemail.com.au/infoxs/tutorials/htmlintr.htm**

Description

This page describes a variety of HTML techniques. An option to bring up a new window enables you to test HTML code. The code is written in one frame in the window, but it is displayed in another frame.

Step-by-Step

The new window is created in the file *htmlintr.htm.* The *window.open* method is used to display the file *try.htm* in a window. The new window is a framed page with the file *input.htm* in the top frame *(frame1)* and the file *output.htm* in the bottom frame *(frame2).* The *output.htm* file contains no data. It is only used to display data written to it by the *input.htm* file.

The top frame in the new window contains a text area object called *txt_try.* This is where you will enter the HTML code that you want to display. Four button objects with *OnClick* event handlers access functions concerning the frames. All of these objects are contained within the same form, called *frm_try.*

At the start of *input.htm* is the command *parent.frame2.document.open().* Using the *open* method, you are then able to use the *write* and *writeln* methods to display to the bottom frame. The *DoHTML()* function demonstrates this. It accesses the value of the *txt_try* text area object and uses the *write* method to display it to *frame2.* The *ClearInput()* function writes a null string to the text area object. The *ClearOutput()* function is used to clear all the data in the bottom frame. The document methods are used to *close* the bottom frame, *open* it again, write a *<P>* tag to it, and *close* it again to clear the frame. The *ClearAll()* function performs the same operations as the *ClearInput()* and *ClearOutput()* functions.

Related Techniques

Accessing Multiple Frames for a Cosmetic Effect

Manipulating Information in Multiple Frames

Checking if All Frames Are Loaded

Creating a Memory Game

Using Variables and Operators: Boolean

Type: JavaScript data type

Used in: JavaScript code

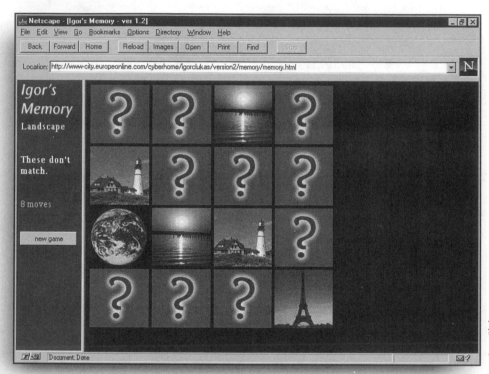

Igor Clukas

```
<SCRIPT language="JavaScript">

// generic object maker prepares an empty array of n items
function makeArray() {
    return this
}
```

```
// create board array
var board = new makeArray()
for (i = 0; i < 8; i++) {
   board[i] = "" + (i+1)
   board[i+8] = "" + (i+1)
}
// shake well (not too many global vars, hope there'll
   be soon random for all platforms)
function shakeBoard() {
   var c = ""
   now = new Date()
   rand = 0

   for (i = 30; i < 150; i++) {
      rand = Math.round(now.getTime() / i) % 16
      for (j = 0; j <= rand; j++) {
         c = board[j % 15]
         board[j % 15] = board[(j+1) % 15]
         board[(j+1) % 15] = c
      }
   }
}

shakeBoard()

// create displayed board array
var displayedBoard = new makeArray()
for (var i = 0; i < 16; i++) {
   displayedBoard[i] = "0"
}

var moves = 0
var oneOpen = false
var done = false
var good = false
var lastCard = 16
var beforeLastCard = 16


// utility function to extract the pathname to the current document
function getPath(URL) {
   return URL.substring(0,(URL.lastIndexOf("/") + 1))
}
```

continues

```
// function checking whether or not to close the last two cards
function checkCard(card) {
   if (oneOpen) {
      good = (board[card] == board[lastCard])
   } else {
      if (board[lastCard] != board[beforeLastCard]) {
         displayedBoard[lastCard] = "0"
         displayedBoard[beforeLastCard] = "0"
      } // end if
   } // end if
}


// function opening the new card
function setCard(card) {

   displayedBoard[card] = board[card]

   // make history
   beforeLastCard = lastCard
   lastCard = card
   oneOpen = !oneOpen
}


// function displaying the actual board
function showBoard() {
   var result = ""
   var baseRef = getPath(self.titlebar.document.location)
   var titleURL = ""

   if (oneOpen) {
      titleURL = "even.html"
   } else {
      titleURL = "odd.html"
   } // end if

   done = true

   result = "<HTML><BODY bgcolor=#000040 text=#FFFFFF>"
   result += "<BASE HREF='" + baseRef + "' target='titlebar'>"
   result += "<TABLE cellpadding=0 cellspacing=3>"
   for (var i = 0; i < 4; i++) {
      result += "<TR>"
      for (var j = 0; j < 4; j++) {
         xy = (i*4+j)
         result += "<TD>"
```

```
                if (displayedBoard[xy] != board[xy]) {
                    result += "<A HREF='" + titleURL + "'"
                    result += " onClick='top.clickCard(" + xy + ")'>"
                } // end if
                result += "<IMG width=100 height=100 border=0 SRC='"
                result += displayedBoard[xy] + ".jpg'>"
                if (displayedBoard[xy] != board[xy]) {
                    result += "</A>"
                    done = false
                } // end if
                result += "</TD>"
            }
            result += "</TR>"
        }
        result += "</TABLE></BODY></HTML>"

        self.disp.document.open()
        self.disp.document.writeln(result)
        self.disp.document.close()
}


// main function evaluating clicked card
function clickCard(coord) {
    checkCard(coord)
    setCard(coord)
    moves++
}

// end script hiding -->
</SCRIPT>
```

Syntax Example

```
if (((year % 4 == 0) && (year % 100 != 0))
    || (year % 400 == 0))
        FebDays = 29
```

Comments

The Boolean data type is the logic data type in JavaScript. Boolean variables have only two values, true or false. A data type is what the format of the variable is. This idea comes from some of the programming languages where you have to specify the data type of a variable before you use it. JavaScript is more forgiving in this manner—it assumes the data type by the way you use it. This example points out some of the Boolean data type's uses.

129

Online Example

"Igor's Memory—ver 1.2," by Igor Clukas, email: **IgorClukas@europeonline.com**

URL: **http://www-city.europeonline.com/cyberhome/igorclukas/version2/memory/memory.html**

Description

This technique implements the game of memory. The mechanical operations of the game are controlled by the client's machine using JavaScript. The user clicks the pictures, which then execute functions in the script.

Step-by-Step

1. A Boolean variable has only two values: true or false.

    There are various comparison operators that evaluate numerical values to a Boolean value. These are

    $x == y$ equals

    $x != y$ does not equal

    $x > y$ greater than

    $x >= y$ greater than or equal to

    $x < y$ less than

    $x <= y$ less than or equal to

    There are other Boolean operators that evaluate Boolean values to a Boolean value. These are

    a && b and—results in true if a and b are true; otherwise false

    a || b or—results in true if a or b is true; otherwise false

    $!a$ not—reverses the value of the variable

2. Boolean variables and operations are used throughout this script. The *oneOpen* variable is used to indicate whether the first of a pair of cards is drawn (*oneOpen* = true) or no cards have been drawn (*oneOpen* = false). The value of *oneOpen* is set in the function *setCard()* that is executed each time a card is clicked. The command to set it is

```
oneOpen = !oneOpen
```

The *not* operator is used to toggle the value between true and false.

3. The *oneOpen* variable is used in the *checkCard()* function.

```
if (oneOpen) {
      good = (board[card] == board[lastCard])
```

If *oneOpen* is true that means the first card of a set has been selected, and the card just clicked upon is the second card. Therefore, a match should be tested for. The *good* variable is another Boolean variable set if a pair of cards match. This is determined by the Boolean equals operator comparing the values of the current card and the previous card.

Related Techniques

Calculating a Formula

Playing Tic-Tac-Toe

Location Object (Search Property)

Type: JavaScript object

Used in: Document object

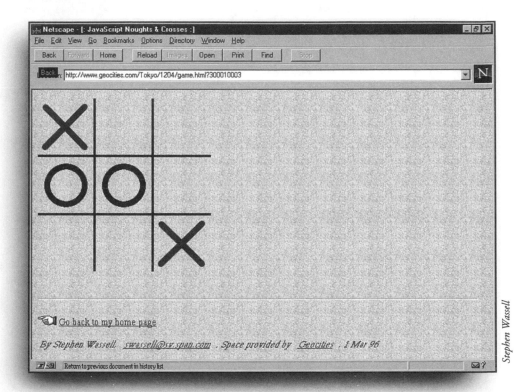

Stephen Wassell

```
function Set (Str, Off, Val) {//equiv. to Str[Off] = Val; return Str
return Str.substring (0, Off) + Val + Str.substring (Off+1, 10)
}
function Sum (Str, a, b, c) { //adds the contents of a, b and c
return (Get (Str, a) + Get (Str, b) + Get (Str, c))
}


function MyMove (Dat) { //do computer's move
var PosLines, Order = '2613', PosCorns
var j, i, a, b, c

 if (Get (Dat, 5) == 1) { //if computer's in centre
  PosLines = '13279817439654652851 9537'
  PosCorns = '124326748968'
 } else {
  PosLines = '519537132798174396546528'
  PosCorns = '542526548586'
 }

Result = ResWin

for (j = 0; j < 4; j++) {
for (i = 0; i < 24; i += 3) {

a = Get (PosLines, i)
b = Get (PosLines, i + 1)
c = Get (PosLines, i + 2)
if (Sum (Dat, a, b, c) == Get (Order, j)) {
if (Get (Dat, a) == 0) return Set (Dat, a, 1)
      if (Get (Dat, b) == 0) return Set (Dat, b, 1)
      if (Get (Dat, c) == 0) return Set (Dat, c, 1)
}
}


     Result = ResNorm

     if (j == 1) { //only between 2nd and 3rd passes
        for (i = 0; i < 12; i += 3) {

        a = Get (PosCorns, i)
        b = Get (PosCorns, i + 1)
        c = Get (PosCorns, i + 2)
        if (Sum (Dat, a, b, c) == 6)
if (Get (Dat, a) == 0) return Set (Dat, a, 1)
    }
   }
}
```

continues

```
Result = ResDraw //no places to go
return Dat
}

function DrawTable (Dat) { //plots the grid
var i, Sqr

for (i = 1; i <= 9; i++) {
Sqr = Get (Dat, i)

if (Sqr == 0) { //it's a blank
if (Result == ResWin) //no more links if it's been won
document.write ('<IMG ALIGN=bottom SRC="gameb.gif">')
else {
document.write ('<A HREF="game.html') //a link for human moves
document.write (Set (Dat, i, '3'))
document.write ('"><IMG ALIGN=bottom BORDER=0 SRC="gameb.gif"></A>')
}

} else if (Sqr == 3) //it's an X
document.write ('<IMG ALIGN=bottom SRC="gamex.gif">')
else //must be an O
document.write ('<IMG ALIGN=bottom SRC="gameo.gif">')

if (i == 9) //finished
document.write ('<P>')
else if (i == 3 || i == 6) //long horizontal line
document.write ('<BR><IMG ALIGN=bottom SRC="gamedh.gif"><BR>')
else //vertical line
document.write ('<IMG ALIGN=bottom SRC="gamedv.gif">')
}

document.write ('<H2>') //make comments

if (Result == ResDraw)
document.write ("It's" + ' a draw!<BR>Want <A HREF="game.html">
another game</A>?')

else if (Result == ResStart)
document.write ("Your go first...")

else if (Result == ResWin)
document.write ('I won!<BR>Like to <A HREF="game.html">
play again</A>?')

document.write ('<BR></H2>')
}

var ResNorm = 0, ResWin = 1, ResDraw = 2, ResStart = 3
var Result = ResStart
```

```
if (location.search.length == 10) //during game
DrawTable (MyMove (location.search))
else //just started

    DrawTable ('?000000000') //draw a load of blanks

// --> <H2>Sorry! You need a <A HREF="http://home.netscape.com/
comprod/products/navigator/version_2.0/">
JavaScript-capable browser</A> to run this.</H2>
</script>
```

Syntax Example

```
document.write("You searched for: " + location.search);
```

Comments

The search section of a URL can be used to transfer information from one page to another. The *location.search* property can be used to identify this section of the URL.

Online Example

": JavaScript Noughts & Crosses :," by Stephen Wassell, email: **swassell@sv.span.com**

URL: **http://www.geocities.com/Tokyo/1204/game.html**

Description

This page implements a game of tic-tac-toe. The search portion of the URL is used to record the current board status.

Step-by-Step

The search portion of the URL is the section that includes and follows a question mark. This portion can be accessed by using the *location.search* property. This page uses a code in which a blank square is represented by a 0; a O is represented by a 1; and an X is represented by a 3. For example, *location.search* for a new game would be *?000000000* , while a game with one X in the middle would be *?000030000.*

135

This page has two main functions. The *MyMove()* function is used to evaluate the computer's move and to return a new search string with the new move. It also determines if the computer has won or if the game is a draw. (Due to the computer algorithm, it is impossible for the user to win.) The *DrawTable()* function is used to write the appropriate images to display the game. It also displays messages to indicate if the game has started, or if it has finished. The remaining functions are often used to identify values in the search string.

Related Techniques

Using Multiple Functions on a Page

Recording Optional Information

Complex Programming Using Loops

Using *for* loops

Type: JavaScript

Used in: Statement

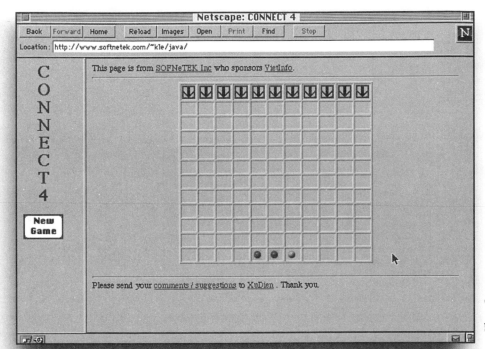

```
<html>
<head><title>CONNECT 4</title></head>
<script language="JavaScript">


function Clear() {
    for (var col = 0; col < 12; col++) {
        for (var row = 0; row < 12; row++)
```

continues

```
          this.table[row][col] = 0;
      this.top[col] = 11;
    }
}


var board = new NewBoard();
var gcol;
</script>

<frameset cols = "100,*">
   <frame src="cn4left.html" name=left noresize>
   <frame src="cn4.html" name=game noresize>
</frameset>
</html>
```

Syntax Example

```
for (var col = 0; col < 12; col++) {
    for (var row = 0; row < 12; row++)
        this.table[row][col] = 0;
    this.top[col] = 11;
}
```

Comments

Teaching a computer to play a game of strategy well is a very difficult task. Not only does this example have a program that can play the game Connect 4; it actually plays it *well*.

How is so much in so few lines of code? Nested *for* loops is used.

Online Example

"Connect 4," by Khang Le, email: **kle@snt1.softnetek.com**

URL: **http://www.softnetek.com/~kle/java/**

Description

The "real" game of Connect 4 consists of a vertical grid that players drop tokens into. They simply try to get four in a row. The catch is that the tokens fall into place; they all have to go at the bottom of the grid, or on top of another token. The grid keeps them in columns.

Step-by-Step

The creator of this example uses every opportunity to compress code. This algorithm is slow, but that is often the price of compact code.

It begins with several very brief functions such as

```
function GetTop(col) {
    return this.top[col];
}
```

These functions do little more than save some keystrokes when you reach the meat of the game.

A concise example of nested *for* loops is the function *Clear*:

```
function Clear() {
    for (var col = 0; col < 12; col++) {
        for (var row = 0; row < 12; row++)
            this.table[row][col] = 0;
        this.top[col] = 11;
    }
}
```

This function actually executes the statement *this.table[row][col] = 0*, 144 times, and the statement *this.top[col] = 11*, 12 times. This concept can be confusing, unless you break it down:

```
function Clear() {
    for (var col = 0; col < 12; col++) {
        DO THIS TWELVE TIMES;
    }
}
```

The statement *DO THIS TWELVE TIMES* is executed twelve times because col starts at 0, goes up to 11, and is increased by one each time. Notice that the *for* statement has three parts, separated by semicolons. The first part defines a variable and sets its starting value; the second sets the end condition of the loop; and the third part determines how the variable will change. Usually the variable goes up by one (thus the expression col++), but sometimes it goes down by one (col—). Feel free to have it change in a more exotic fashion if you want.

Now, let's replace *DO THIS TWELVE TIMES* with the following:

```
for (var row = 0; row < 12; row++)
    this.table[row][col] = 0;
```

This statement, another *for* loop, does something else twelve times. Repeat the process twelve times, where that process involves doing something twelve times. You do it 144 times, because 144 is 12 × 12. Got it?

Notes

Your homework: Figure out the rest of the game!

Related Techniques

Evaluating String Expressions

Creating a Memory Game

Evaluating String Expressions

Using the *eval* Function

Type: JavaScript

Used in: Function

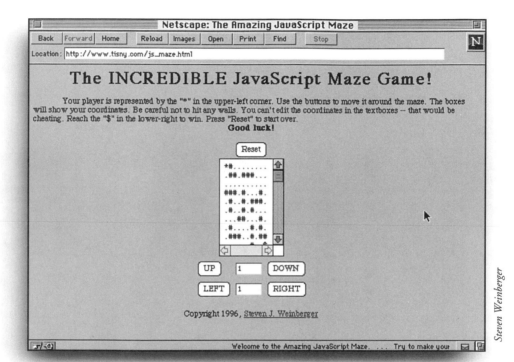

Steven Weinberger

```
<html>
<head>
<title>The Amazing JavaScript Maze</title>
<!-- begin Script here

     Copyright 1996 by Steven Weinberger of
Transaction Information
     Systems. All rights reserved.

<script>
```

continues

```
function makeboard() {
        for (var i=1; i<= 10; i++)
                this[i] = new makeRow();
        return this;
}
function fillBoard (form) {
    // Clear board buffer
        line = "";
        form.grid.value = "";
    // Fill board buffer
        for (var i=1; i<= 10; i++)
                for (var j=1; j<= 10; j++)
                        line += theBoard[i][j];
    // Move buffer contents to board
        form.grid.value=line;
}

function update(form) {
        var horiz = eval(form.xval.value);
        var vert = eval(form.yval.value);
    plot(vert,horiz);
        fillBoard(form);
        return;
}

function incx(form) {
        fill = blank;
        update(form);
        checkx = eval(1 * form.xval.value + 1);
        checky = form.yval.value;
        if (form.xval.value < 10) {
            if (theBoard[checky][checkx] != wall) {
              form.xval.value=eval(1 * form.xval.value + 1);
            }
            else {
                alert("THUD!\nYou hit a wall.");
            }
            if (theBoard[checky][checkx] == goal) {
                alert("YOU WIN!");
                        location.href="http://www.tisny.com/js_demo.html";
            }
        }
        fill = full;
        update(form);
}

</script>
```

```
<body>
<center>
<h1>The INCREDIBLE JavaScript Maze Game!</h1>
</center>
<form method="post" name="board">
<input type='button' value='Reset' onClick=
'clearBoard(this.form);update(document.board);'>
<br>
<textarea name="grid" rows="9" cols="10"
wrap=virtual></textarea><br>

<table>
<tr>
  <td><input type='button' value='UP'
onClick='decy(this.form)'></td>
  <td><input type='text' value='1' size=5 name='yval'
onChange='cheater(this.form);'></td>
  <td><input type='button' value='DOWN'
onClick='incy(this.form)'></td>
<tr>
  <td><input type='button' value='LEFT'
onClick='decx(this.form)'></td>
  <td><input type='text' value='1' size=5 name='xval'
onChange='cheater(this.form);'></td>
  <td><input type='button' value='RIGHT'
onClick='incx(this.form)'></td>
</table>
</form>
</center>
</body>
</html>
```

Syntax Example

```
form.xval.value=eval(form.xval.value - 1)
```

Comments

The Incredible JavaScript Maze Game has become part of the new folklore of JavaScript. The creator was truly pushing the limits of JavaScript at the time he developed this example.

Evaluating String Expressions

Online Example

"The Amazing JavaScript Maze," by Steven Weinberger, email:
steve@garcia.tisny.com

URL: **http://www.tisny.com/js_maze.html**

Description

A maze in a *TEXTAREA* form element enables you to navigate the maze by clicking buttons. Hitting a wall yields a resounding *THUD*, and reaching the goal yields an appropriate reward.

Cheaters beware: Changing the maze has no effect, and trying to change your location in the maze earns you a scolding and resets your game.

Step-by-Step

The important part of this game is the function that moves the player in a direction. Four functions were created for moving in each direction, although they could have been combined into one.

Here is one of these functions:

```
function incx(form) {
   update(form);
   checkx = eval(1 * form.xval.value + 1);
   checky = form.yval.value;
   if (form.xval.value < 10) {
      if (theBoard[checky][checkx] != wall) {
         form.xval.value=eval(1 * form.xval.value + 1);
         }
   else {
         alert("THUD!\nYou hit a wall.");
         }
      if (theBoard[checky][checkx] == goal)
         alert("YOU WIN!");
   }
   update(form);
}
```

First, *update(form)*, which redraws the maze (just in case you changed it), is called. Next, it calculates where you are going. In the case of the variable *checkx*:

```
checkx = eval(1 * form.xval.value + 1);
```

Eval is a function that takes a string representation of an expression, and evaluates the expression it represents. But what about the expression *1 * form.xval.value + 1*? Even if *form.xval.value* is a string, won't the entire expression evaluate to a number, because it begins with a number? Don't count on it. If there is any doubt in your mind whether an expression that should yield a number actually will, use the *eval* function. It seems that all you have to do is breathe on an expression and it turns into a string.

The example then proceeds to refer to the maze itself and determine whether you are trying to move into a wall:

```
if (theBoard[checky][checkx] != wall) {
    form.xval.value=eval(1 * form.xval.value + 1);
    }
```

If the square you are moving to is not a wall, then the function moves you to that square. Notice first that the *eval* function is used again to make sure a number is passed to *form.xval.value*; and second, the variables *checky* and *checkx* are used as indices of an array. The point here is that this array *must* have whole numbers as indices.

It then proceeds to check whether you have won, and if not, *update(form)* is called once more to display your new position.

Notes

If an expression contains only numbers or variables that have been assigned numbers, you don't need the eval function. If any term in an expression might be a string—in particular, the value property of an object—then use the eval function if you want the result to be a number.

Related Techniques

Complex Programming Using Loops

Creating a Memory Game

Using Radio Buttons to Create Special Effects

Using the Radio Object

Type: JavaScript

Used in: Object, property of form

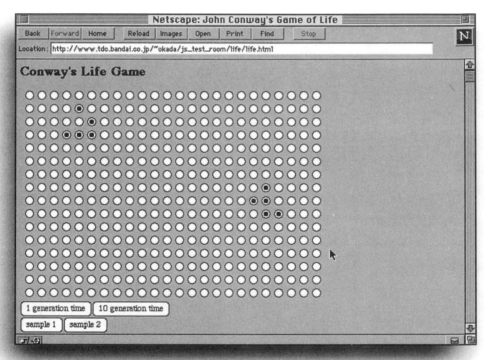

Hiroshi Okada

```
<HTML>
<HEAD>
    <TITLE>John Conway's Game of Life</TITLE>
<SCRIPT LANGUAGE="JavaScript">
<!--
// -- by Hiroshi Okada      okada@tdc.bandai.co.jp


// ---- World size
var wsize_x =24;
```

```
var wsize_y = 16;
var wsize = wsize_x * wsize_y;
var onoff = new MakeArray( wsize, false);
var count = new MakeArray( wsize, 0);

// ---- Turn over clicked cell.
function reverce( obj, n){
   obj.checked = (onoff[ n] = ( onoff[ n] == false));
}

    // ---- Birth, Survival, Death
    for( n=1; n<=wsize; n++){
        onoff[ n] = ( ( count[n] == 3) ¦¦ ( count[n] == 12)
¦¦ ( count[n] == 13));
        document.form1.elements[ n-1].checked = onoff[ n];
     }


}

// ---- Set x y
function setXY( x, y){
    var n = y*wsize_x + x;

    document.form1.elements[ n].checked = onoff[ n+1] = true;
}

// ---- Make world
document.write( "<H2>Conway's Life Game</H2>");
document.write( "<FORM NAME='form1'>");
document.write( "<TABLE>");
for( var y=0; y<wsize_y;y++){
    document.write( "<TR><TD>" );
    for( var x=0; x<wsize_x; x++){
        document.write( "<INPUT TYPE='radio'
onClick='reverce( this, ");
        document.write(  y*wsize_x + x + 1);
        document.write(  ")'>" );
    }
    document.write(  "</TD></TR>" );
}
document.write( "</TABLE>");
;
document.write( "</FORM>");

// -->
</SCRIPT>

</HEAD>
</HTML>
```

Syntax Example

```
document.form1.elements[ n-1].checke'd = onoff[ n]
```

Comments

The game of life is part of the folklore of computer science. Given a grid with dots on it and some simple algorithms about how many neighbors a dot has to have to survive, die, or breed, you can develop ongoing patterns that take on a life of their own—hence the name.

This example illustrates a novel approach to the game. Radio buttons are used, not because they work in sets, but simply because they are dots that can be turned on and off with JavaScript.

Online Example

"John Conway's Game of Life," by Hiroshi Okada, email: **okada@tdc.bandai.co.jp**

URL: **http://www.tdc.bandai.co.jp/~okada/js_test_room/life/life.html**

Description

The screen is filled with radio buttons, in a rectangular 24×16 grid. Play the game for one or ten generations. Two sample "automata" are provided, in case you can't create any you like.

Place your dots; start the game; and watch your critters grow, move, and die.

Step-by-Step

This document has no body at all; all HTML is generated by scripts. Clearly, you wouldn't want to draw 384 radio buttons any other way!

1. The *document.write* function is used to start a table. Then the following statements are used to create the buttons:

```
for( var y=0; y<wsize_y;y++)
   {
   document.write(   "<TR><TD>" );
   for( var x=0; x<wsize_x; x++)
           {
           document.write( "<INPUT TYPE='radio'
onClick='reverce( this, ");
           document.write(   y*wsize_x + x + 1);
           document.write(   ")'>" );
           }
   document.write(   "</TD></TR>" );
   }
```

Each iteration through the outer loop produces a row of buttons. In each row the inner loop creates a radio button. Every button is the same; that is, they are not assigned names or values. The only difference is the second argument being sent to the function "reverce" in the *onClick* event handler, which distinguishes the button from its neighbors.

2. *Function reverce* is very simple:

```
function reverce( obj, n){
   obj.checked = (onoff[ n] = ( onoff[ n] == false));
}
```

onoff is an array of boolean values. This function checks to see if the nth element in array *onoff* is false. If it is, it becomes true; if not, it becomes false. This is a very complicated way of saying it switches its value.

3. Next, the checked property of the object *obj* (namely, a particular radio button), is also assigned the new value of *onoff[n]*. This shortcut takes advantage of a property in JavaScript statements: the expression x=7 assigns the value of 7 to x, but it also assigns the value of 7 to the expression *itself*. Therefore, if you write y = (x=7), then both x and y are set to 7.

4. The next generation is made with the function next_gen.

Notes

If you think the expression *obj.checked = (onoff[n] = (onoff[n] == false))* is awkward, you're not alone. Here are some other ways of accomplishing the same thing:

```
obj.checked = (onoff[n] = !onoff[n])
```

or more explicitly:

```
onoff[n] = !onoff[n];
obj.checked = onoff[n]
```

Related Techniques

Programming Buttons

Creating Animated Radio Buttons

Programming Buttons

Using the Button INPUT Type

Type: JavaScript

Used in: Object; property of the form object

Voth Communications

```
<HTML>
<HEAD>

<TITLE>Voth Communications - Javascript Examples</TITLE>
<LINK REV="made" HREF="mailto:vothcom@pobox.com">

<SCRIPT LANGUAGE="LiveScript">
<!-- hide this script tag's contents from old browsers

// keep track of whether we just computed display.value
```

continues

```
var computed = false
var destination = "http://www.seercom.com/vothcom/"
var decimal = 0

function convert (entryform, from, to)

{
     convertfrom = from.selectedIndex
     convertto = to.selectedIndex
     entryform.display.value = (entryform.input.value *
     from[convertfrom].value / to[convertto].value )
}

function addChar (input, character)
{

     if((character=='.' && decimal=="0") || character!='.')

     {
          (input.value == "" || input.value == "0") ? input.value
           character : input.value += character

          convert(input.form,input.form.measure1,input.form.measure2)

          computed = true

          if (character=='.')
          {
                  decimal=1
          }
     }
}

function openVothcom()
{
   window.open("","Display window","toolbar=no,directories=no,menubar=no");
}

function clear (form)
{
     form.input.value = 0
     form.display.value = 0
     decimal=0
}

function changeBackground(hexNumber)
{
     document.bgColor=hexNumber
}

<!-- done hiding from old browsers -->
</SCRIPT>
```

```
</HEAD>
<BODY>

<H1 ALIGN="CENTER">Javascript Page</H1>

<P>The following are a couple examples that make use of Netscape's
new scripting language 'Javascript' available in Netscape 2.0. </P>
<P><EM>The following is for demonstration purposes and no guarantees
regarding the accuracy of the calculations are made.</EM></P>

<H2>Metric Converter</H2>

<FORM METHOD="POST" NAME="calculator">
<TABLE BORDER="3" CELLPADDING="3">
<TR><TH>Convert from:</TH>
<TD><INPUT SIZE="15" NAME="input" ONCHANGE="convert(this.form,
form.measure1, form.measure2)"></TD>
<TD>
<SELECT NAME="measure1" ONCHANGE="convert(this.form,this, form.measure2)">
<OPTION VALUE="0.01" SELECTED>cm
<OPTION VALUE="1">m
<OPTION VALUE="1000">km
<OPTION VALUE="0.3048">feet
<OPTION VALUE="0.9144">yds
<OPTION VALUE="1610">mi
</SELECT>
</TD>
<TR><TH>Convert to:</TH>
<TD><INPUT SIZE="15" NAME="display"></TD>
<TD>
<SELECT NAME="measure2" ONCHANGE="convert(this.form,form.measure1, this)">
<OPTION VALUE="0.01">cm
<OPTION VALUE="1">m
<OPTION VALUE="1000">km
<OPTION VALUE="0.3048" SELECTED>feet
<OPTION VALUE="0.9144">yds
<OPTION VALUE="1610">mi
</SELECT>
</TD>

</TABLE>
<TABLE BORDER="3" CELLPADDING="3">

<TR><TD><INPUT TYPE="button" VALUE="7" ONCLICK="addChar(this.form.input,'7')">
</TD>
<TD><INPUT TYPE="button" VALUE="8" ONCLICK="addChar(this.form.input,'8')"></TD>
<TD><INPUT TYPE="button" VALUE="9" ONCLICK="addChar(this.form.input,'9')"></TD>

<TR><TD><INPUT TYPE="button" VALUE="4" ONCLICK="addChar(this.form.input,'4')">
</TD>
```

continues

153

```
<TD><INPUT TYPE="button" VALUE="5" ONCLICK="addChar(this.form.input,'5')"></TD>
<TD><INPUT TYPE="button" VALUE="6" ONCLICK="addChar(this.form.input,'6')"></TD>

<TR><TD><INPUT TYPE="button" VALUE="1" ONCLICK="addChar(this.form.input,'1')">
</TD>
<TD><INPUT TYPE="button" VALUE="2" ONCLICK="addChar(this.form.input,'2')"></TD>
<TD><INPUT TYPE="button" VALUE="3" ONCLICK="addChar(this.form.input,'3')"></TD>

<TR><TD><INPUT TYPE="button" VALUE="0" ONCLICK="addChar(this.form.input,'0')">
</TD>
<TD><INPUT TYPE="button" VALUE="." ONCLICK="addChar(this.form.input,'.')"></TD>
<TD ROWSPAN=""><INPUT TYPE="button" VALUE="C" ONCLICK="clear(this.form)"><TD>
</TABLE>

</FORM>
<HR SIZE="4">

<H2>Background Selector</H2>

<FORM METHOD="POST" NAME="background">
<TABLE BORDER="3" CELLPADDING="3">
<TR><TD><INPUT TYPE="button" VALUE="blue"
ONCLICK="changeBackground('#B2B5FB')"></TD>
<TD><INPUT TYPE="button" VALUE="red" ONCLICK="changeBackground('#FAB7B2')"></TD>
<TD><INPUT TYPE="button" VALUE="white" ONCLICK="changeBackground('#FFFFFF')">
</TD>
</TABLE>
</FORM>


<HR SIZE="4">

<H2>Traverse History</H2>

<FORM METHOD="POST" NAME="history">
<TABLE>
<TR><TD><INPUT TYPE="button" VALUE="3 Pages back" ONCLICK="history.go(-3)"></TD>
<TD><INPUT TYPE="button" VALUE="Previous Page" ONCLICK="history.go(-1)"></TD>
<TD><INPUT TYPE="button" VALUE="Next Page" ONCLICK="history.go(1)"></TD>
<TD><INPUT TYPE="button" VALUE="3 Pages forward" ONCLICK="history.go(3)"></TD>
</TABLE>
</FORM>


<HR SIZE="4">

<P>Contact <A HREF="http://www.seercom.com/vothcom">Voth Communications</A>
for your world wide web needs<BR>
<A HREF="mailto:vothcom@uniserve.com">vothcom@uniserve.com</A></P>

<!--#include file="copyright.html"-->

</BODY>
</HTML>
```

Syntax Example

```
<INPUT TYPE="button" VALUE="7" ONCLICK="addChar(this.form.input,'7')">
```

Comments

Because buttons are so flexible, one of the first projects every budding JavaScript programmer attempts is a calculator.

Online Example

"Javascript Examples," by Voth Communications, email: **vothcom@pobox.com**

URL: **http://www.seercom.com/vothcom/convert.html**

Description

This example has a unit converter that features a calculator-style keyboard for entering numbers, and buttons that enable you to select background colors and traverse the history of the window.

Step-by-Step

HTML provides for an *<INPUT TYPE="button">* form element, which looks just like a submit button, except, yes, it doesn't submit. In fact, without JavaScript, the button type would not do anything at all.

1. Now, however, you can make buttons do whatever you want:

```
<INPUT TYPE="button" VALUE="5"
ONCLICK="addChar(this.form.input,'5')">
```

The value contains what you want to display on the button. It is usually a good idea to name a button so that you can refer to it by name in your scripts. Clicking the button simply executes the contents of the *onClick* event handler.

Programming Buttons

Note that *onClick* is spelled *ONCLICK*. This is incorrect, and may cause the script to fail for some users. JavaScript is case sensitive, and if that weren't bad enough, many terms have capital letters in the middle only, like *onClick*. (Your second grade teacher would just die!)

This button is part of the Metric Converter form, named "calculator," which contains 16 elements: two text fields named "input" and "display," two pull-down menus named "measure1" and "measure2," and the 12 calculator keys that they don't bother to name.

So what does this.form.input refer to? "this" is a special JavaScript term that refers to the current object. In this case, "this.form" refers to "document.calculator." It is probably easier to just use "document.calculator"!

2. Clicking this button sends the field "input" and the number corresponding to the button to addChar, which places the number in the field. The details of the unit conversion process are not very enlightening, but there is one statement in *addChar* that is worth looking at:

```
(input.value == "" ¦¦ input.value == "0") ?
input.value = character : input.value += character
```

This statement is an unusual use of a conditional expression. Usually, a conditional expression is used to assign one of two values to a variable, depending upon whether some expression is true or false:

```
Dinner = (fridge == empty) ? "EatOut" : "EatIn";
```

In this expression, if fridge equals empty, Dinner is assigned the value *"EatOut"*; otherwise, it is assigned the value *"EatIn"*.

3. This example uses the conditional expression a little differently. If the expression in parentheses is true, the statement *input.value = character* is executed; otherwise, the statement *input.value += character* is executed. Take a look at a more standard conditional expression that had the same result:

```
input.value = (input.value == "" ¦¦ input.value == "0") ?
character : input.value + character
```

You may prefer the original script better because it uses the cool += assignment operator.

Notes

In case you are rusty on your assignment operators, *value += number* is equivalent to *value = value + number*.

Also note the difference between = and ==; == is a test for equality, while = assigns a value to a variable. Thus, the expression a == b is a boolean expression (either true or false), while the statement a = b assigns the value of b to the variable a. Using a = where a == belongs is a common syntax error.

Related Techniques

Programming Your Own "Back" and "Forward" Buttons

Blinking Radio Buttons

Creating Animated Radio Buttons

Using the Radio Object

Type: JavaScript object

Used in: Form objects

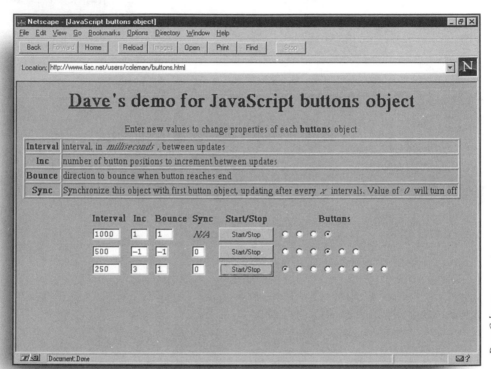

Dave Coleman

```
<HTML>
<HEAD>
<TITLE>JavaScript buttons object</TITLE>
</HEAD>

<SCRIPT LANGUAGE='JavaScript'>
<!-- Use comment to hide from browsers not supporting JavaScript
//==========================================================
//
//    buttons object
//
// Author: Dave Coleman (coleman@faxint.com)
// Date: 96/02/27
```

```
// Abstract: A JavaScript object which provides properties and
//  methods to simulate blinking lights by using RADIO form
//  objects.
//
// Comments: This is intended as an example of JavaScript objects.
//  There are more efficient ways to do it without all the
//  features provided by this example.
//  This example provides advanced features and can be used
//  to support multiple buttons objects in the same page.

// NOTE: First parameter is name, which must match the name of the
// object.  Is there any way to determine this with JavaScript??
// This is used for the setTimeout, which can't pass an object
// To use status window, specify output parameter as null
function buttons (name, output, interval, increment, bounce, offset){
// Initialize with default values
this.name = name  // object name, needed for setTimeout
this.output = null  // output area
this.interval = 1000 // milliseconds
this.increment = 1  // skip characters
this.bounce = 1  // direction to bounce when message wraps
this.offset = 0
this.timeout = null
this.syncCount = 0
this.syncName = new array ()
this.syncInterval = new array ()
this.syncCountdown = new array ()

// Define object methods
this.update = buttonsUpdate
this.start = timerAppStart
this.stop = timerAppStop
this.toggle = timerAppToggle
this.loop = timerAppLoop
this.setOutput = timerAppSetOutput
this.setInterval = timerAppSetInterval
this.sync = timerAppSync
this.unsync = timerAppUnsync
this.setIncrement = timerAppSetIncrement
this.setBounce = timerAppSetBounce
this.setOffset = timerAppSetOffset

// Initialize with specified values
this.setOutput (output)
this.setInterval (interval)
this.setIncrement (increment)
this.setBounce (bounce)
this.setOffset (offset)

this.start()
}
```

continues

159

```
function buttonsUpdate () {
if (this.output) {
 var newOffset = this.offset + this.increment
 if ((newOffset < this.output.length)
     && (newOffset >= 0)) {
     this.offset = newOffset
 } else {
     this.increment *= this.bounce
     if (this.increment >= 0) {
this.increment = modRange (this.increment, 0, this.output.length-1)
     } else {
  this.increment = 0 - modRange (Math.abs (this.increment),
    0, this.output.length-1)
     }
     this.offset += this.increment
     this.offset = modRange (this.offset, 0, this.output.length-1)
 }

 this.output[this.offset].checked = true
}
}


/////////////////////////////////////////////////////////////
//
// Common functions
//

// return value as modulo value between min and max range
function modRange (value, min, max) {
if (min == max) {
 return (min)
}
var low = Math.min (min, max)
var high = Math.max (min, max)
var range = high - low + 1
var valOff = parseInt (value) - low
var mod = range * Math.floor (valOff / range)
result = low + valOff - mod
if (result < low) {
 result += high
}
if (result > high) {
 result = low
}
return (result)
}
// array must be created as an object,
// does not work as inline statement
function array () {
this[0] = null
}
```

```
/////////////////////////////////////////////////////////////
//
// timerApp functions, common for all timer applications
//
function timerAppStart () {
this.stop ()
this.loop ()
}

function timerAppStop () {
clearTimeout (this.timeout)
this.timeout = null
}

function timerAppToggle () {

if (this.timeout) {
 this.stop ()
} else {
 this.start ()
}
}

function timerAppLoop () {
this.update ()
command = this.name + '.loop()'
for (var i = 0; i < this.syncCount; i++) {
 if (this.syncName[i] != "") {
     if (--this.syncCountdown[i] <= 0) {
  this.syncCountdown[i] = this.syncInterval[i]
  command += ";" + this.syncName[i] + '.update()'
     }
 }
}
this.timeout = setTimeout (command, this.interval)
}

function timerAppSetOutput (output) {
if (! this.output) {
 this.output = output
}
}

function timerAppSetInterval (interval) {
if (interval) {
 var newInterval = parseInt (interval)
 if (newInterval > 0) {
     this.interval = newInterval
 } else {
alert ('Interval value must be a positive number: ' + interval)
 }
```

continues

161

```
}
}

function timerAppSync (name, interval) {
if (! interval) {
 interval = 1
}
if (interval <= 0) {
 eval (this.name + '.unsync("' + name + '")')
 return
}
var newIndex = this.syncCount
for (var i = 0; i < this.syncCount; i++) {
 if (this.syncName[i] == name) {
     newIndex = i
     break
 }
}
if (newIndex == this.syncCount) {
 this.syncCount++
}
this.syncInterval[newIndex] = interval
this.syncCountdown[newIndex] = interval
this.syncName[newIndex] = name
}

function timerAppUnsync (name) {
for (var i = 0; i < this.syncCount; i++) {
 if (this.syncName[i] == name) {
     this.syncName[i] = ""
     if (i == (this.syncCount - 1)) {
  this.syncCount--
     }
 }
}
}

function timerAppSetIncrement (increment) {
if (increment) {
 var newIncrement = parseInt (increment)
//*Unix only* if (! isNan (newIncrement)) {
 if (newIncrement != 0) {
     this.increment = newIncrement
 } else {
alert ('Increment value must be a number: ' + increment)
 }
}
}
```

```
function timerAppSetBounce (bounce) {
if (bounce) {
 var newBounce = parseInt (bounce)
//*Unix only* if (! isNan (newBounce)) {
 if (newBounce != 0) {
    this.bounce = newBounce
 } else {
    alert ('Bounce value must be a number: ' + bounce)
 }
}
}

function timerAppSetOffset (offset) {
if (offset) {
 var newOffset = parseInt (offset)
 if ((newOffset > 0)
    && (newOffset <= this.output.length)) {
    this.offset = newOffset
 } else {
warnMessage = 'Value of offset must be a valid index (0 - '
   + this.output.length + '): ' + offset
    alert (warnMessage)
 }
}
}
<!-- done hiding from old browsers not supporting JavaScript -->
</SCRIPT>

<BODY onLoad='
demoButtons = new buttons ("demoButtons",
    document.demo.buttonsRadio,
    document.demo.interval.value,
    document.demo.increment.value)
;demoButtons1 = new buttons ("demoButtons1",
    document.demo.buttonsRadio1,
    document.demo.interval1.value,
    document.demo.increment1.value)
;demoButtons2 = new buttons ("demoButtons2",
    document.demo.buttonsRadio2,
    document.demo.interval2.value,
    document.demo.increment2.value)
' onUnload='
demoButtons.stop()
; demoButtons1.stop()
; demoButtons2.stop()
'>
```

continues

163

```
<CENTER>
<H1><A HREF="./dmc_bio.html">Dave</A>'s demo for JavaScript
 <B>buttons</B> object</H1>
<TABLE BORDER=1>
<CAPTION> Enter new values to change properties of each
<B>buttons</B> object
</CAPTION>
</TR><TR><TH> Interval</TH>
<TD> interval, in <EM>milliseconds</EM>, between updates</TD>
</TR><TR><TH> Inc</TH>
<TD> number of button positions to increment between updates</TD>
</TR><TR><TH> Bounce</TH>
<TD> direction to bounce when button reaches end</TD>
</TR><TR><TH> Sync</TH>
<TD> Synchronize this object with first button object, updating after
 every <EM>x</EM> intervals.  Value of <EM>0</EM> will turn off</TD>
</TR></TABLE>

<FORM NAME='demo' ACTION=''>
<TABLE NOBORDER>
<TR>
<TH>Interval</TH>
<TH>Inc</TH>
<TH>Bounce</TH>
<TH>Sync</TH>
<TH>Start/Stop</TH>
<TH>Buttons</TH>
</TR>
<TR><TD>
<INPUT TYPE='text' SIZE=5 NAME='interval' VALUE=1000
onChange='demoButtons.setInterval (this.value)'>
</TD><TD>
<INPUT TYPE='text' SIZE=3 NAME='increment' VALUE=1
onChange='demoButtons.setIncrement (this.value)'>
</TD><TD>
<INPUT TYPE='text' SIZE=3 NAME='bounce' VALUE=1
  onChange='demoButtons.setBounce (this.value)'>
</TD><TD>
<EM>N/A</EM>
</TD><TD>
<INPUT TYPE='button' VALUE='Start/Stop'
onClick='demoButtons.toggle ()'>
</TD><TD>
<INPUT TYPE='radio' NAME='buttonsRadio'>
<INPUT TYPE='radio' NAME='buttonsRadio'>
<INPUT TYPE='radio' NAME='buttonsRadio'>
<INPUT TYPE='radio' NAME='buttonsRadio'>
</TD></TR>
<TR><TD>
<INPUT TYPE='text' SIZE=5 NAME='interval1' VALUE=500
onChange='demoButtons1.setInterval (this.value)'>
```

```
</TD><TD>
<INPUT TYPE='text' SIZE=3 NAME='increment1' VALUE=-1
onChange='demoButtons.setIncrement (this.value)'>
</TD><TD>
<INPUT TYPE='text' SIZE=2 NAME='bounce' VALUE=-1
  onChange='demoButtons1.setBounce (this.value)'>
</TD><TD>
<INPUT TYPE='text' SIZE=2 VALUE='0'
onChange='demoButtons.sync ("demoButtons1", this.value)'>
</TD><TD>
<INPUT TYPE='button' VALUE='Start/Stop'
onClick='demoButtons1.toggle ()'>
</TD><TD>
<INPUT TYPE='radio' NAME='buttonsRadio1'>
<INPUT TYPE='radio' NAME='buttonsRadio1'>
<INPUT TYPE='radio' NAME='buttonsRadio1'>
<INPUT TYPE='radio' NAME='buttonsRadio1'>
<INPUT TYPE='radio' NAME='buttonsRadio1'>
<INPUT TYPE='radio' NAME='buttonsRadio1'>
</TD></TR>
<TR><TD>
<INPUT TYPE='text' SIZE=5 NAME='interval2' VALUE=250
onChange='demoButtons2.setInterval (this.value)'>
</TD><TD>
<INPUT TYPE='text' SIZE=3 NAME='increment2' VALUE=3
onChange='demoButtons.setIncrement (this.value)'>
</TD><TD>
<INPUT TYPE='text' SIZE=2 NAME='bounce' VALUE=1
  onChange='demoButtons2.setBounce (this.value)'>
</TD><TD>
<INPUT TYPE='text' SIZE=2 VALUE='0'
onChange='demoButtons.sync ("demoButtons2", this.value)'>
</TD><TD>
<INPUT TYPE='button' VALUE='Start/Stop'
onClick='demoButtons2.toggle ()'>
</TD><TD>
<INPUT TYPE='radio' NAME='buttonsRadio2'>
<INPUT TYPE='radio' NAME='buttonsRadio2'>
<INPUT TYPE='radio' NAME='buttonsRadio2'>
<INPUT TYPE='radio' NAME='buttonsRadio2'>
<INPUT TYPE='radio' NAME='buttonsRadio2'>
<INPUT TYPE='radio' NAME='buttonsRadio2'>
<INPUT TYPE='radio' NAME='buttonsRadio2'>
<INPUT TYPE='radio' NAME='buttonsRadio2'>
</TD></TR>
</TABLE>
</FORM>
</CENTER>

</BODY>
</HTML>
```

Syntax Example

```
<FORM>
<INPUT TYPE="radio" onClick='alert("Hi!")'> click me!
</FORM>
```

Comments

A radio object is another form object in which you can give the user a choice to make from a list. It is a useful tool when one of multiple selections is made. You can let the radio buttons stand alone so you can select as many as you want. You can also set up the radio buttons so that they are part of one set, in which only one button can be selected at a time.

Online Example

"JavaScript buttons object," by Dave Coleman, email: **coleman@faxint.com**

URL: **http://www.tiac.net/users/coleman/buttons.html**

Description

This page uses radio buttons to illustrate animation. A set of radio buttons is clicked on and off from the JavaScript to create the effect. Various timer functions are used to control the animation. The *setTimeout* method is used within the timer functions to control the speed, starting and stopping functions of the animation.

Step-by-Step

1. The radio object is in the form of:

```
<INPUT TYPE="radio" NAME="radioName" VALUE="buttonValue" [CHECKED]
[onClick="handlerText"]> textToDisplay
```

NAME will give the select object a name such that it can be referred to in the JavaScript. In a set of radio buttons, they will all have the same name.

VALUE is the value associated with the object that can be accessed in the JavaScript.

CHECKED will specify if the radio button is selected.

OnClick is an event handler that will execute if the button is selected by the user.

The properties of the radio object are

checked	This allows the radio button to be checked in the JavaScript.
defaultChecked	This reflects the *CHECKED* attribute in *INPUT* tag.length
name	This is the number of radio buttons in a set of radio buttons.
value	This is the NAME defined in the INPUT tag. This is the VALUE defined in the INPUT tag.

The method of the radio object is

click()	This simulates the user clicking a radio button.

2. In this page, three sets of radio buttons are created. Each set is given a different name. The *onLoad* event handler in the *<BODY>* tag of the page initializes all of the sets of radio buttons. Objects of the type *buttons* are created and initialized to the values in the *demo* form object. An *OnUnload* event handler is used to execute methods which stop the script from executing. In the function *buttons*, which is used as an object, the parameters and methods are defined. All of the methods are defined to timer application functions. Some of the methods are initialized to values specified when the object was created. Within the page there are various parameters displayed in text forms that affect the properties of the moving radio buttons. The parameters are modified by using the *onClick* event handler in these text objects.

Related Techniques

Implementing a Game Using Form Objects

Displaying Repeating Information on a Page

Creating a Multiple Choice Test

Creating a Remote in a Separate Window

Programming Your Own "Back" and "Forward" Buttons

Using the History Object

Type: JavaScript

Used in: Object, property of document

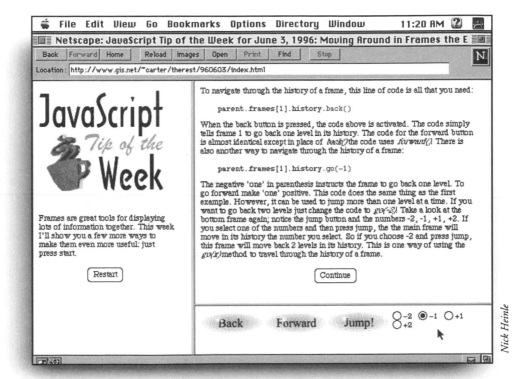

Nick Heinle

File: index.html

```
<HTML>
<HEAD>
<TITLE>Moving Around in Frames With JavaScript</TITLE>
</HEAD>
    <FRAMESET COLS="225,*">
    <FRAME NAME = "a" SRC="side.html">
```

continues

```
        <FRAMESET ROWS="*,70">
        <FRAME NAME = "b" SRC="main01.html">
        <FRAME NAME = "c" SRC="bottom.html">
        </FRAMESET>
    </FRAMESET>


bottom_nav_jump.html:

<HTML>
<HEAD>
<SCRIPT LANGUAGE = "JavaScript">

var num = 0;
function jump(){
        parent.frames[1].history.go(num);
        }
</SCRIPT>
</HEAD>

<BODY>
<A HREF = "JavaScript:parent.frames[1].history.back()">
<IMG HEIGHT=29 WIDTH=85 BORDER=0 SRC="back.gif"></A>

<A HREF = "JavaScript:parent.frames[1].history.forward()">
<IMG HEIGHT=29 WIDTH=85 BORDER=0 SRC="forward.gif"></A>
</BODY>
</HTML>
```

Syntax Example

```
parent.frames[1].history.back()
parent.frames[1].history.go(num)
```

Comments

In Netscape 2.0, the "Back" button takes you to the previous page loaded into the browser window. If the current page has frames, then "Back" takes you back beyond any navigation you might have done in the frames.

In Netscape 3.0, the Back button will back you up, frame by frame, in the reverse order that you navigated the frames. Although this may be an improvement, it may still have unexpected effects. That is why it is so important to be able to program your own Back (and Forward) buttons to work just the way you want.

Online Example

"Moving around in frames the easy way," by Nick Heinle, email: **carter@gis.net**

URL: **http://www.gis.net/~carter/therest/960603/index.html**

Description

This is a rather complex example because the frames are used to contain the explanation as use of the custom "back" and "forward" buttons is demonstrated.

There are three frames: the left one contains the introductory graphic and text, and the start (or restart) button; the top-right frame contains the explanatory text; and the lower-right frame contains the history buttons. As you navigate the site, the history buttons change. This example begins with the two basic buttons, but a "jump" button, which moves through the history depending on the value of a radio button is soon added.

Step-by-Step

The idea of the history is simply the term for what appears under the *"go"* menu. To be more specific, the *go* menu contains the history of the current browser window. In fact, each frame has its own history, and it is that history that you will be navigating.

Let's begin with the back and forward buttons:

```
<A HREF = "JavaScript:parent.frames[1].history.back()">
<IMG SRC = "back.gif"></A>


<A HREF = "JavaScript:parent.frames[1].history.forward()">
<IMG SRC = "forward.gif"></A>
```

These statements are in the file *bottom_nav_jump.html*, which is a file that loads into the lower-right frame. The parent of this page is the outermost frameset, *index.html*. The parent has three frames, which are indexed 0, 1, and 2 (remember, counting always begins with 0 in JavaScript). In this example you want to navigate the history of frame number 1, which is the upper-right frame. That frame's history, then, is called *parent.frames[1].history* because history is a property of both frames and windows. History, in turn, has its own properties: the functions *back* and *forward*.

In order to have clickable images call these functions, the *<A HREF = "JavaScript: ...* structure is used. This is the easiest way to have an anchor execute a script, when you don't want it to do anything else.

The other property of the history object used here is the *go* function:

```
parent.frames[1].history.go(num)
```

This function goes forward or backward in the history of frames[1], depending on whether *num* is positive or negative.

Notes

History is also a property of the window object, so you can navigate the window's history with the statement *window.history.go()*.

If you had wanted to load a new URL into the current frame while you moved through the history of the top-right frame, your anchor could have read:

```
<A HREF = "new.html" onClick="parent.frames[1].history.back()">
<IMG SRC = "back.gif"></A>
```

Related Techniques

Programming Buttons

Creating Animated Radio Buttons

Creating a Remote in a Separate Window

OnClick Event Handler

Type: JavaScript event handler

Used in: Button, checkbox, radio, link, reset, and submit objects

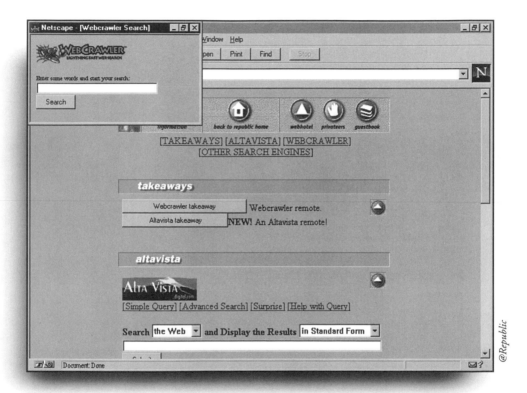

@Republic

```
<SCRIPT LANGUAGE="javascript">
<!-- Helpers for JSI page...
var palwin = null;
function RepPal() {
palwin=open("","PalOff","width=290,height=150");
if (palwin != null) {
palwin.rootWin = self;
palwin.location = "http://www.republic.se/search/webcrawler.html";
}
}
```

continues

```
var altwin = null;
function AltPal() {
altwin=open("","altOff","width=290,height=150");
if (altwin != null) {
altwin.rootWin = self;
altwin.location = "http://www.republic.se/search/altavista.html";
}
}
// end Helpers -->
</SCRIPT>



<FORM>
<INPUT TYPE="button" VALUE="Webcrawler takeaway"
   ONCLICK="RepPal()"> Webcrawler remote.<BR>
<INPUT TYPE="button" VALUE="Altavista takeaway"
ONCLICK="AltPal()"><B><BLINK>NEW!</BLINK></B> An Altavista remote!
</FORM>
```

Syntax Example

```
<FORM>
<INPUT TYPE="checkbox" NAME="box1" onClick='alert("Hi!")'> Click Me!
</FORM>
```

Comments

OnClick is an event handler that executes JavaScript when a button, radio, link or any similar type of object is pressed. Buttons on this page are used with the event handler to create remotes. A remote is a new window spawned for the main page. The window is typically small in size and used to load new pages into the main page.

Online Example

"search," by @Republic, email: **webmaster@republic.se**

URL: **http://www.republic.se/search/search.html**

Description

This page allows access to various search engines. It also has buttons that enable the user to open a new window with a remote to access the search engines. Because the remote is in a different window, it will be easily accessible after accessing pages. A remote can perform any JavaScript function that a main page can. Typically the functions of remotes are used purely for page navigation.

Step-by-Step

This page uses buttons to contain the *OnClick* event handler that will access the remote function. The button object is a property of form objects so the button tags need to be contained within *<FORM>* tags.

```
<INPUT TYPE="button" VALUE="Altavista takeaway" ONCLICK="AltPal()">
```

The event handler in this case executes the *AltPal()* function.

```
function AltPal() {
altwin=open("","altOff","width=290,height=150");
if (altwin != null) {
altwin.rootWin = self;
altwin.location = "http://www.republic.se/search/altavista.html";
}
}
```

The *AltPal()* function uses the *open* method open a new window of a specific size. The *open* method is assigned to *altwin*, which is the name of the new window object. The name of the new window (NOT the object name) is "*altOff*". *altwin* is tested for a null value to see if the *open* method was successful and the new window was created. If successful, the location object of the new window is set to the URL to display the forms for the search.

The function *RepPal()* and the button associated with it work in exactly the same manner.

Related Techniques

HTML Practice Window

Fade In/Fade Out Technique

OnUnload Event Handler

Type: JavaScript event handler

Used in: Window objects, frame objects

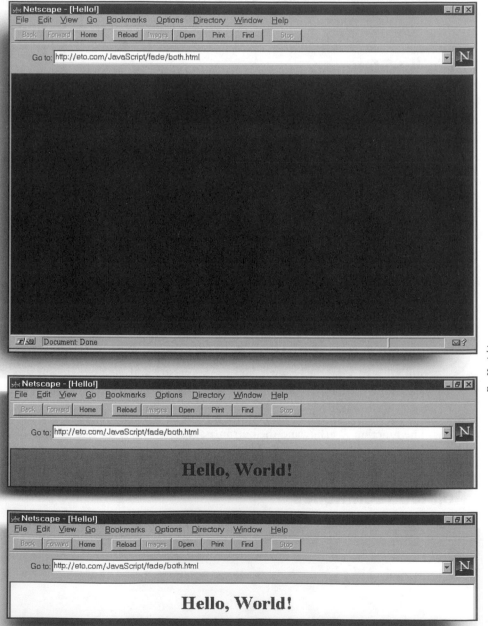

```
<html>
<head>
<title>Hello!</title>
<script language="JavaScript">
<!--
/*****************************************************************
 * fade script ver0.1 by Kouichirou@Eto.com 1996/02/20
 * Copyright (c) 1996 Kouichirou Eto. All Rights Reserved.
 * You can freely copy, use, modify this script,
 * if the credit is given in the source.
 * If you would like to get information for this script,
 * please access <http://eto.com/JavaScript/>
 */
function makearray(n) {
    this.length = n;
    for(var i = 1; i <= n; i++)
        this[i] = 0;
    return this;
}
hexa = new makearray(16);
for(var i = 0; i < 10; i++)
    hexa[i] = i;
hexa[10]="a"; hexa[11]="b"; hexa[12]="c";
hexa[13]="d"; hexa[14]="e"; hexa[15]="f";

function hex(i) {
    if (i < 0)
      return "00";
    else if (i > 255)
      return "ff";
    else
      return "" + hexa[Math.floor(i/16)] + hexa[i%16];
}

function setbgColor(r, g, b) {
    var hr = hex(r); var hg = hex(g); var hb = hex(b);
    document.bgColor = "#"+hr+hg+hb;
}

function fade(sr, sg, sb, er, eg, eb, step) {
    for(var i = 0; i <= step; i++) {
      setbgColor(
      Math.floor(sr * ((step-i)/step) + er * (i/step)),
      Math.floor(sg * ((step-i)/step) + eg * (i/step)),
      Math.floor(sb * ((step-i)/step) + eb * (i/step)));
    }
}
```

continues

```
/* Usage:
 *    fade(inr,ing,inb, outr,outg,outb, step);
 * example.
 *    fade(0,0,0, 255,255,255, 255);
 * fade from black to white with very slow speed.
 *    fade(255,0,0, 0,0,255, 50);
 *    fade(0xff,0x00,0x00, 0x00,0x00,0xff, 50); // same as above
 * fade from red to blue with fast speed.
 * step 2 is very fast and step 255 is very slow.
 */

function fadein() {
    fade(0,0,0, 255,255,255, 64);
}
function fadeout() {
    fade(255,255,255, 0,0,0, 64);
}
/* do fadein */
fadein();
/***** end fade script *****/
// -->
</script>
</head>

<body bgcolor="#ffffff" onUnLoad="fadeout()">
<h1 align="center">Hello, World!</h1>
</body>
</html>
```

Syntax Example

```
<FRAMESET ROWS="20%,*" onUnLoad="fadeout()"
```

Comments

OnUnload is an event handler that executes JavaScript when the page is cleared. Any action that the user does to leave the page will cause *OnUnload* to execute. Possible uses of this event handler include displaying a good-bye message, or saving users information to a cookie before they leave the page.

Online Example

"Hello!," by Eto Kouichirou, email: **Kouichirou@Eto.com**

URL: **http://eto.com/JavaScript/fade/both.html**

Description

This is a good attention-grabbing script that manipulates the *document.bgColor* property to cause a fading effect on the page. The background color is rapidly changed in steps from black to white when the page is loaded and from white to black as the user leaves the page.

Step-by-Step

1. The *onUnload* event handler is similar to the *onLoad* event handler, it just operates when the page is cleared. In this page, *onUnload* spawns a function that changes the background color from white to black. The *onUnload* event handler on this page executes the *fadeout()* function. This function performs the white to black change by executing the command:

```
fade(255,255,255, 0,0,0, 64);
```

2. The function to create the effects is the *fade()* function.

```
function fade(sr, sg, sb, er, eg, eb, step) {
```

The first three parameters to *fade* specify the RGB values, in decimal, of the starting background color. The next three specify the RGB values of the background color to end on. The last parameter specifies how fast the function should execute the fade. The fastest speed is two while the slowest is 255.

```
for(var i = 0; i <= step; i++) {
   setbgColor(
   Math.floor(sr * ((step-i)/step) + er * (i/step)),
   Math.floor(sg * ((step-i)/step) + eg * (i/step)),
   Math.floor(sb * ((step-i)/step) + eb * (i/step)));
     }
```

A *for* loop is used to step through as many values as specified by *step*. The loop index *i* and *step* are used in a formula to calculate the intermediate values for RGB colors. The values determined by this formula are converted to integers by the *Math.floor* method. These integers are passed to the function *setbgColor()*, which displays the color to the background.

Related Techniques

Flashing Color Over Frames

Accessing Multiple Frames for a Cosmetic Effect

Automating a Web Page Tour

Using the Location Object

Type: JavaScript object

Used in: Document objects

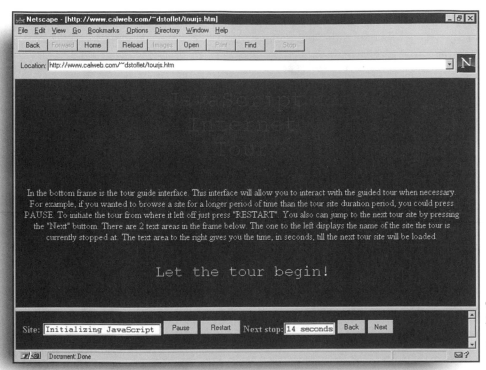

Darryl Stoflet

```
<HTML>
<HEAD>
<SCRIPT LANGUAGE = "JavaScript">


<!-- Hide this from browsers that can't read JavaScript
var timerID = null
var timerRunning = falsevar loc = 1
var sec = 21
```

continues

```
var counter = 1000
halt = false;

function stopclock(){
// cannot directly test timerID
if(timerRunning)
clearTimeout(timerID)
timerRunning = false
}

function startclock(){
// Make sure the clock is stopped
stopclock()
showtime()
}

function showtime(){
sec = sec - 1
if(sec <= 0 & loc == 1){
parent.frames.main.location.href =  "http://www.freqgrafx.com/411/";
document.tour.timeleft.value = "loading...";
document.tour.countdown.value = "JavaScript 411";
sec = 40;
loc = loc + 1;
}
if(sec <= 0 & loc == 2){
parent.frames.main.location.href =
        "http://tanega.com/java/java.html";
document.tour.timeleft.value = "loading...";
document.tour.countdown.value = "JavaScript Examples";
sec = 40;
loc = loc + 1;
}


    ...
    ...
    ...

if(sec <= 0 & loc == 12){
parent.frames.main.location.href =
"http://www.webconn.com/java/javascript/intro/index.htm";
document.tour.countdown.value = "Voodoo's Intro to JavaScript";
document.tour.timeleft.value = "loading...";
sec = 40;
loc = loc + 1;
}
```

```
if (halt == true){
document.tour.timeleft.value = "PAUSED";
}
else{
if(sec < 31){
document.tour.timeleft.value = sec + " seconds";
}
}

timerID = setTimeout("showtime()", counter)
timerRunning = true

if(loc > 13){
document.tour.countdown.value = "The tour is over";
document.tour.timeleft.value = "Tour over";
}
}


function pause(){
halt = true
stopclock();
document.tour.timeleft.value = "PAUSED";
}

function restart(){
if (halt == false){
alert("You have not paused the tour so it is not necessary
      to press RESTART")
}
else{
halt = false;
document.tour.timeleft.value = "Restarting";
startclock();
}
}
function retrace(){
if(loc > 2){
sec = 1;
loc = loc - 2;
}
else{
alert("You are at the first site. There is no site to go back to");
}
}
```

continues

```
function forward(){
sec = 1;
}
//-->


</SCRIPT>
</HEAD>
<BODY   BGCOLOR=#000000   TEXT=#c0c0c0
      onLoad = setTimeout("startclock()",1000)>

<FORM NAME = "tour">
<b>Site:</b>
<INPUT TYPE = "text" VALUE = "Initializing JavaScript Tour"
                 NAME = "countdown"
SIZE = 24>
<INPUT TYPE = "button" VALUE = "Pause" onClick = "pause()">
<INPUT TYPE = "button" VALUE = "Restart" onClick = "restart()">
<b>Next stop:<INPUT TYPE = "text" VALUE = "" NAME = "timeleft"
               SIZE = 10></b>
<INPUT TYPE = "button" VALUE = "Back" onClick = "retrace()">
<INPUT TYPE = "button" VALUE = "Next" onClick = "forward()">
</FORM>
</BODY>
</HTML>
```

Syntax Example

```
parent.frames.main.location.href =   "http://www.yahoo.com/";
```

Comments

A JavaScript guided tour can be used to present a group of Web pages. The tour automatically loads a variety of pages sequentially into your browser. Because the computer is doing the work, you do not need to continuously consult a hot list or menu page.

Online Example

By Darryl Stoflet, email: **dstoflet@calweb.com**

URL: **http://www.calweb.com/~dstoflet/who.htm**

Description

A script in one frame is used to present a series of Web pages in a different frame. This Web tour is set on a timer to load a new page every 40 seconds. Buttons included on the JavaScript frame enable you to navigate manually through the tour.

Step-by-Step

This frame has various controls that manipulate the tour. There is a text object called *countdown* which indicates the current site in the tour. Another text object called *timeleft* is used display the time until the next site is loaded. Four buttons control the tour. Two buttons are used to pause and restart the clock. The other two are used to move to the previous and next site in the tour. An *OnLoad* event handler in the body tags calls the *startclock()* function, which in turn calls the *showtime()* function.

The main function in this JavaScript tour is the recursive *showtime()* function.

```
function showtime(){
sec = sec - 1
if(sec <= 0 & loc == 1){
parent.frames.main.location.href =  "http://www.freqgrafx.com/411/";
document.tour.timeleft.value = "loading...";
document.tour.countdown.value = "JavaScript 411";
sec = 40;
loc = loc + 1;
}
```

The variable *sec* is used to keep track of the number of seconds left in each call of the function. It is decremented by one at the start of function. The variable *loc* is used to note the current location in the tour. A series of *if* statements is used to check if *sec* is zero or less and to check the value of *loc*. If one of the *if* conditions is satisfied, the *href* property of the location object of the other frame is assigned a new URL.

Also, the string *"loading..."* is assigned to the *timeleft* text object, whereas a description of the new URL is assigned to the *countdown* text object. The *sec* variable is reset to 40 to enable the next page to load after 40 seconds. The *loc* variable is incremented to keep track of the next page to be loaded. After these *if* statements, whether a new page has been loaded or not, the *halt* variable is checked to see if the tour has been paused.

```
if (halt == true){
document.tour.timeleft.value = "PAUSED";
}
else{
if(sec < 31){
document.tour.timeleft.value = sec + " seconds";
}
}

timerID = setTimeout("showtime()", counter)
timerRunning = true

if(loc > 13){
document.tour.countdown.value = "The tour is over";
document.tour.timeleft.value = "Tour over";
}
}
```

If *halt* is true, *"PAUSED"* is displayed on the *timeleft* text object. Otherwise, if *sec* is less than 31, the number of seconds left is displayed there. Then, the *setTimeout* method is used to call the *showtime()* function again after one second. The *loc* value is checked to display messages to the text objects if the tour is over.

Related Techniques

Automatically Moving to an Updated Page

Using Time-Dependent Web Page Properties

Using Multiple Functions on a Page

Using JavaScript Functions (Advanced Techniques)

Type: JavaScript structure

Used in: Page organization

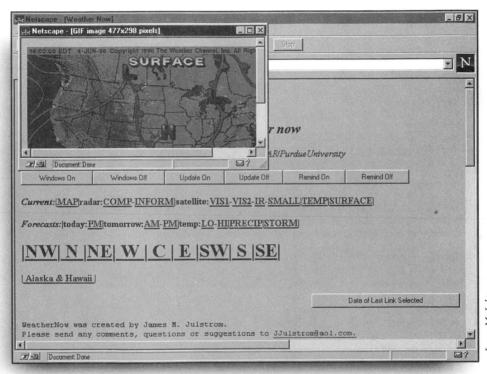

James M. Julstrom

```
function map(){
linkwindow(1,"http://www.weather.com/images/curwx.gif",
 "map","497","328")
}
function comp(){
 linkwindow(0,"http://www.intellicast.com/weather/usa/radar/",
 "comp","550","400")
}
```

continues

```
function inform(){
 linkwindow(0,"http://www.intellicast.com/weather/usa/radsum/",
 "inform","550","400")
}


function nwssm(state){
 nws(state, "summary")
 }
function nwszn(state){
 nws(state, "zone")
 }
function nwsfr(state){
 nws(state, "state")
 }
function nws(astate,filen){
nwsref="http://iwin.nws.noaa.gov/iwin/"+astate+"/"+filen+".html"
 wnws="nws"+astate+filen
 linkwindow(1,nwsref,wnws,"620","200")
}


function linkwindow(mdate, uniformrl, windowname, wid, hei){
windowconfig="status,scrollbars,resizable,width="+wid+",height="+hei
 moddate=mdate
 if (onoff==1){
  if (isupdate==0){
windowvar=window.open(uniformrl, windowname, windowconfig)
   if (windowvar.history.length>=1){
    del=-windowvar.history.length
    windowvar.history.go(del)
   }
   if (remind==1){
windowvar.alert('For date, click Date of Last Link Selected
 button.  May not work with 2.01 or 2.02.  To disable this message,
 click the Remind Off button.')
   }
  }
  else{
   upwindowname=windowname+"control"
if (navigator.appVersion.substring(0,4)=="2.0 "){
    controlwin(uniformrl)
   }
   else{
if (navigator.appVersion.substring(0,4)=="2.01"){
    alert("The update feature does not work with Navigator version
2.01.  Please use 2.02, or click the Update Off button.")
   }
```

```
    else{
     windowvar1=window.open("http://members.aol.com/weathernow/
control.htm", upwindowname,"width=220,height=215")
     if (remind==1){
      windowvar1.alert("For auto-updates, set your browser to verify
 documents EVERY TIME, and leave this small control window open.
  Enter different values in this window if desired.  To disable this
 message, click the Remind Off button.")
     }
     windowvar1.defaultStatus=uniformrl
    }
   }
  }
 }
 else {
  window.location.href=uniformrl
 }
}


<P><B><I>Current:</I>¦
<A HREF="javascript:map()">MAP</A>¦radar:
<A HREF="javascript:comp()">COMP</A>-
<A HREF="javascript:inform()">INFORM</A>


<A HREF="javascript:nwssm('wy')">Sm</A>
<A HREF="javascript:nwszn('wy')">Zn</A>
<A HREF="javascript:nwsfr('wy')">Fr</A>
```

Syntax Example

```
function display(string1,string2) {
 document.write(string1,string2);
  }
```

Comments

JavaScript functions can be used to arrange the structure of the page for easy programming and debugging instead of having the code in one large block. They are also
useful for code that is continuously repeated. Passing variables to a function makes this
possible by allowing the same section of code to operate on different variables.

Online Example

"Weather Now," by James M. Julstrom, email: **JJulstrom@aol.com**

URL: **http://members.aol.com/tujulstrom/jscript.html**

Description

This page uses JavaScript functions to access various weather map information on the Internet. Many of the groups of map pictures come from the same location with similar filenames. Various functions contain the partial URL of the locations. The functions need only to pass the section of the filename requested to identify the full URL. The functions insert the specific file information into a URL and display the requested picture.

Step-by-Step

The main function used in this page is the *linkwindow()* function. This function is a generalized function that will accept a URL along with other function parameters. The function will display that URL in a user specified format.

You can specify whether the picture is to be displayed in a different window or on the original window according to the *onoff* variable. You can also specify if the date the picture was last modified is to be displayed. Another option is to choose whether the function should return control to the main page after the picture is displayed.

A few of the functions such as *map()*, *comp()*, and *inform()* are used to display whole maps of the United States. These functions are accessed directly from links on the page. The URLs of these pictures are constant so the *linkwindow()* function is called with the same parameters.

The functions for the local maps are accessed from links such as:

```
<A HREF="javascript:nwssm('wy')">Sm</A>
```

In this case, the *nwssm()* function calls another function *nws()* passing the state ("wy") and the type of map ("summary"). The *nws()* function creates an URL by concatenating this information into a text string. This URL calls the *linkwindow()* function to display the appropriate map.

Related Techniques

Creating a Remote in a Separate Window

Recording Optional Information

Automatically Moving to an Updated Page

Navigator Object

Type: JavaScript object

Used in: Window objects

```
<SCRIPT LANGUAGE = "JavaScript">
<!--
if (navigator.appCodeName == "Mozilla")
{
alert('We noticed that you have Netscape 2.0 or greater so we will
take you to the Java enhanced site, hope you approve.  If not, just
go to http://homedirections.com');
location="http://netmart.com/homedirections/hdfram.html";
}
// -->
</script>
```

Syntax Example

```
document.write('Version: ' + navigator.appVersion)
```

Comments

The navigator object is an object that allows JavaScript to detect various properties of the user's browser. The properties can detect the name, version number, OS, and other properties of a browser. You can use this to specialize your JavaScript to specific browser types.

Online Example

"Home Directions," by Home Directions, email: **gorsline@ix.netcom.com**

URL: **http://world.std.com/~gorsline/kwg2.html**

Description

This page is a new form of the "We have moved" type of pages. If the JavaScript version of Netscape is detected, it will automatically take you to a certain version of a new page.

Step-by-Step

The navigator object has the following read-only properties:

```
appCodeName
```

The *appCode Name* property specifies the code name of the version. In the case of Netscape 2.0, the code name is "Mozilla."

```
appName
```

appName is the name of the browser.

```
appVersion
```

appVersion specifies a string in the form of: *"releaseNumber (platform; country)"*.

releaseNumber is the version number of the browser.

platform indicates the OS that this version runs on.

country is either "I" for the international version or "U" for the U.S. version.

`userAgent`

userAgent is a value used by servers to identify the client. It is in a form similar to the *appVersion* property.

The navigator object has no methods and uses no event handlers.

An *if* statement, such as if the *appCodeName* is "Mozilla," will display an alert message indicating a new page is being loaded. The loaded page uses frames, JavaScript, and other techniques specific to that version of Netscape. If another browser is used, either the JavaScript will not be detected or the *if* statement condition will be false. In either case you can click the link on the page to move to a new page.

Related Techniques

Detecting the User's Type of Browser

Examining Form Data

Responding to Multiple Selected Items

Using the With Statement

Type: JavaScript command

Used in: Page navigation

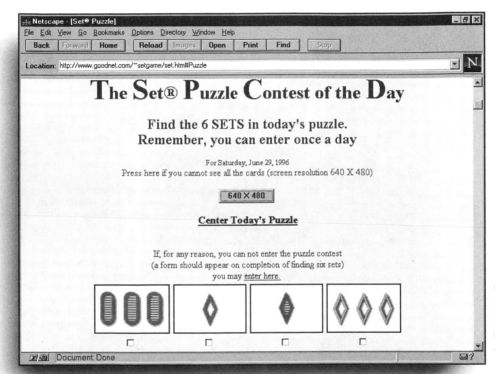

Set Enterprises, Inc.

```
<Script language="JavaScript">
<!-- No reason to see this
var total=0;
var found=0;
var set1=false;
var set2=false;
var set3=false;
var set4=false;
var set5=false;
var set6=false;
// If someone knows a better way to create an array please tell me!
```

```
function zero(){
var i=1;
with (window.document){
for (i=1;i<13;i++){card[i].checked = 0}}}

function mess(on_off){
if (on_off==1){message='GREAT! \n'+found+' Sets Found'}
else {message='You already found that one! \nStill have '+
      (6-found)+' to find'}}

function callset(dancing){
var setexist = false;
if (dancing=='A1912') {setexist = true;if (set1==false){set1=true;
      found++;mess(1)}else {mess(2)}}
if (dancing=='A4612') {setexist = true;if (set2==false){set2=true;
      found++;mess(1)}else {mess(2)}}
if (dancing=='A4711') {setexist = true;if (set3==false){set3=true;
      found++;mess(1)}else {mess(2)}}
if (dancing=='A569') {setexist = true;if (set4==false){set4=true;
      found++;mess(1)}else {mess(2)}}
if (dancing=='A789') {setexist = true;if (set5==false){set5=true;
      found++;mess(1)}else {mess(2)}}
if (dancing=='A81011') {setexist = true;if (set6==false){set6=true;
      found++;mess(1)}else {mess(2)}}
if (setexist==true) {alert(message)}
else {alert('NOT A SET!')}
if (found==6){window.open('sixfound.htm','newWin','scrollbars=1,
      width=450,height=450');found=0}}

function Count(){
total = 0
var dance='A';
var i = 1;
with (window.document){for (i=1;i<13;i++){
if (card[i].checked == 1) {total++;dance=dance+i}}}
if (total == 3)
    {total = 0;callset(dance);zero()}
if (total > 3)
    {zero()}}

<!--Done-->
</Script></HEAD>


<FORM NAME="card" method="post">
<TABLE><TR>
<TH><A HREF="#Puzzle" Border=0
onClick="with(window.document.card.A1){ if (checked == 1){checked=0}
      else {checked = 1}};Count()" >
```

```
<IMG SRC="graphics/51.gif"height=80 width=123 Border="2"></A></TH>
<TH><A HREF="#Puzzle" Border=0
onClick="with(window.document.card.A2){ if (checked == 1){checked=0}
     else {checked = 1}};Count()" >
<IMG SRC="graphics/67.gif"height=80 width=123 Border="2"></A></TH>
<TH><A HREF="#Puzzle" Border=0
onClick="with(window.document.card.A3){ if (checked == 1){checked=0}
     else {checked = 1}};Count()" >
<IMG SRC="graphics/37.gif"height=80 width=123 Border="2"></A></TH>
<TH><A HREF="#Puzzle" Border=0
onClick="with(window.document.card.A4){ if (checked == 1){checked=0}
     else {checked = 1}};Count()" >
<IMG SRC="graphics/72.gif"height=80 width=123 Border="2"></A></TH>
</TR>
<TR><TH><input type="checkbox" name="A1" onclick="Count()"></TH>
<TH><input type="checkbox" name="A2"  onClick="Count()"></TH>
```

Syntax Example

```
with(Math) {
        sqrt( cos(PI) )
}
```

Comments

The *with* statement can help simplify your JavaScript code. Given a large amount of data to be accessed from the same object, the *with* statement can specify that object so it will not have to be repeated in the code.

Online Example

"Set® Puzzle," by Set Enterprises, Inc., email: **setgame@goodnet.com**

URL: **http://www.goodnet.com/~setgame/set.htm**

Description

This page implements a puzzle game in which the user needs to find sets of three images within a grid of 12 images. The user can click either the pictures or checkboxes under the pictures to select them. When the user finds six correct sets, the page will display a form in which the user can enter a contest.

Step-by-Step

1. Within the page the 12 images are displayed with 12 checkboxes underneath. The checkboxes are given names *A1* through *A12*. When each checkbox is checked, the *onClock* event handler executes the *Count()* function. To make it so the user is able to click the images, the images are set up as links. The links all point to the same anchor in the page. The links are used for the *onClick* event handler that executes statements such as:

```
"with(window.document.card.A1){ if (checked == 1){checked=0}
    else {checked = 1}};Count()"
```

The use of the *with* statement allows the properties enclosed in the braces to be accessed from the same object. The same group of statements could be also written without the *with* statement:

```
"if (window.document.card.A1.checked == 1)
        { window.document.card.A1.checked=0}
    else { window.document.card.A1.checked = 1};Count()"
```

You can see how this can simplify the code. What these statements do is toggle the checkmark of the checkbox associated with the image. They then execute the *Count()* function just as if the checkbox was checked directly.

2. The function *Count()* creates a string called *dance* with the checkbox values so that they may be checked to see whether a set has been selected. The string is started with the 'A' character. A *for* loop is used to check through all the checkbox's *checked* property.

If one of the checkboxes is checked, the number of the checkbox is appended to the string. If three checked checkboxes are found, the *callset()* function is called passing *dance*. This function checks the string to see whether it is a valid set. It displays *alert* messages indicating if a set was found, or previously found, or not a set at all. If all six sets are found, the *window.open* method opens a new window with the file *sixfound.htm*—here the users can enter their names in a contest.

Related Techniques

Blinking Radio Buttons

Tic-Tac-Toe Game

Detecting the User's Operating System

Using the String Object (Substring Method)

Type: JavaScript object

Used in: Window objects

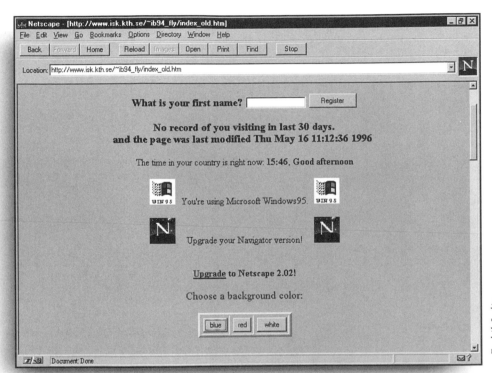

Fredrik Lydén

```
var theVersion = navigator.appVersion;
var platform = "";
var nversion = "";
var i = 1;
if (theVersion.substring(0,4) == "2.02") {
     nversion="22"
}
else
{
```

continues

```
        nversion="2"
}

while (i < theVersion.length) {
if (theVersion.substring(i,i+1) == "(") {
if (theVersion.substring(i+1,i+4) == "Mac") {
platform="Mac";
}
else if (theVersion.substring(i+1,i+4) == "Win") {
platform="Win";
}
else {
platform = "X";
}
if (theVersion.substring(i+1,i+6) == "Win95") {
platform="Win95";
}
break;
}
i = i + 1;
}


if (platform == "Mac") {
imageSrc = '<A HREF="http://www.apple.com" target="_top">
<img src="Media/Apple.jpg" height=24 width=24 align=absmiddle
hspace=5></A>'
   htmlOut += imageSrc + "</td><td align=center>You're using
Macintosh.</td><td>" + imageSrc
}
else if (platform == "Win") {
imageSrc = '<A HREF="http://www.microsoft.com" target="_top">
<img src="win.gif" height=44 width=44 hspace=10 border=0></A>'
   htmlOut += imageSrc + "</td><td align=center>You're using
Microsoft Windows.</td><td>" + imageSrc
}
else if (platform == "Win95") {
imageSrc = '<A HREF="http://www.windows95.com" target="_top">
<img src="win95.gif" height=44 width=44 hspace=10 border=0></a>'
   htmlOut += imageSrc + "</td><td align=center>You're using
Microsoft Windows95.</td><td>" + imageSrc
}
else {
imageSrc = '<img src="x.gif" height=34 width=34 hspace=5>'
   htmlOut += imageSrc + "</td><td align=center>You're using
UNIX.</td><td>" + imageSrc
}
```

Syntax Example

```
FirstInitial = name.substring(0,1)
```

Comments

The *string* object has a number of methods to manipulate strings. The *substring* method is used to extract a section of a string. This page uses the method on string properties of the navigator object. The method checks to see whether portions of the string properties contain codes indicating the operating system of the browser.

Online Example

By Fredrik Lydén, email: **ib94_fly@isk.kth.se**

URL: **http://www.isk.kth.se/~ib94_fly/index_old.htm**

Description

This page uses the navigator object to determine what type of operating system the user has and displays a message indicating it.

Step-by-Step

The *substring* method of the string object is used as:

```
StringPortion = StringName.substring(index1,index2)
```

The portion of *StringName* between characters at position *index1* and *index2* is stored in *StringPortion*.

The *naviagtor.appversion* property is used to obtain the string that contains the operating system information. It is in the form *releaseNumber (platform; country)*.

First, the number of characters in the string is obtained using the *length* string property. A *while* statement is used to increment the variable *i* until the string length is reached. If the substring of i and i+1 is the left parenthetical mark, the next section of letters will specify the operating system. Each possible choice is checked, and if found, it is stored in the variable *platform*. If a browser does not use the navigator object, *navigator.appName* will be *null* and *platform* will also be *null*.

The *platform* variable is used later in the page to display the operating system name with an appropriate graphic to the user.

Related Techniques

Automatically Moving to an Updated Page

Detecting the User's Type of Browser

Filtering Out Links

Document Object (Referrer Property)

Type: JavaScript object

Used in: Browser documents

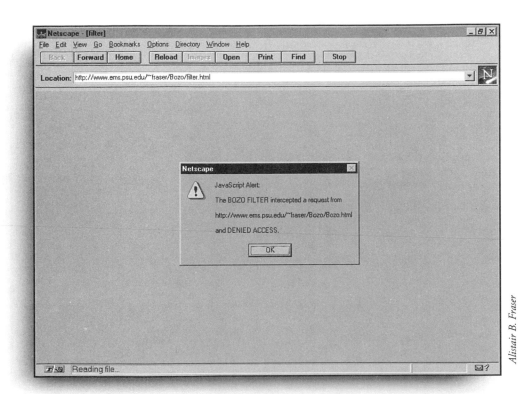

Alistair B. Fraser

```
<script language="JavaScript">
<!--- hide script from old browsers
// this BOZO filter was created by Alistair B. Fraser: abf1@psu.edu

var caller = document.referrer    // this discovers the calling page

var msg1 = "The BOZO FILTER intercepted a request from\n\n"
var msg2 = "\n\nand DENIED ACCESS."
// these form the
// message in the
```

continues

```
// alert window
if (caller=="") {
msg1 = "The BOZO FILTER intercepted a request which did not come
from a page, "
msg2 = "and DENIED ACCESS. \n\nYou must branch to here from a
recognizable page."
}

var numb =2          // set value to the number of bozos listed below

function Bozo(numb) {
for (var i =1;  i <= numb; i++) {
this[i] = i
}
}

bozo = new Bozo(numb)

// List the URLs of as many bozos as you wish following
//      the formate of those shown immediately below.
// The (1st) empty bozo blocks attempts to circumvent the filter by
//      accessing the page through the Open File dialogue box.


bozo[1] = "";
bozo[2] = "http://www.ems.psu.edu/~fraser/Bozo/Bozo.html";


for (var i in bozo) {

if (bozo[i] == caller){
alert("\n"+msg1 + bozo[i] + msg2); //delete line to remove
history.back();                     // alert dialogue
break;}
}

// end hiding from old browsers -->
</script>
```

Syntax Example

```
var caller = document.referrer    // this discovers the calling page
```

Comments

The *document.referrer* property can be used to see what URL was used to link to the current page. A popular use of this property is to detect which search engine found a page, if one was used.

Online Example

"Filter," by Alistair B. Fraser, email: **abf1@psu.edu**

URL: **http://www.ems.psu.edu/~fraser/Bozo/Bozo.html**

Description

This page will deny access from certain specified links. It will automatically return you to the previous page. This can prevent access from sites that you would like to avoid. For example, a nude art site may not want to be associated with a pornographic site.

Step-by-Step

This script first stores the *document.referrer* property in a string variable named *caller*. The property will contain the URL of the page that the current page was linked from. If the current page was not linked to (accessed by typing in the URL directly), the property will contain a null string (""). Defined messages will display in a dialog box if the URL is to be denied access. Special messages are defined if *caller* is a null string.

Then an array called *Bozo[]* is defined that will contain all the URLs you want to deny. A null string can be put in the array if you only want the page to be linked to and not through (using the Open Location command in the user's browser).

A *for* loop is used to cycle through all the values in the *bozo[]* array. If one of the entries in the array is equal to the *caller* variable, it means the page is to be denied access. A dialog box appears with the message defined earlier and the URL that was detected in the *bozo[]* array. The *history.back* method is then used to take you back to the previous page, before this page is displayed.

Notes

This method is in no way secure. A non-JavaScript enabled browser can be used to access the page, or JavaScript can be disabled in the current browser. You can obtain the URL from the "banned" link and create that link in one of your own pages. However, it will prevent most users from accessing a page from a certain link.

Related Techniques

User-Customized Links in a Frame

Controlling Interaction Among Open Windows

Detecting the User's Type of Browser

Using the Navigator Object

Type: JavaScript object

Used in: Window object

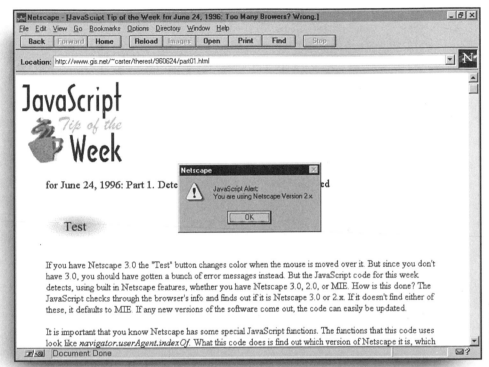

Nick Heinle

```javascript
var version = 0;

if(navigator.appName.indexOf("Netscape") != -1){

        if(
        navigator.userAgent.indexOf("Mozilla/3.0b3") != -1 ||
        navigator.userAgent.indexOf("Mozilla/3.0b4") != -1 ||
        navigator.userAgent.indexOf("Mozilla/3.0b5") != -1 ||
        navigator.userAgent.indexOf("Mozilla/3.0b6") != -1 ||
        navigator.userAgent.indexOf("Mozilla/3.0") != -1) {
        version = 3;
```

continues

```
        active = new Image(105, 42);
        active.src = "test_active.jpg";
        inactive = new Image(105, 42);
        inactive.src = "test_inactive.jpg";
          if (navigator.userAgent.indexOf("Macintosh") != -1) {
          version = 4;
          }
        }

        else if(
        navigator.userAgent.indexOf("Mozilla/2.0") != -1 ||
        navigator.userAgent.indexOf("Mozilla/2.01") != -1 ||
        navigator.userAgent.indexOf("Mozilla/2.02") != -1) {
        version = 2;
        }

        else version = 2;
        }

else {
version = 1;
}


function which_one(){

if (version == 4) return "Netscape Version 3.0 for Macintosh.";

if (version == 3) return "Netscape Version 3.0.";

if (version == 2) return "Netscape Version 2.x.";

if (version == 1) return "Microsoft Internet Explorer 3.0.";

}
```

Syntax Example

```
if (navigator.userAgent.indexOf("Macintosh") != -1) {
```

Comments

Occasionally, it may be useful to know which browser is being used to view your page. For example, one might want to use a function allowed by an advanced browser, but it causes an error in the previous browser version. JavaScript can be used to display the function only to the advance browser.

Online Example

"JavaScript Tip of the Week for June 24, 1996: Too Many Browers? Wrong.," by Nick Heinle, email: **carter@gis.net**

URL: **http://www.gis.net/~carter/therest/960624/part01.html**

Description

This page uses the Navigator object to determine which browser is being used. The object can also be used to find the version number, operating system, and other information about the browser.

Step-by-Step

Two of the Navigator object's properties are used in this script: *appName* and *userAgent*. The name of the browser is stated in *appName*, while special codes identifying the browser are present in *userAgent*. The string method *indexOf* is used to determine if various parts of strings are present in the navigator properties. If the method's parameter is not present in the navigator object's property, a -1 is returned.

Throughout this script, the *version* variable is used to store a number that refers to the browser type. First, the *appName* property is checked to see if Netscape is being used. If not, *version* is set to 1 (indicating MicroSoft Internet Explorer 3.0 or some other non-Netscape JavaScript capable browser). If Netscape is being used, the *userAgent* property is checked to see if the browser is a 2.x, 3.0, or Macintosh version.

The function *which_one()* has a series of *if* statements which test the *version* number. The function returns a string indicating what type of browser the previous script has detected.

Related Techniques

Automatically Moving to an Updated Page

Detecting the User's Operating System

Determining the Data Type of a Parameter

Using the typeof Function

Type: JavaScript

Used in: Functions

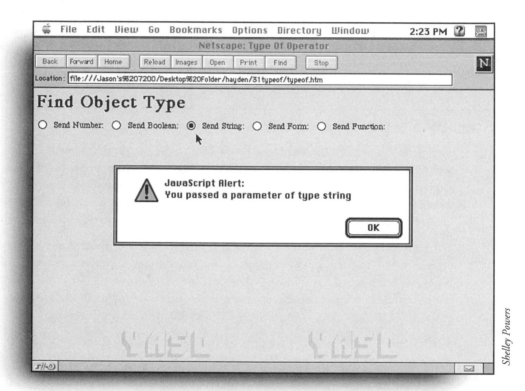

Shelley Powers

```
<HTML>
<HEAD><TITLE> Type Of Operator</TITLE>

<SCRIPT LANGUAGE="JavaScript">
<!--- hide script from old browsers

function FindTypeOf(vParameter) {
    var sTypeOf = typeof vParameter
    alert("You passed a parameter of type " + sTypeOf)
    }
```

```
// end hiding from old browsers -->
</SCRIPT>

</HEAD>

<body BACKGROUND="nmbk2.gif">

<H1> Find Object Type </H1>

<FORM NAME="TypeForm">
<INPUT TYPE="radio" Name="Type"
     onClick="FindTypeOf(1.0)"> Send Number: 

<INPUT TYPE="radio" Name="Type"
     onClick="FindTypeOf(true)"> Send Boolean: 

<INPUT TYPE="radio" Name="Type"
     onClick="FindTypeOf('test')"> Send String: 

<INPUT TYPE="radio" Name="Type"
     onClick="FindTypeOf(TypeForm)"> Send Form: 

<INPUT TYPE="radio" Name="Type"
     onClick="FindTypeOf(FindTypeOf)"> Send Function: 
</FORM></BODY>
</HTML>
```

Syntax Example

```
sTypeOf = typeof vParameter
```

Commments

The *typeof* operator is new to Netscape 3.0. It helps clear up the confusion caused by JavaScript's loose typing of variables.

Online Example

"Type of Operator," by Shelley Powers of YASD, email: **shelleyp@yasd.com**

URL: **http://www.yasd.com/javascrpt/typeof.htm**

Description

This example illustrates the simple, straightforward use of the *typeof* operator. Click a button that says "send number," and you are alerted that you sent a number. Looking at the JavaScript is the point of this example.

Step-by-Step

Clicking the button executes the following statements:

```
var sTypeOf = typeof vParameter
alert("You passed a parameter of type " + sTypeOf)
```

Notice that you don't write *typeof (vParameter)*. You just write *typeof vParameter* because *typeof* is not a function. It is an operator, such as return.

Notes

As this is being written, Netscape 3.0 is still in beta, so it is not clear just how this operator will work.

Related Techniques

Grouping Variables Together

Using Multiple Functions on a Page

Grouping Variables Together

Using JavaScript Arrays

Type: JavaScript technique

Used in: Arrays

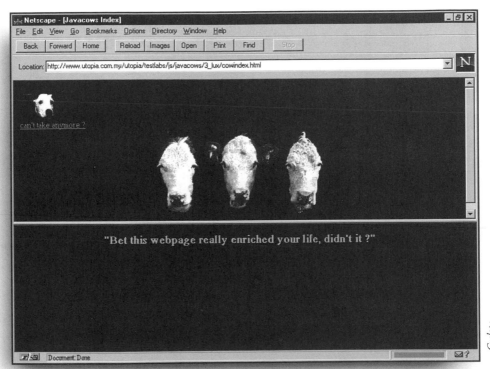

Cyclops

```
<!-- This script was created by Chas Sweeting, Medusa + Cyclops  -->

function makearray (x) {
    this.length = x
    for (var i=1; i<= x; i += 1){
        this[i] = 0;
        }
}

cowa = new makearray (7);
cowb = new makearray (12);
cowc = new makearray (8);
```

continues

```
   cowa[1] = "What do you make of this mad cow's thing ?";
   cowa[2] = "It will all blow over... then they will eat us again.
<BR> People have already started to forget about it."
   cowa[3] = "Remember the salmonella scare 6 years ago and people
stopped <BR>eating eggs, even though they had eaten them all
their lives ?<BR> Look how long that lasted.";


   .
   .
   .

function speak(id,thecow,arrayel){
     if (last_cow == id) {
             return;
             }
             arrayel += 1;
             if (arrayel > thecow.length) {
                     arrayel = 1;    }
             output = thecow[arrayel];

             // set the control variables
             last_cow = id;
             if (id == "aaaa") {
                     alastsaid = arrayel;
                     }
             if (id == "bbbb") {
                     blastsaid = arrayel;
                     }
             if (id == "cccc") {
                     clastsaid = arrayel;
                     }


<A HREF = "#top" onMouseOver = "speak('aaaa',cowa, alastsaid);
 return true"> <IMG SRC = "../images/cowb150.gif" BORDER = "0"
 HEIGHT = "150" WIDTH = "84"></A>

<A HREF = "#top" onMouseOver = "speak('bbbb',cowb, blastsaid);
 return true"> <IMG SRC = "../images/cowa150.gif" BORDER = "0"
 HEIGHT = "150" WIDTH = "131"></A>

<A HREF = "#top" onMouseOver = "speak('cccc',cowc, clastsaid);
 return true"> <IMG SRC = "../images/cowc150.gif" BORDER = "0"
 HEIGHT = "150" WIDTH = "74"></A>
```

Syntax Example

```
item[j] = j * Math.PI
```

Comments

Arrays are a useful tool to link groups of variables together. An array is a collection of data that is indexed by an integer. This way specific elements of the array can be accessed in the JavaScript by a number.

Using arrays for your groups of variables enables you to more easily search through the data, or pick out an ordered element. For example, for a search one could use a *for* loop to loop through the values of an array. The loop variable can then be used as the index of the array and be checked for a value. Here is an example that searched for a specific string in an array:

```
for (j=1 ; j<N ; j++)
        if (Country[j] == "Canada")
                alert('Canada is present in the array.')
```

Online Example

"Javacows Index," by Cyclops, email: **cyclops@utopia.com.my**

URL: **http://www.utopia.com.my/utopia/testlabs/js/javacows/3_lux/cowindex.html**

Description

This page has a group of "talking cows" by display text from *onMouseOver* event handlers. The quotes from each of the three cows are stored in three arrays. The use of arrays allow the quotes from each cow to be displayed in order. All of the quotes can be displayed through one function. Without arrays, you would probably need a large number of *if* statements to achieve the same effect. The code would be much longer and less efficient.

Step-by-Step

1. The *makearray()* function is used to create a generic array of a specific size. The *new makearray(x)* command creates an array with *x* number of elements. The function uses a *for* loop to initialize every element in the new array to zero. This sets away a certain amount of space for the array.

2. This script creates three arrays of varying sizes called *cowa, cowb* and *cowc* using the *new makearray(x)* command. Then strings are assigned to every element of these arrays in the desired order in which they are to be displayed. Now all of the strings can be accessed from the arrays. To access the third string from the second cow, you would use the statement *cowb[3]*.

3. The images of the three cows in the page are created as links. The links just link to a dummy anchor on the page. They are used to access the *onMouseOver* event handler. The event handler accesses the *speak()* function. Passed to this function are three parameters: a code indicating which cow, the array of strings for that cow, and the index of the last message displayed:

```
arrayel += 1;
if (arrayel > thecow.length) {
        arrayel = 1;    }
output = thecow[arrayel];
```

What *speak()* does is take the index of the last message displayed called *arrayel*, and increments it by one. If *arrayel* is greater that the number of values in the array it is set to one. The variable output, which will later be used to display the quote, is assigned the string at position *arrayel* in the array. The value of *arrayel* is stored in a global variable specific to the cow that called the function, so the index of the last message displayed can be stored for later use.

Related Techniques

Displaying a Calendar Month

Client-Side Search

Creating Random Phrases

Using a Random Number Generator

Type: JavaScript process

Used in: Throughout the page

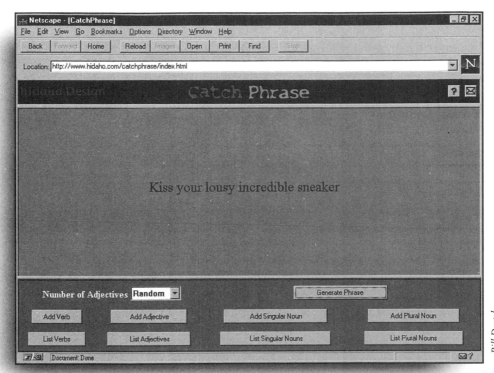

Bill Dortch

continues

```
  else
    this.seed = test + this.M;
  return (this.seed * this.oneOverM);
}
function RandomNumberGenerator() {
  var d = new Date();
  this.seed = 2345678901 +
    (d.getSeconds() * 0xFFFFFF) +
    (d.getMinutes() * 0xFFFF);
  this.A = 48271;
  this.M = 2147483647;
  this.Q = this.M / this.A;
  this.R = this.M % this.A;
  this.oneOverM = 1.0 / this.M;
  this.next = NextRandomNumber;
  return this;
}


function DarkColor () {
  this.red = Math.round (127 * rand.next());
  this.green = Math.round (127 * rand.next());
  this.blue = Math.round (127 * rand.next());
  this.toString = ColorString;
  return this;
}
function LightColor () {
  this.red = Math.round (127 * rand.next()) + 128;
  this.green = Math.round (127 * rand.next()) + 128;
  this.blue = Math.round (127 * rand.next()) + 128;
  this.toString = ColorString;
  return this;
}


var rand = new RandomNumberGenerator();
if (rand.next() >= .5)
    body = new BodyColor (new DarkColor(), new LightColor());
  else
    body = new BodyColor (new LightColor(), new DarkColor());
```

218

Syntax Example

```
var rand = new RandomNumberGenerator();
die=Math.ceil(6 * rand.next)
```

Comments

No useful random number method exists in JavaScript. There is a *Math.random* method, but it works only on UNIX platforms. This was an oversight that will probably be corrected in future browser versions. To create random numbers, you must include a function based on the current time or some other seed.

Online Example

"Catch Phrase," by Bill Dortch, email: **feedback@hidaho.com**

Pseudo-Random Number Generator code by David N. Smith

URL: **http://www.hidaho.com/catchphrase/index.html**

Description

Random numbers are used throughout the page to generate the phrase, the number of adjectives, the font size, the font style, and other aspects. This section of code examines how random numbers are used to generate random colors for the phrase and background.

Step-by-Step

The *RandomNumberGenerator()* function uses the current number of minutes and seconds to create a seed for a random number generator algorithm. It also sets some of the variables needed for the algorithm. The *this.next = NextRandomNumber* command sets the next number in the pseudo-random number series by calling the *NextRandomNumber* function. To use these functions, a random number object must be declared, as in *var rand = new RandomNumberGenerator()*. You can use *rand.next()* to create a random floating-point number from 0 to 1.

The two functions *DarkColor()* and *LightColor()* create a random color. In *DarkColor()*, the red, green, and blue components are assigned a random number from 0 to 127 using the command *Math.round (127 * rand.next())*. In *LightColor()*, numbers from 128 to 255 are created using the command *Math.round (127 * rand.next()) + 128*. These values are used in other functions to create the colors on-screen.

Notes

The *Math.round* method is used to find a random integer using the random number functions. This technique works in such a way that the integer does not result in an even distribution. For example, consider finding an integer from 0 to 2 using *Math.round(2 * rand.next)*. The probability of getting 0 is $^1/_4$, 1 is $^1/_2$, and 2 is $^1/_4$. To achieve an even distribution you could use *Math.floor(3 * rand.next)*. Using the *Math.floor* and *Math.ceil* methods results in an even distribution.

Related Techniques

Using Time-Dependent Web Page Properties

Displaying Random Images

Implementing a Game Using Form Objects

Encrypting Text in a Page

Using String Variables

Type: JavaScript data type

Used in: String variables

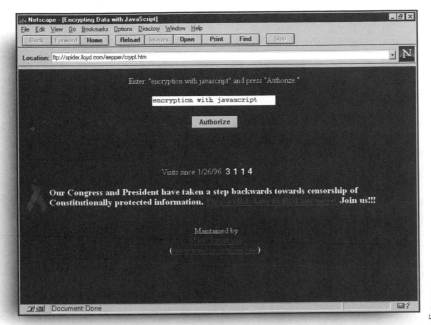

```
<script Language="JavaScript">
<!-- Password protected page!
// Copyright (c) Mark Epperson 1996. (epperson@ix.netcom.com)

// this list of characters MUST be 2^N in length (32, 64, 128, 256)
var charsLen = 64;
var chars=" #$%&'()*+,-./0123456789:;{=}?@abcdefghijklmnopqrstuv
wxyz[\]^_'¦~";

// these characters are translated into escape sequences
// using '^' for the escape char
// example: "A" gets translated into "^a"
var uCase="ABCDEFGHIJKLMNOPQRSTUVWXYZ<>";
var escapeChar = "^";
var escapeIndex = chars.indexOf(escapeChar);
var kSum = 0; var prev = 0; var lCaseA = 0; var pass=charsLen-1;

// gather information about the key to incorporate into the
// encryption. The idea here is to incorporate the length of the key
// and information about each individual character into the key.
// This makes the encrypted output dependent  on the changing
// even a single character in the key or length of the key.
// Also note that two characters from the key are used
// to encrypt each character of the data.

function PreProcessKey() {
  key = document.authorize.pass.value;
  key = key.toLowerCase();
  kSum = 0;

  // get the (sum % number of chars)
  for (var ix = 0; ix < key.length; ix++) {
    var keyChar  = key.charAt(ix);
    kSum += chars.indexOf(keyChar);
  }
  kSum %= charsLen;

  // xor in the length and -1 for good measure
  kSum ^= key.length ^ (charsLen-1);

  prev = chars.indexOf(key.charAt(key.length - 1));
  lCaseA = chars.indexOf("a");
}

// This function implements reversable XOR encryption. Each character
// of the data is XOR'ed with two characters from the key,
// the checksum of the key, the length of the key, the middle
// character of the key, and the current position within the key
// (not starting at the beginning of the key). Mixed case is
// accomplished by dynamically translating upper-case characters
// into escaped sequences using '^' as the escape character
// (eg. "M" gets translated into "^m" and visa versa).
```

```
function Scramble(data) {
  var outData = "";
  var prevValue = 0 + prev;

  var ixK; var ixD; var dataChar; var dataValue;
  var keyChar; var keyValue; var outValue; var outChar;

  // get more info on the key, use the middle character
  // in the encryption
  dataChar = data.charAt(key.length / 2);
  var offset = chars.indexOf(dataChar);
  var shift = false;  var dCodeChar = "";

  // process each character in the input data, wrap the key when
  // it gets to the end.
  ixK = (Math.floor(key.length/3) + pass) % key.length;
  pass++;

  for (ixD = 0; ixD < data.length; ixD++, ixK++) {
    if (ixK >= key.length)
      ixK = 0;

    // check for shifted chars
    if (dCodeChar != "") {
      // second pass of shifted char, insert the lower case character
      dataChar = dCodeChar;
      dCodeChar = "";
      dataValue = chars.indexOf(dataChar);
      if (dataValue == -1)
        return ""; // fail
    } else {
      // normal processing, just get character from the chars array
      dataChar = data.charAt(ixD);
      dataValue = chars.indexOf(dataChar);
    }

    if (dataValue == -1) {
      // character not found in the chars array, try to generate
      // a shifted char
      dataValue = lCaseA + uCase.indexOf(dataChar);
      dCodeChar = chars.charAt(dataValue);

      // two passes are required to encode a shifted char, insert
      // the "^" first
      ixD--;
      dataValue = escapeIndex;
    }
```

continues

223

```
    // do the actual encryption here
    keyChar = key.charAt(ixK);
    keyValue = chars.indexOf(keyChar);
    outValue = ((((dataValue ^ keyValue) ^ prevValue) ^
     ((ixK + offset) % charsLen)) ^ kSum);

    // if shifted get the data from the uppercase array,
    // otherwise use the normal array
    if (shift)
    {
      outChar = uCase.charAt(outValue - lCaseA);
      if (outChar == "")
      {
        // not a shifted character after all, put the escape
        // character back in
        shift = false;
        outData += escapeChar;
      }
    }

    if (!shift)
      outChar = chars.charAt(outValue);

    // treat "^" as the first character of an escape sequence,
    // in the next pass if we cannot find the escaped character
    // in the shifted characters list then we
    // will put this character in then.
    prevValue = keyValue;
    shift = (outChar == escapeChar);
    if (!shift )
      outData += outChar;
  }
  return outData;
}

// this is where you write out the HTML for your page. Note that a
// single quote should be used instead of a double quote.
// The way this is normally done is to first write this function with
// the NON encrypted data and run the page with the password you want
// to use. Then copy and paste the result over the original data.

function WriteData() {
  document.write( "<BODY TEXT=#FFFFFE BGCOLOR=#000000>" );
  document.write("<center><Font size=+4>Encrypting data with
JavaScript<br><br></Font></Center>");
  document.write("<Font size=+2>");
  document.write("<pre>");
  document.write("This is the decrypted data:<br>");
```

```
// Uncomment these lines to generate the encrypted data.
// The encryption changes EACH
// TIME IS IS CALLED so the lines MUST me in exactly the same order.
//  document.write("document.write(Scramble( '"
+ Scramble( "Your Name" ) + "' );<br>");
//  document.write("document.write(Scramble( '"
+ Scramble( "Street address" ) + "' );<br>");
//  document.write("document.write(Scramble( '"
+ Scramble( "City, State zip" ) + "' );<br>");
//  document.write("document.write(Scramble( '"
+ Scramble( "(800) 555-1212" ) + "' );<br>");

 //comment these lines out when the above lines are not commented out
  document.write(Scramble( ".v3#'j)f*[n" ) + "<br>");
  document.write(Scramble( "c/ '-a]9/ozwnxl" ) + "<br>");
  document.write(Scramble( "r54{-$9k¦j{`f=k}/" ) + "<br>");
  document.write(Scramble( "5eht19#}+0 96#" ) + "<br>");

  document.write("<br><hr>");
  document.write("This is what you put in your page:<br>");
  document.write("document.write(
Scramble( \".v3#'j)f*[n\" ));<br>");
  document.write("document.write(
Scramble( \"c/ '-a]9/ozwnxl\" ));<br>");
  document.write("document.write(
Scramble( \"r54{-$9k¦j{'f=k}/\" ));<br>");
  document.write("document.write(
Scramble( \"5eht19#}+0 96#\" ));<br>");

  document.write("<hr></pre></Font>");
}

// write out the encrypted page.
function Authorize() {
  PreProcessKey();
  WriteData();
}
<!-- done hiding from old browsers -->
</script></HEAD>

<BODY TEXT=#FFFFFE BGCOLOR=#000000>
<form name='authorize' onSubmit='Authorize()'><div><Center>
Enter: "encryption with javascript" and press "Authorize."<br><br>
<input type='text' name='pass' size=30 value=''>
<br><br>
<input type='button' value='Authorize' onClick='Authorize()'><br>
</Center></div></form>
```

225

Syntax Example

```
Scramble( ".v3#'j)f*[n" )
```

Comments

Sometimes you would like the data in your Web pages to be encrypted. You can limit your page so it can be read only by people who have a password. Another use is to encrypt the answers to a quiz in the page. This way no one can use the "View Source" command to cheat.

Online Example

"Encrypting Data with JavaScript," by Mark Epperson, email: **epperson@ix.netcom.com**

URL: **http://spider.lloyd.com/aepper/crypt.htm**

Description

There is encrypted data within this page. This page has a text form that enables the user to enter a password to display the encrypted data. The encryption algorithm is based on the password, so if a wrong password is entered, the data will not be displayed in a readable format.

Step-by-Step

There are two main functions used in the encryption, the *PreProcesKey()* function and the *Scramble()* function:

- The *PreProcessKey()* function takes a password and creates an encryption key from the password. This key must be created to be used in the encryption process.

- The second function, *Scramble()* is used to perform the encryption process. The function receives a string, and performs an encryption algorithm using the key obtained from the *PreProcessKey()* function. The processed string is then returned by the function.

To create your own encrypted page you must first find the encrypted text. This is easy to do because the *Scramble()* function uses the same process to encrypt data as to decrypt data. For example, *Scramble(Scramble("xyz"))* would return *"xyz"*.

1. First, you create preliminary code in JavaScript. This would display the results of the *Scramble()* function of the unencrypted text you wish to display:

```
document.write(Scramble("My dog has fleas."));
```

2. Then you would execute the JavaScript using a password you have chosen. Using the password "cat" with this example you will obtain:

```
*kw2bqw$f1u$vjc1u0
```

3. Now you can replace the unencrypted text in the JavaScript with what you have obtained:

```
document.write(Scramble("*kw2bqw$f1u$vjc1u0"));
```

4. When you execute the JavaScript with the password "cat" you will obtain the original string:

```
My dog has fleas.
```

You can string together multiple statements in this fashion to create your whole page. HTML tags can also be included in the encrypted data.

Related Techniques

Creating a Multiple Choice Test

Creating a Memory Game

Storing Information Using a Custom Object

Displaying an Image via a Selection List

Using the Select Object

Type: JavaScript object

Used in: Form objects

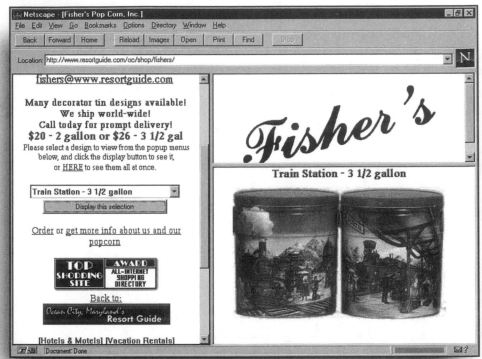

Fisher's Pop Corn, Inc.

File: index.html

```html
<html><head>
<title>Fisher's Pop Corn, Inc.
</title>

</head>
<frameset cols="7*,9*">
<frame src="idx.html" name=title1 marginwidth=1 marginheight=1>
<frameset rows="160,*">
<frame src="title.html" name=menu marginwidth=1 marginheight=1>
<frame src="body.html" name="display" marginwidth=1 marginheight=1>
</frameset></frameset>
```

File: idx.html

```
<script>

function select_item(name, value) {
this.name = name;
this.value = value;
}

function get_selection(select_object) {
contents = new select_item();

for(var i=0;i<select_object.options.length;i++)
if(select_object.options[i].selected == true) {
contents.name = select_object.options[i].text;
contents.value = select_object.options[i].value;
}

return contents;
}

function display_image(form) {

selection = get_selection(form.imagename);
    var result = "";
result += ("<HTML><BODY BGCOLOR=FFFFFF TEXT=000000>");
   result += ("<CENTER><B><FONT SIZE=+1>" + selection.name
+ "</FONT></B><br>");
   result += ("<IMG
SRC='http://www.resortguide.com/oc/shop/fishers/pix/"
+ selection.value + "' vspace=12 hspace=12>");
    result += ("</CENTER></BODY></HTML>");
parent.display.document.close(); // just to be safe
parent.display.document.open("text/html");
parent.display.document.writeln(result);
parent.display.document.close();
}

function display (form) {
var frame = frames["display"]
if(frame != null)
display_image (form);
}
</SCRIPT>


<FORM NAME="previewForm">
<CENTER>
<select NAME="imagename">
```

continues

```
<option value="bday.jpg">Happy Birthday - 2 Gallon
<option value="potpourri.jpg">Potpourri - 2 Gallon
<option value="thanks.jpg">Thank You - 2 Gallon
<option value="sports.jpg">Sports - 2 Gallon
<option value="holidays.jpg">Holidays - 2 Gallon
<option value="berries.jpg">Holly and Berries - 2 Gallon
<option value="bears.jpg">Polar Bears - 2 Gallon
<option value="roofSanta.jpg">Rooftop Santa - 2 Gallon
<option value="hugbear.jpg">Hugging Bear - 3 1/2 gallon
<option value="mountain.jpg">Mountain Majesty - 3 1/2 gallon
<option value="train.jpg">Train Station - 3 1/2 gallon
<option value="pheasants.jpg">Pheasants - 3 1/2 gallon
<option value="pigout.jpg">Pig Out - 3 1/2 gallon
<option value="kidsChrismas.jpg">Childrens' Christmas - 3 1/2 gallon
<option value="nutcrkr.jpg">Nutcracker - 3 1/2 gallon

</select>
<input type=button value="Display this selection"
onClick="display(this.form)">
<p><a href="order.html" target="_top">Order</a> or
<a href="caramel.html" target="_top">
get more info about us and our popcorn</a>
</CENTER>

</FORM>
```

Syntax Example

```
<FORM>
<SELECT name="list" SIZE="2" MULTIPLE>
<OPTION SELECTED> item1
<OPTION> item2
<OPTION> item3
</SELECT>
</FORM>
```

Comments

The *select* object on this page is used to create a popup list. You can use a popup selection list to accept a choice from the user. The main advantage to using a popup list is that it can display many options without taking a lot of real estate on the page.

Online Example

"Fisher's Pop Corn, Inc.," by Fisher's Pop Corn, Inc., email:
fishers@www.resortguide.com

URL: **http://www.resortguide.com/oc/shop/fishers/**

Description

The *select* object on this page enables you to select a certain image. The image is displayed on a different frame of the page. This enables you to view exactly what you want to see, without having to wait for all of the images to load.

Step-by-Step

In this page, all the options are given values in which the name of the respective image is stored. When the button is pushed, a function called *display()* passes *this.form* as a parameter. This function checks to see if the frame named *"display"* exists, and if so, calls the function *display_image()*. This function first uses the command:

```
selection = get_selection(form.imagename);
```

After this command is called, the option text and associated image name will be stored in *selection.name* and *selection.value*. Using a string variable called *result*, HTML code is generated using these variables. This code is displayed on the frame named *display* using the *document.open* and *document.writeln* methods.

Related Techniques

Loading a Page via a Selection List

Displaying Random Images

Implementing a Scientific Calculator

Using the Math Object

Type: Built-in JavaScript object

Used in: Because Math is an object, it can be used in any JavaScript statement

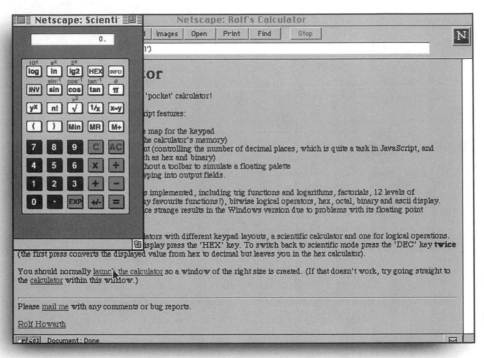

Rolf Howarth

```
<HTML>
<HEAD>
<TITLE>Scientific Calculator</TITLE>
<script language=javascript>
//<!--
 // Javascript scientific calculator   (4 March 1996)
 // (C) Copyright Rolf Howarth 1996
 // rolf@insect.demon.co.uk

 function push(value,op,prec)
 {
     if (level==STACKSIZE)
         return false;
     for (i=level;i>0; --i)
     {
```

```
                stack[i].value = stack[i-1].value;
                stack[i].op = stack[i-1].op;
                stack[i].prec = stack[i-1].prec;
        }
        stack[0].value = value;
        stack[0].op = op;
        stack[0].prec = prec;
        ++level;
        return true;
}

function pop()
{
        if (level==0)
                return false;
        for (i=0;i<level; ++i)
        {
                stack[i].value = stack[i+1].value;
                stack[i].op = stack[i+1].op;
                stack[i].prec = stack[i+1].prec;
        }
        --level;
        return true;
    }
}

 function enter()
 {
        if (exponent)
                value = value * Math.exp(expval * Math.LN10);
        entered = true;
        exponent = false;
        decimal = 0;
        fixed = 0;
 }


function func(f)
{
        enter();
         if (f=='n!')
        {
                if (value<0 || value>200 || value !=
Math.round(value))
                        value = "NAN";
                else
                {
                        var n = 1;
                        var i;
                        for (i=1;i<=value;++i)
                                n *= i;
```

continues

```
                        value = n;
                }
        }
        else if (inverse)
        {
                if (f=="sin")
                        value = Math.asin(value)*180/Math.PI;
                else if (f=="cos")
                        value = Math.acos(value)*180/Math.PI;
                else if (f=="tan")
                        value = Math.atan(value)*180/Math.PI;
                else if (f=="log")
                        value = Math.exp(value * Math.LN10);
                else if (f=="pi")
                        value = Math.E;
        }
        else
        {
                if (f=="sin")
                        value = Math.sin(value/180 * Math.PI);
                else if (f=="cos")
                            value = Math.cos(value/180 * Math.PI);
                else if (f=="tan")
                        value = Math.tan(value/180 * Math.PI);
                else if (f=="log")
                        value = Math.log(value)/Math.LN10;
                else if (f=="pi")
                        value = Math.PI;
        }
        refresh();
 }

// -->
</script>
</HEAD>

<BODY onLoad="refresh()" bgcolor=#808080>

<center>
<FORM name=result>
 <INPUT size=18 name=result
onFocus="refresh(); this.blur();">
</FORM>
<IMG SRC="scalc.gif" width=159 height=224
usemap="#map" border=0>
<MAP name="map">
<AREA SHAPE=rect HREF="javascript:digit(0)"
COORDS="12,191,32,209">
<AREA SHAPE=rect HREF="javascript:period()"
COORDS="40,191,60,209">
</MAP>

</BODY>
</HTML>
```

Syntax Example

```
value = Math.asin(value)*180/Math.PI
```

Comments

The *Math* object has eight properties, some of which are the fundamental constants of mathematics, like pi. It has 17 methods, including trigonometric and logarithmic functions.

The eight properties are

Math.E (Euler's constant, e)

Math.LN10 (the natural log of 10)

Math.LN2 (the natural log of 2)

Math.LOG2E (the log base 2 of e)

Math.LOG10E (the common log — log base 10 — of e)

Math.SQRT1_2 (the reciprocal of the square root of 2, which happens to be the sine or cosine of 45 degrees)

Math.SQRT2 (the square root of 2)

Math.PI (pi)

The trigonometric methods (all expressed in radians) are

Math.sin

Math.cos

Math.tan

Math.asin

Math.acos

Math.atan

The logarithmic and exponential methods are

Math.exp (e raised to the given power)

Math.log (natural logarithm)

235

Math.pow (which takes two arguments, and returns the first argument raised to the power of the second)

The remaining methods are

Math.max and *Math.min*, which each take two arguments, and yield the greater or lesser argument, respectively

Math.abs (absolute value)

Math.sqrt (square root)

Math.random (a pseudo-random number between zero and one; only works on UNIX platforms in Navigator versions before 3.0)

Math.round (rounds a number to the closest integer)

Math.ceil (the smallest integer greater than the argument)

Math.floor (the largest integer smaller than the argument)

Online Example

"Rolf's Calculator," by Rolf Howarth, email: **rolf@insect.demon.co.uk**

URL: **http://www.parallax.co.uk/~rolf/Calculator**

Description

This scientific calculator keyboard is very similar to most real scientific calculators; it includes memory, an inverse button, and hexadecimal arithmetic functions.

Step-by-Step

```
else if (inverse)
{
    if (f=="sin")
        value = Math.asin(value)*180/Math.PI;
else if (f=="cos")
        value = Math.acos(value)*180/Math.PI;
else if (f=="tan")
        value = Math.atan(value)*180/Math.PI;
else if (f=="log")
        value = Math.exp(value * Math.LN10);
else if (f=="log2")
```

```
            value = Math.exp(value * Math.LN2);
else if (f=="ln")
            value = Math.exp(value);
else if (f=="sqrt")
            value = value*value;
else if (f=="pi")
            value = Math.E;
}
else
{
    if (f=="sin")
            value = Math.sin(value/180 * Math.PI);
else if (f=="cos")
            value = Math.cos(value/180 * Math.PI);
else if (f=="tan")
            value = Math.tan(value/180 * Math.PI);
else if (f=="log")
            value = Math.log(value)/Math.LN10;
else if (f=="log2")
            value = Math.log(value)/Math.LN2;
else if (f=="ln")
            value = Math.log(value);
else if (f=="sqrt")
            value = Math.sqrt(value);
else if (f=="pi")
            value = Math.PI;
}
```

The Math object is mostly used in the *func()* function. This function checks to see if the inverse button was pushed; then it evaluates the expression that you entered. Note that the function automatically converts radians to degrees for all the trigonometric functions.

```
        var frac = Math.floor(valFrac * mult + 0.5);

        valInt = Math.floor(Math.floor(value * mult + .5) / mult);
```

Math.floor is also used to truncate the decimal portion of certain values.

```
if (exponent)
      value = value * Math.exp(expval * Math.LN10);
```

When the exponent key is implemented, the *Math.exp* is used to calculate the exponent, and the constant *Math.LN10* is used to change the base of the exponent from e to 10. (If you don't remember Algebra II, this won't mean much to you!)

Notes

Cookies keep track of the calculator's memory. This means that you can shut down your computer, go to lunch, and when you return, your calculator will still remember the value you put in its memory!

A client-side imagemap is used instead of input buttons for the interface. This way, it has the desired appearance.

Also note that a stack is implemented, which is a construct familiar to anyone with any computer science background. When you click certain keys, they are "pushed" into the stack. At the appropriate time, they are "popped" off of the stack, in the reverse order they were pushed.

Related Techniques

Recording Optional Information in a Cookie

Creating Client-Side Imagemaps in JavaScript

Changing Images Dynamically

Using the Images Object

Type: JavaScript

Used in: Object; property of the document object

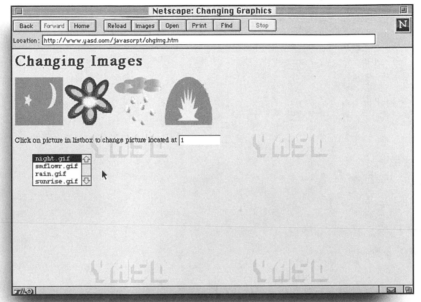

```
<HTML>
<HEAD><TITLE> Changing Graphics </TITLE>
<SCRIPT LANGUAGE="JavaScript">
<!-- hide script from old browsers
/* Copyright (C)1996 YASD   All Rights Reserved.
   This code can be re-used or modified, if credit is given
   in the source code.*/

function ChangeGraphic(GrphForm) {
   var iIndex = GrphForm.Picture.value
   sSelected = GrphForm.Graphic.options
[GrphForm.Graphic.selectedIndex].text

   var sImage = ""
   sSelected = "http://www.yasd.com/javascrpt/" + sSelected
   iIndex--
   document.images[iIndex].src = sSelected
   }

// end hiding from old browsers -->
</SCRIPT>
</HEAD>

<body BACKGROUND="nmbk2.gif">

<H1> Changing Images </H1>
<p>
<IMG SRC="night.gif" width=75 height=75>
<IMG SRC="smflowr.gif" width=75 height=75>
<IMG SRC="rain.gif" width=75 height=75>
<IMG SRC="sunrise.gif" width=75 height=75>
<p>

<FORM NAME="FormValue" >
<INPUT TYPE="text" Name="Picture" Value=1 size=10>
<p>


<SELECT SIZE=4 NAME="Graphic"
onChange="ChangeGraphic(this.form)">

<OPTION SELECTED> night.gif
<OPTION> smflowr.gif
<OPTION> rain.gif
<OPTION> sunrise.gif
</SELECT>

</FORM></BODY></HTML>
```

Syntax Example

```
document.images[iIndex].src = sSelected
```

Comments

The images property of the document object is new to Netscape 3.0. It enables you to change an image in a document without reloading the document. This feature opens worlds of animation possibilities using JavaScript.

Online Example

"Changing Graphics," by Shelley Powers of YASD, email: **shelleyp@yasd.com**

URL: **http://www.yasd.com/javascrpt/chgimg.htm**

Description

This simple example illustrates the capability to change images. It contains four images, a scrolling list of the images, and a text field. Enter a number from 1 to 4 into the text field and select an image; that image loads into the position you selected.

Notice that in the figure shown here, one image shows through the other. This is a bug in Netscape 3.0b4 for the Macintosh. It does not appear in the Windows version, and hopefully, won't be in the Mac version by the time you read this.

Step-by-Step

1. Selecting the name of an image executes the following function:

```
function ChangeGraphic(GrphForm) {
   var iIndex = GrphForm.Picture.value
   sSelected = GrphForm.Graphic.options
[GrphForm.Graphic.selectedIndex].text
   sSelected = "http://www.yasd.com/javascrpt/"
 + sSelected
   iIndex--
   document.images[iIndex].src = sSelected
   }
```

2. First, the *iIndex* is set to the number that you entered in the text field. Then, the *sSelected* is set to the text in the option list that you selected; it puts text in front of it to make it into a URL.

241

3. Next, the *iIndex* is reduced by one. Why, you ask? Because even though you enter a number from 1 to 4, JavaScript counts from 0 to 3!

4. Finally, the key statement:

```
document.images[iIndex].src = sSelected
```

In Netscape 3.0, the *document* object has the property images, which is an array that refers to all the images in a document, from top to bottom. Hence, the first image is called *document.images[0]*, and the number of images in a document is *document.images.length*.

5. In turn, each image object has its own properties: src, lowsrc, height, width, border, vspace, hspace, and complete. All but the last correspond to familiar HTML attributes. Complete indicates whether the browser has finished loading the image.

Notes

As this is being written, Netscape 3.0 is still in beta, so it is not clear just how this object will work.

Related Techniques

Using Client-Side Imagemaps in JavaScript

Creating Special Graphical Effects

Creating Special Graphical Effects in JavaScript

Controlling the <HEIGHT> and <WIDTH> Attributes of the <IMG> Tag

Type: JavaScript

Used in: Complex JavaScript routine

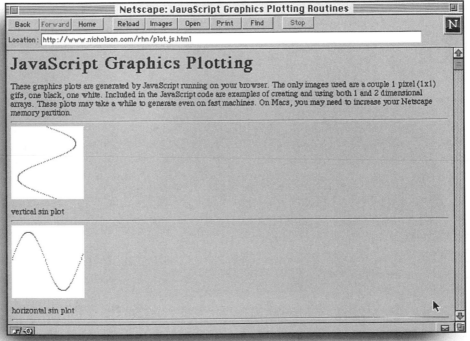

Ronald H. Nicholson, Jr.

```
<HTML>
<HEAD>

<TITLE>JavaScript Graphics Plotting Routines</TITLE>

<script language=JavaScript>
<!--hide
```

continues

```
   function plot_vertical(aa, size) {
     var j, w1, w2
     for (var i=0;i<size;++i) {
      j = aa[i]
      w1=parseFloat(j-1);
      w2=parseFloat(size-j);
      document.write (
        "<img src=sw.gif height=1 width=" +w1+">")
      document.write (
        "<img src=sb.gif height=1 width=1>")
      document.write (
        "<img src=sw.gif height=1 width=" +w2+"><br>");
     }
   } // plot_vertical

// -->
</script>
</HEAD>

<BODY bgcolor="c0c0c0">
<h1>JavaScript Graphics Plotting</h1>

<script language=JavaScript>
<!--hide

  // vertical plotting only requires a one dimensional array
  var a = new make_1d_array(100)
  var j
  for (var i=0;i<100;++i) {
   j = 50 + 40 * Math.sin(i/15);
   a[i] = j ;
  }
  plot_vertical(a, 100)
  document.write("<br>vertical sin plot")

// -->
</script>

</BODY>
</HTML>
```

Syntax Example

```
document.write ("<img src=sw.gif height=1 width=" +w1+">")
```

Comments

Because of the variability of the appearance of text and the need to reload a page to change its appearance, HTML does not lend itself to creating graphs. However, this example demonstrates a slick way to graph using the smallest graphical images possible.

Online Example

"JavaScript Graphics Plotting Routines," by Ronald H. Nicholson, Jr., email:
rhn@nicholson.com

URL: **http://www.nicholson.com/rhn/plot.js.html**

Description

This example illustrates how to graph various curves by exhibiting some standard trigonometric functions. The graphs themselves aren't important here; it is the flexibility of the technique that deserves some attention.

Step-by-Step

The key to this technique is to use single pixel images, and then expand them with the *<WIDTH>* and *<HEIGHT>* attributes of the <IMG> tag. The black dot is called sb.gif, and the white dot is called sw.gif (their names are bigger than they are!).

It begins with a vertical graph, like the ones you typically saw in high school. The values to be graphed, (in this case, a sine curve) are calculated first:

```
var a = new make_1d_array(100)
for (var i=0;i<100;++i)
        {
        j = 50 + 40 * Math.sin(i/15);
        a[i] = j ;
        }
```

Begin by creating one instance of an array object with 100 elements with the "new" operator. Then 100 values of the function are calculated, and those values are placed into the array:

```
plot_vertical(a, 100)
```

The function *plot_vertical*, which plots the values in the array, is then called:

```
function plot_vertical(aa, size)
        {
        for (var i=0;i<size;++i)
                {
                j = aa[i]
                w1=parseFloat(j-1);
                w2=parseFloat(size-j);
                document.write
("<img src=sw.gif height=1 width=" +w1+">")
                document.write
("<img src=sb.gif height=1 width=1>")
                document.write
("<img src=sw.gif height=1 width=" +w2+"><br>");
                }
        }
```

parseFloat is a built-in function that changes an expression into a floating-point real number, which guarantees that w1 and w2 are numbers that can be worked with.

Notice that one line is drawn horizontally across the screen 100 times. First, the values are *parseFloated.* Then a white bar that is w1 pixels wide (and one pixel tall) is drawn. Next, a single black dot is drawn. Finally, a white bar that goes the rest of the way across the graph is drawn. Repeat 99 more times, and you have a sine graph (on its side).

The key to this procedure is the *document.write* statement, which writes HTML onto the page:

```
document.write ("<img src=sw.gif height=1 width=" +w1+">")
```

This statement actually writes three strings, which taken together, form a valid IMG tag expression. Note that the *value* of the variable w1 will appear in the HTML, not the variable w1 itself.

Notes

All browsers draw the page by starting in the upper-left corner of the window, following all the way across to the right, and then moving down one pixel and doing the same, until the entire screen is drawn. As a result, all graphing routines must follow this pattern. If you want to create, say, a bar graph with the bars drawn vertically, you must calculate the positions of all the bars and slice your graph horizontally, because you always have to paint your page with horizontal strokes.

Related Techniques

Changing Images Dynamically

Using Client-Side Imagemaps in JavaScript

Displaying Random Images

Using Client-Side Imagemaps in JavaScript

Map Object

Type: JavaScript object

Used in: Images

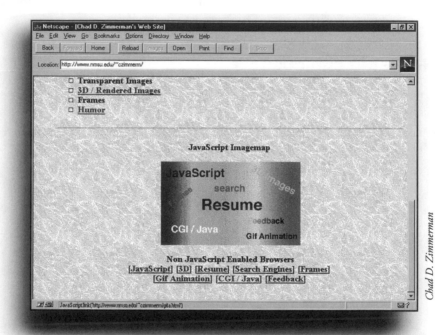

Chad D. Zimmerman

```
function link (uuu)  {
        location = uuu;
}



<h3 align=center>
JavaScript Imagemap
<map name="imap">
<area shape=rect coords=8,10,136,37
href="JavaScript:link('http://www.nmsu.edu/~czimmerm/javascript')">
<area shape=rect coords=182,5,282,68
href="JavaScript:link('http://www.nmsu.edu/~czimmerm/3D/')">
```

```
<area shape=rect coords=10,52,69,96
href="JavaScript:link('http://www.nmsu.edu/~czimmerm/frames/')">
<area shape=rect coords=107,47,177,65
href="JavaScript:link('http://www.nmsu.edu/~czimmerm/search.html')">
<area shape=rect coords=83,74,214,103
href="JavaScript:link('http://www.nmsu.edu/~czimmerm/resume1.html')">
<area shape=rect coords=12,127,123,150
href="JavaScript:link('http://www.nmsu.edu/~czimmerm/cgi-java/')">
<area shape=rect coords=176,113,258,131
href="JavaScript:link('mailto:czimmerm@nmsu.edu')">
<area shape=rect coords=175,144,285,163
href="JavaScript:link('http://www.nmsu.edu/~czimmerm/gifa.html')"
onMouseOver="window.status='Gif Animation' ; return true">
</map>

<h1 align=center><img src="./javascript/imap.gif" usemap="#imap"
 border=0></h1>
```

Syntax Example

```
<area shape=circle coords=20,30,5 href="file.html">
```

Comments

A client-side imagemap is often a better choice than a server-side imagemap. It is more efficient with fewer server accesses, and can provide information about various parts of the map. Also, because it is not dependent on the server, the map and associated code can be moved anywhere.

Online Example

"Chad D. Zimmerman's Web Site," by Chad D. Zimmerman, email:
czimmerm@nmsu.edu

URL: **http://www.nmsu.edu/~czimmerm/**

Description

This page has a JavaScript imagemap used to navigate this Web site. The map tag is used to define areas in an image. These areas are associated with JavaScript functions to display messages on the status bar and to link the user to a new page.

Step-by-Step

1. To create an imagemap, it needs to be of the form:

```
<MAP NAME="MapName">
<AREA SHAPE=(polygon,circ,rect,default)  COORDS="xcoord,ycoord,…"
 HREF="url" [OnMouseOver="handlerText"]>
</MAP>
```

2. Every map needs a name. The map can then be referenced in the image tag as follows:

```
<IMG SRC="image.gif" USEMAP="#MapName">
```

For all the shapes, the coordinates are referenced with (0,0) in the upper-left corner of the image. The *polygon* option can be used to specify any type of area with the coordinates specified at the corners of the polygon. The *rect* option needs only two sets of coordinates, one for the upper-left corner and one for the lower-right corner. The *circ* option has three numbers on the *<COORDS>* parameter.

The first two numbers set the center of the circle and the third sets the radius. The *default* option can be used to account for any space in the imagemap not specified by an area. For overlapping areas, the first area presented in the list takes precedence.

Within the *HREF* parameter, the contained URL will be loaded in the clicked area. JavaScript functions can be executed in this matter by using *javascript:* as the protocol in the URL.

3. An *OnMouseOver* event handler can be used within the *<AREA>* tags to execute JavaScript functions. For example, messages can be displayed on the status bar.

This page creates an imagemap called *imap*. It uses rectangular areas, in which all of them access the function *link()* passing a URL. In the function *link()*, the value passed is assigned to the window location property, which loads the URL to the page. The last area in the list uses the *OnMouseOver* event handler to display text on the status bar. An *<IMG>* tag is used to display the image, and the *usemap="#imap"* parameter is used to assign the imagemap to it.

Related Techniques

Status Line Display for Selected Links

Displaying MouseOver Information to a Form

Displaying Random Images

Using the Document Object (*WriteIn* Method)

Type: JavaScript object

Used in: Browser windows

```
<SCRIPT LANGUAGE="JavaScript">
<!-- to hide from other browsers

function showimg() {
img = new Object();
width = new Object();
height = new Object();

img[0] = "-1.jpg"; width[0]="120"; height[0]="96"
img[1] = "-2.jpg"; width[1]="120"; height[1]="80"
img[2] = "-3.jpg"; width[2]="120"; height[2]="80"
```

continues

```
img[51] = "h2.jpg"; width[51]="80"; height[51]="120"
img[52] = "h3.jpg"; width[52]="120"; height[52]="85"
img[53] = "h4.jpg"; width[53]="85"; height[53]="130"
var now = new Date();
var mytime=Math.floor(now.getTime()/1000)
var rand = Math.floor(mytime % 57)
document.writeln('<A href="../expanded/'+ img[rand] + '">'
+ '<IMG SRC="../icons/' + img[rand] + '" width="' + width[rand]
+ '" height="' + height[rand] + '" ALT="JavaScript"></A><br>');
if (rand < 7) document.writeln('<b>
<A href="gbartolomucci.html" target= "_top">Giovanni Bartolomucci
</A></b>')
else if (rand >= 7 && rand < 14) document.writeln('<b>
<A href="stefanelli.html" target= "_top" >Myriam Stefanelli</A></b>')
else if (rand >= 14 && rand < 21) document.writeln('<b>
<A href="provino.html" target= "_top" >Salvatore Provino</A></b>')
else if (rand >= 21 && rand < 23) document.writeln('<b>
<A href="collective.html" target= "_top" >Gianni Methz</A></b>')
else if (rand >= 23 && rand < 29) document.writeln('<b>
<A href="veschini.html" target= "_top" >Antonio Veschini</A></b>')
else if (rand >= 29 && rand < 36) document.writeln('<b>
<A href="gombacci.html" target= "_top" >Alice Gombacci</A></b>')
else if (rand >= 36 && rand < 43) document.writeln('<b>
<A href="fait.html" target= "_top" >Camillo Fait</A></b>')
else if (rand >= 43 && rand < 50) document.writeln('<b>
<A href="delsal.html" target= "_top" >Luigi Del Sal</A></b>')
else if (rand >= 50 && rand < 57) document.writeln('<b>
<A href="pasto.html" target= "_top" >Alessandro Past&ograve;
</A></b>')
document.writeln('<p>') }
//-->
</SCRIPT>
```

Syntax Example

```
document.writeln('<img src="image.gif" height=20 width=30>')
```

Comments

JavaScript can be used to write HTML or text to a page. In most cases, this is unnecessary. However, if random or user-specified elements need to be put into the page, JavaScript should be used.

Online Example

"ArtNet Italia," by ArtNet Italia, email: **arte@thru.com**

URL: **http://www.thru.com/art/uk/index.html**

Description

This page presents a random picture with the artist's name when the page is loaded. This shows how JavaScript can be used to change the look of your page on every visit.

Step-by-Step

The *document.writeln* method will simply display the parameters of the method to the document window followed by a newline character. Text, HTML tags, and JavaScript variables are some of the elements that can be displayed using this method.

The *showimg()* function is called within the body of the page to display the image:

```
function showimg() {
img = new Object();
width = new Object();
height = new Object();

var now = new Date();
var mytime=Math.floor(now.getTime()/1000)
var rand = Math.floor(mytime % 57)
document.writeln('<A href="../expanded/'+ img[rand] + '">'
+ '<IMG SRC="../icons/' + img[rand] + '" width="' + width[rand]
+ '" height="' + height[rand] + '" ALT="JavaScript"></A><br>');
```

First, three array variables are defined in the function. For each number in each array, *img* contains the filename of the image; *width* and *height* contain the size parameter of the image. A semi-random number from 0 to 57 is obtained by using the remainder operator on the *getTime* method from the current date.

That number is used to index the three image array variables. Then the *document.writeln* method is used to write HTML code to the page including these variables. This is done by writing out the HTML tags as strings and appending the array variables to "fill in the blanks." Finally, a series of *if-else* statements is used with the random number to determine the artist of the image. Then the *document.writeln* method is used again to display a link containing the artist's name.

Related Techniques

Grouping Variables Together

Creating Random Phrases

Using Time-Dependent Web Page Properties

Creating a Multiple Choice Test

Using the Form Object

Type: JavaScript object

Used in: Document object

Zoltan Schreter

```
<script language="JavaScript">
<!-- hide this script tag's contents from old browsers

var N=1
var nr_correct=0.0
var question1="Cherry's(1953) experiment utilised a technique called"
var answer11="dichotic listening"
var answer12="dichotic response"
var answer13="bitopic listening"
var answer14="monotopic listening"
```

continues

```
var correct1=1
var question2="Gray and Wedderburn's (1960) results pose a problem
for Broadbent's theory because"
var answer21="they indicate low level processing"
var answer22="they indicate early processing"
var answer23="they indicate processing of meaning"
var answer24="they indicate syntactic processing"
var correct2=3


function answer1 (form)
{
   var current_correct

   if (N==1)
   current_correct=correct1
   if (N==2)
   current_correct=correct2
   if (N==3)
   current_correct=correct3
   if (N==4)
   current_correct=correct4
   if (N==5)
   current_correct=correct5

   if (current_correct==1){
    form.feedback.value="Correct!";
    form.correct_answer.value=" "
    nr_correct++
    }
   else{
    form.feedback.value="Sorry, not correct"
    form.correct_answer.value=current_correct
    }
   if (N==5){
   form.correct_answers.value=nr_correct
   form.percentage_correct_answers.value=100*nr_correct/N
   }
}
function answer2 (form)
{
   var current_correct

   if (N==1)
   current_correct=correct1
   if (N==2)
   current_correct=correct2
   if (N==3)
   current_correct=correct3
```

```
    if (N==4)
    current_correct=correct4
    if (N==5)
    current_correct=correct5

    if (current_correct==2){
     form.feedback.value="Correct!";
     form.correct_answer.value=" "
     nr_correct++
     }
    else{
     form.feedback.value="Sorry, not correct"
     form.correct_answer.value=current_correct
     }
    if (N==5){
    form.correct_answers.value=nr_correct
    form.percentage_correct_answers.value=100*nr_correct/N
    }
}


function next_question (form)
{
    if (N==1)  {
    form.question.value=question2
    form.a1.value=answer21
    form.a2.value=answer22
    form.a3.value=answer23
    form.a4.value=answer24
    form.feedback.value=" "
    form.correct_answer.value=" "
    }
    else
    if (N==2)  {
    form.question.value=question3
    form.a1.value=answer31
    form.a2.value=answer32
    form.a3.value=answer33
    form.a4.value=answer34
    form.feedback.value=" "
    form.correct_answer.value=" "
    }
    else
    if (N==3)  {
    form.question.value=question4
    form.a1.value=answer41
    form.a2.value=answer42
    form.a3.value=answer43
```

continues

257

```
    form.a4.value=answer44
    form.feedback.value=" "
    form.correct_answer.value=" "
    }
    else
    if (N==4)  {
    form.question.value=question5
    form.a1.value=answer51
    form.a2.value=answer52
    form.a3.value=answer53
    form.a4.value=answer54
    form.feedback.value=" "
    form.correct_answer.value=" "
    }
    else{
    form.feedback.value="No more questions"
    form.correct_answer.value=" "
    }
    N++
}

function start (form)
{
    form.question.value=question1
    form.a1.value=answer11
    form.a2.value=answer12
    form.a3.value=answer13
    form.a4.value=answer14

    form.feedback.value=" "
    form.correct_answer.value=" "

    form.correct_answers.value=" "
    form.percentage_correct_answers.value=" "

    nr_correct=0

    N=1
}

// done hiding from old browsers -->
</script>
```

```
<form method="post">
<input type="button" value="Start this test"
 onClick="start(this.form)">
<table border="1">
<tr>
<td align=right>Question:</td><td><textarea name="question"
cols=60 rows=1 value=" "></textarea></td>
</tr>
<tr>
<td align=right><input type="button" value="1:"
onClick="answer1(this.form)"></td><td><input name="a1"
size=60 value=" "></td>
</tr>
<tr>
<td align=right><input type="button" value="2:"
onClick="answer2(this.form)"></td><td><input name="a2"
size=60 value=" "></td>
</tr>
<tr>
<td align=right><input type="button" value="3:"
onClick="answer3(this.form)"></td><td><input name="a3"
size=60 value=" "></td>
</tr>
<tr>
<td align=right><input type="button" value="4:"
onClick="answer4(this.form)"></td><td><input name="a4"
size=60 value=" "></td>
</tr>

<td align=right><input type="button" value="Next question"
onClick="next_question(this.form)"></td>
<td align=center>Feedback:<input name="feedback" size=20 value=" ">
Correct answer:<input name="correct_answer" size=3 value=" "></td>

</tr>
</table>
The number of correct answers during the test:
<input name="correct_answers" size=4 value=" ">
This corresponds to a % of
<input name="percentage_correct_answers" size=6 value=" ">
</table>
</form>
```

Syntax Example

```
form.correct_answer.value=current_correct
```

Comments

An interactive quiz is an application that is well-suited for JavaScript. Because of all the user input in a quiz, a server-side implementation would be inconvenient. JavaScript can immediately respond to an answer, with no need to contact a server. Avoiding this delay for the user makes the quiz more efficient.

Online Example

"Multiple choice test," by Zoltan Schreter, email: **Z.Schreter@psychol.utas.edu.au**

URL: **http://info.utas.edu.au/docs/psychology/cognition/l4/l4_tute.htm**

Description

This page uses a form to provide an interactive quiz to the user. Text objects are used to display the current question and its answers, whereas button objects are used to accept input from the user.

Step-by-Step

The form of this page contains a table with various form elements. A *textarea* object named *question* is used to display the question. There are four text objects named *a1* through *a4* which hold answers, and four button objects which correspond to those answers. A button is used to access the next question, and another is used to start the test. Other text objects named *feedback* and *correct_answer* acknowledge if an answer is correct; if the answer is not correct, they display the correct answer. At the end of the test the *correct_answers* and *percentage_correct_answers* text objects are used to display what they are named for.

All of the questions, answers, and other related variables are defined in the start of the script. The start button begins the quiz by executing a function called *start()*. The function assigns the question and answers to the *question* textarea object and to the *a1*, *a2*, *a3*, and *a4* text objects respectively. The other text objects are cleared, and the *nr_correct* variable, which records the number correct, is set to 0. The *N* variable, which keeps track of the question number, is set to 1.

The *next_question()* function is a similar function. It is executed by the Next Question button on the page. It checks the *N* variable in a series of if-else statements to display the next question and answer. The *N* variable is incremented by 1 at the end of the function.

Each answer button calls a different function using an *OnClick* event handler. The functions are named *answerX()* with X being the answer number. The functions are similar in form. If statements are first used with the variable *N* to find and store the correct answer in *current_correct*. If the answer is correct, it is stated so in the *feedback* text object and *nr_correct* is incremented. Otherwise, an incorrect message and the correct answer are displayed. If *N* = 5 (the last question), the number correct and the percentage correct are displayed.

Notes

Using JavaScript does not present a secure way of administering a quiz. Any clever test taker can use the view source command in the browser to find the answers.

This code tends to be lengthy in nature. Using arrays for the questions and answers and combining the answer function into one function may reduce the size of the code.

Related Techniques

Responding to User Form Data

Displaying MouseOver Information to a Form

JavaScript Question Examples

Responding to User Form Data

Using the Text Object

Type: JavaScript object

Used in: Form objects

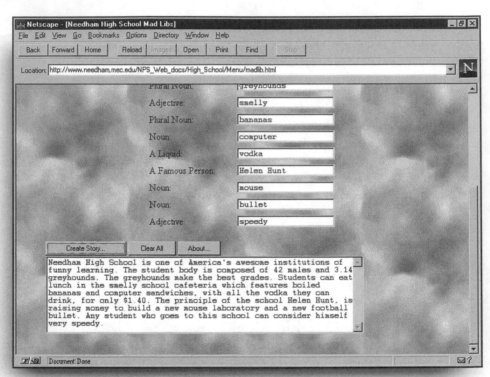

Nick Heinle

```
<HTML>
<HEAD>
<TITLE>Needham High School Mad Libs</TITLE>
<SCRIPT LANGUAGE="JavaScript">
<!-- hide the script
function create(form) {
        if (confirm("Are you sure?"))
                {
```

```
form.story.value = ("Needham High School is one of America's " +
form.input1.value+ " institutions of " +form.input2.value+
" learning. The student body is composed of " +form.input3.value+
" males and " +form.input4.value+ " " +form.input5.value+ ".");
form.story.value = (form.story.value + " The " +form.input5.value+
" make the best grades." + " Students can eat lunch in the " +
form.input6.value+ " school cafeteria which features boiled " +
form.input7.value+ " and " +form.input8.value+ " sandwiches,");
form.story.value = (form.story.value + " with all the " +
form.input9.value+ " they can drink, for only $1.40.
The principle of the school " +form.input10.value
+ ", is raising money to build a new " +form.input11.value
+ " laboratory and a new football ");
form.story.value = (form.story.value + form.input12.value
+ ". Any student who goes to this school can consider himself very "
+form.input13.value+ ".");
                }
        }
function about() {
msg=open("about.html","DisplayWindow","toolbar=no,width=280,
height=420,directories=no,status=no,scrollbars=yes,resize=no,
menubar=no");
        }


// end hiding contents from old browsers  -->

</SCRIPT>
</HEAD>
<BODY BGCOLOR = "#FFFFFF" BACKGROUND = "bluesky.jpg"
LINK = "#00008B" ALINK = "#0000FF" TEXT = "#00008B">
<CENTER>
<FONT COLOR = "#00008B" SIZE = 6>N<FONT SIZE = 5>EEDHAM</FONT>
<FONT SIZE = 6>H<FONT SIZE = 5>IGH</FONT>
<FONT SIZE = 6>S<FONT SIZE = 5>CHOOL</FONT>
</FONT></FONT></FONT>
<BR><FONT SIZE = 6 COLOR = "#C71585">
<TT><B>Mad Libs</B></TT></FONT></CENTER>
<HR WIDTH = 65% SIZE = 4>
<CENTER>By Nick Heinle</CENTER>
<FORM>
<CENTER>
<TABLE BORDER = 0 CELLPADDING = 2>
<TR><TD>
Adjective (Superlative):<TD><INPUT TYPE="text" NAME="input1" SIZE=20>
<BR><TR><TD>
Adjective:<TD><INPUT TYPE="text" NAME="input2" SIZE=20 >
<BR><TR><TD>
Number:<TD><INPUT TYPE="text" NAME="input3" SIZE=20 >
<BR><TR><TD>
```

continues

```
Different Number:<TD><INPUT TYPE="text" NAME="input4" SIZE=20 >
<BR><TR><TD>
Plural Noun:<TD><INPUT TYPE="text" NAME="input5" SIZE=20 >
<BR><TR><TD>
Adjective:<TD><INPUT TYPE="text" NAME="input6" SIZE=20 >
<BR><TR><TD>
Plural Noun:<TD><INPUT TYPE="text" NAME="input7" SIZE=20 >
<BR><TR><TD>
Noun:<TD><INPUT TYPE="text" NAME="input8" SIZE=20 >
<BR><TR><TD>
A Liquid:<TD><INPUT TYPE="text" NAME="input9" SIZE=20 >
<BR><TR><TD>
A Famous Person:<TD><INPUT TYPE="text" NAME="input10" SIZE=20 >
<BR><TR><TD>
Noun:<TD><INPUT TYPE="text" NAME="input11" SIZE=20 >
<BR><TR><TD>
Noun:<TD><INPUT TYPE="text" NAME="input12" SIZE=20 >
<BR><TR><TD>
Adjective:<TD><INPUT TYPE="text" NAME="input13" SIZE=20 ><BR>
</TABLE>
</CENTER>

<BLOCKQUOTE>
<INPUT TYPE="button" VALUE="Create Story..."
ONCLICK="create(this.form)">
<INPUT TYPE="reset" VALUE="Clear All">
<INPUT TYPE="button" VALUE="About..." ONCLICK="about()">
<TEXTAREA WRAP NAME="story" ROWS = "8" COLS = "65">
</TEXTAREA>
</BLOCKQUOTE>
</FORM>
<I></I></BODY>
</HTML>
```

Syntax Example

```
<FORM>
<TEXTAREA NAME="box" ROWS="5" COLS="60">SampleText</TEXTAREA>
</FORM>
```

Comments

A *textarea* object is very similar to a text object. The only differences is that a *textarea* object can have multiple rows. You can use this object when your string input or output needs multiple lines.

Online Example

"Needham High School Mad Libs," by Nick Heinle.

URL: **http://www.needham.mec.edu/NPS_Web_docs/High_School/Menu/madlib.html**

Description

Forms can be used to retrieve information from a user and to post information to a user. JavaScript can use the information from a form immediately, with no need to load a new page (as a CGI script would). This page uses different types of form objects to implement a story. Text objects are used to receive the information, button objects are used to execute the JavaScript functions, and a textarea object is used to display the information from the functions.

Step-by-Step

To display the text obtained from the JavaScript function, a form called a *textarea* object is used. The *textarea* form is in the form of:

```
<TEXTAREA [NAME="textareaName"] [WRAP= "off"|"virtual"|"physical"]
[ROWS="integer"] [COLS="integer"] [onBlur="handlerText"]
[onChange="handlerText"] [onFocus="handlerText"]
[onSelect="handlerText"]>  textToDisplay </TEXTAREA>
```

NAME will give the textarea object a name such that it can be referred to in the JavaScript.

WRAP indicates if word wrapping will occur in the form. If it is *"off"* or not specified, no word wrapping will occur.

ROWS and *COLS* will specify the size of the form.

TextToDisplay will be the text that initially appears in the textarea.

The rest of the parameters are event handlers that can be used to execute JavaScripts.

The methods and properties of the textarea object are the same as for the text object.

When the "Create Story..." button is pushed, the create *(this.form)* function is executed. Using the *this.form* object will specify all the form information to be sent to the function. This function will simply concatenate the text form values with some other text to create the story. Note how the values are accessed: *form.input1.value*, for example. This indicates the string *value*, from the text object named *input1*, which is from the form object *form*. The name of the form is called *form*, since that what was named in the function statement *create(form)*. The completed text is displayed by assigning the text to the statement *form.story.value*. This will assign the text to the object named *story*, which happened to be the textarea object.

Related Techniques

Displaying MouseOver Information to a Form

Saving Form Values for Future Visits

Submitting a Form

Calculating a Formula

Variables and Operators: Numerical

Type: JavaScript data type

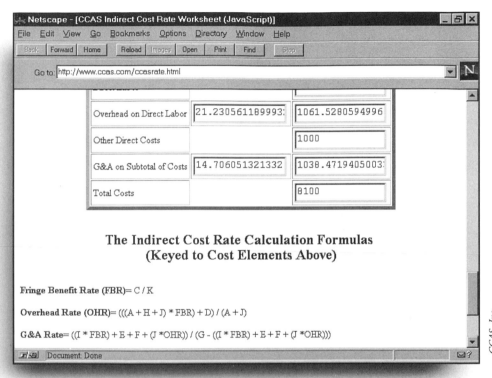

CCAS, Inc.

```
function computeForm(form)
{
if ((form.DL.value == null || form.DL.value.length == 0) ||
      (form.ODC.value == null || form.ODC.value.length == 0) ||
      (form.TFB.value == null || form.TFB.value.length == 0) ||
      (form.TOH.value == null || form.TOH.value.length == 0) ||
      (form.TGA.value == null || form.TGA.value.length == 0) ||
      (form.TBP.value == null || form.TBP.value.length == 0) ||
      (form.OHL.value == null || form.OHL.value.length == 0) ||
      (form.GAL.value == null || form.GAL.value.length == 0) ||
      (form.BPL.value == null || form.BPL.value.length == 0)) {
      form.FBR.value = "Incomplete data";
```

continues

```
        form.OHR.value = "Incomplete data";
        form.GAR.value = "Incomplete data";
        return;
    }

    if (!checkNumber(form.DL, 1,99999999, "Direct Labor") ||
!checkNumber(form.ODC, 0,99999999, "Other Direct Costs") ||
        !checkNumber(form.TFB, 1,99999999, "Total Fringe Benefits")||
        !checkNumber(form.TOH, 1,99999999, "Total Overhead") ||
        !checkNumber(form.TGA, 0,99999999, "Total G&A") ||
        !checkNumber(form.TBP, 0,99999999, "Total B&P") ||
        !checkNumber(form.OHL, 1,99999999, "Total Overhead Labor")||
        !checkNumber(form.GAL, 0,99999999, "Total G&A Labor") ||
        !checkNumber(form.BPL, 0,99999999, "Total B&P Labor")) {
        form.FBR.value = "Invalid";
        form.OHR.value = "Invalid";
        form.GAR.value = "Invalid";
        return;
    }

    var i=form.DL.value *1
    var j=form.ODC.value*1
    form.TOTDIR.value=i + j
            form.DLL.value=i

    var k=form.TFB.value *1
    var l=form.TOH.value *1
    var m=form.TGA.value *1
    var n=form.TBP.value *1
    form.TOTIND.value=k + l + m + n
    var z=i + j + k + l + m + n
    form.TC.value=z

    var o=form.OHL.value *1
    var p=form.GAL.value *1
    var q=form.BPL.value *1
       var r=i + o + p + q
    form.TOTLAB.value= r

    var s=(k /  r)
    form.FBR.value=s * 100

    var t=(((i + o + q) * s) + l) / (i + q)
    form.OHR.value= t * 100

            var u=(m + n+ (p * s) + (t * q))
    var z=z - u
            var z= u / z
    form.GAR.value=z * 100
```

```
    form.DLB.value=i
       var v=i * t
    form.OHRB.value=v
    form.OHRR.value=t * 100
    form.ODCB.value=j
    form.GARR.value=z * 100
    var w=(i + v + j) * z
    form.GARB.value=w
    form.TCB.value=w + i + v + j
}
```

Syntax Example

```
var t=(((i + o + q) * s) + 1) / (i + q)
```

Comments

The numeric data type provides the calculating capabilities in JavaScript. You can do all the typical calculations, such as add, subtract, and divide. You can also use the Math object with this data type to perform functions such as sin, log, and sqrt. Both integer and floating point values can be represented. The difference between these values is that a floating point value requires a decimal point whereas an integer value does not.

Online Example

"CCAS Indirect Cost Rate Worksheet (JavaScript)," by CCAS, Inc., email: **info@ccas.com**

URL: **http://www.ccas.com/ccasrate.html**

Description

This page implements a financial worksheet in JavaScript. Numerical variables and operators are necessary to calculate the desired values. The values are obtained from the user entering data in text objects. Event handlers are used in the text objects to take the values, check to see if they are valid numerical variables, calculate a result from the variables, and store the result in another text object.

Step-by-Step

Numerical variables have two forms: integer or floating point. Typically, using operators on an integer will result in an integer value, except for the division (/) operator. Floating point and mixed operations always result in a floating point value.

Here are the arithmetic operators for the numeric data type:

$x + y$ add—returns the sum of x and y

$x - y$ subtract—returns the difference of x and y

$x * y$ multiply—returns the product of x and y

x / y divide—returns the quotient of x and y

$x \% y$ modulo—returns the remainder of x / y

x++ postfix increment—returns x and adds 1 to x

++x prefix increment—adds 1 to x and returns new x (x + 1)

x-- postfix decrement—returns x and subtracts 1 to x

--x prefix decrement—subtracts 1 to x and returns new x (x - 1)

$-x$ negate—returns x times -1

Other numerical operators are used as assignment operators:

$y = x$ assigns the value of x to y

y += x assigns the value of x + y to y

y -= x assigns the value of x - y to y

$y *= x$ assigns the value of x * y to y

$y /= x$ assigns the value of x / y to y

$y \%= x$ assigns the value of x % y to y

On this page, a series of text objects obtain and display the financial values. The text objects are given names such as *BPL* and *FBR*. The *computeForm()* function is used to calculate and display the desired values. First, the function uses two *if* statements to determine if all the needed values are given, and in the correct format. If the values are OK, the text object values are assigned to variables with statements such as *var i=form.DL.value *1*. Numerical operators are then used to calculate the desired values according to the necessary formulas. The calculated values are then displayed to the text objects with a statement such as *form.GARB.value=w*.

Related Techniques

Performing Calculations in Forms

Implementing a Real-Time Clock

Displaying MouseOver Information to a Form

Using the Text Object

Type: JavaScript object

Used in: Form objects

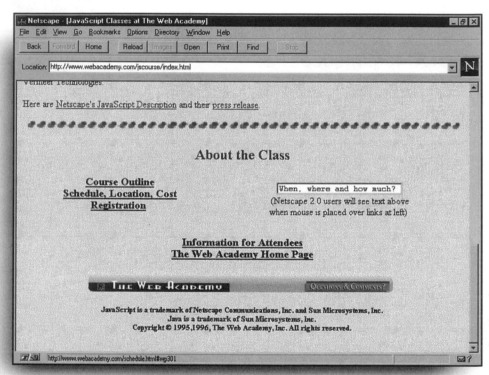

```
<form>
<h3 align="center">
<a href="/outline.html#wp301"
onMouseOver="document.forms[0].hint.value
='  What will be covered?';">
   Course Outline</a><br>
<a href="/schedule.html#wp301"
onMouseOver="document.forms[0].hint.value
```

```
='When, where and how much?';">
   Schedule, Location, Cost</a><br>
<a href="/register.html"
onMouseOver="document.forms[0].hint.value
='    OK, sign me up!';">
   Registration</a>
</h3>
<td>
<div align="center">
<input type="text" name="hint" size="26"><br>
(Netscape 2.0 users will see text above<br>
when mouse is placed over links at left)
</div>
</table>
</form>
```

Syntax Example

```
<FORM>
<input type="text" name="display" value="hi!" size="5">
</FORM>
```

Comments

A text object is normally used for receiving user entered text. In this case, it is being used to display text. The variety of event handlers available to this object make it very useful to JavaScripts. The different event handlers can execute when the object is focused upon, focused away from, selected, or changed.

Online Example

"JavaScript Classes at The Web Academy," by The Web Academy, email: **webacad@webacademy.com**

URL: **http://www.webacademy.com/jscourse/index.html**

Description

This page has a series of links. The *onMouseOver* event handler on these links are used to execute a JavaScript statement. The statement displays a string describing the link to a text object on the page.

Step-by-Step

The forms in which the data is input on this page are text objects. Text forms are created in the form of:

```
<INPUT TYPE="text" [NAME="textName"] [VALUE="textValue"]
[SIZE="integer"] [onBlur="handlerText"] [onChange="handlerText"]
  [onFocus="handlerText"]  [onSelect="handlerText"]>
```

NAME will give the text object a name such that it can be referred to in the JavaScript.

VALUE is an optional parameter that will give an initial value to the text object.

SIZE will specify the number of characters in length that the form will be.

The rest of the parameters are event handlers that can be used to execute JavaScripts.

The properties of the text object are:

defaultValue	This represents the initial value of the object. Setting this value will not update the value of the object.
name	This is the name of the object.
value	This is the current value of the object.

The methods of the text object are:

blur()	This removes focus from the object.
focus()	This gives focus to the object.
select()	This selects the input area of the object.

When the mouse is moved over the links, the *onMouseOver* event handler executes a command of the form *document.forms[0].hint.value=' <string>'*. The *value* is the property of the text object; *hint* is the name of the text object which is a property of the form object. *forms[0]* identifies the first form object, which is the property of the *document* object. Thus, assigning a string to the object-oriented path will display text in the text object.

Related Techniques

Responding to User Form Data

Status Line Display for Selected Links

Examining Form Data

Window Object (Alert and Prompt Methods)

Type: JavaScript object

Used in: Forms

Zoegas

```
function doState(){
 var ss = document.f1.STAT.value;
 if(document.f1.STAT.value.length < 2){
ss = (prompt("Enter your 2-character State code",
         "CA")).toUpperCase();
   document.f1.STAT.value = ss;
   }
   if (ss.toUpperCase() == "CA")
return true;
return false;
}
function checkList(){
var msg = " . . . Please check item and then resubmit.";
doUpdate();
if( !(document.f1.NAME.value.length > 3 ||
 document.f1.CCNA.value.length > 3)){
alert("Name?" + msg);
return false;}
if( document.f1.ADDR.value.length < 6){
alert("Address?" + msg);
return false;}
if( document.f1.CITY.value.length < 3){
alert("City?" + msg);
return false;}
if( document.f1.STAT.value.length < 2){
alert("State?" + msg);
return false;}
if( document.f1._ZIP.value.length < 5){
alert("ZipCode?" + msg);
return false;}
if( document.f1._CCN.value.length < 12){
alert("Credit Card Number?" + msg);
return false;}
if( document.f1.ExDT.value.length < 4){
alert("Credit Card Expiration Date?" + msg);
return false;}
return true;
}
```

Syntax Example

```
zip = prompt("Please enter your zip code","10118")
```

277

Comments

A dialog box can be used to send information to a user or to receive information from a user. You can display dialog boxes to display text, ask a yes or no question, or ask a question with a form for the answer. These methods are available through the window object.

Online Example

"Sweden ZORGAS ON-LINE ORDER USA," by Zoegas, email: **zoegas@mcn.org**

URL: **http://www.mcn.org/A/Zoegas/Orderform.html**

Description

This online order form is JavaScript enhanced. The JavaScript code is used to calculate tax and totals from the input information. It is also used to warn the user of possible incorrect form data.

Step-by-Step

The format of the prompting dialog box is:

```
prompt(message, [inputDefault])
```

This method will display a dialog box with the *message* string and a form containing the *inputDefault* string. It will return a string containing what is displayed in the form if you press OK, or it will return a null string if you press Cancel.

The warning messages have the following format:

```
alert("message")
```

This method simply calls up a dialog box with a warning symbol, the *message* string, and an OK button. It is best used to convey important information to the user.

Another window method that displays a dialog box is:

```
confirm("message")
```

This method calls up a dialog box with the message, an OK, and a Cancel button. It will return a Boolean value depending on which button was pressed.

Related Techniques

JavaScript Question Examples

Responding to User Form Data

Loading a Page via a Selection List

Using the Select Object

Type: JavaScript object

Used in: Form objects

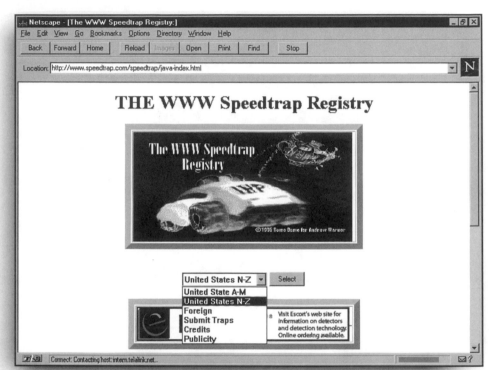

Andrew Warner

```
<SCRIPT LANGUAGE="LiveScript">
<!-- Hide JavaScript code from older browsers
function update(form){
if(form.select1[0].selected){
top.location.assign('
http://www.speedtrap.com/speedtrap/usam.html')}
if(form.select1[1].selected){
  top.location.assign('
http://www.speedtrap.com/speedtrap/usnz.html')}
if(form.select1[2].selected){
  top.location.assign('
http://www.speedtrap.com/speedtrap/foreign.html')}
```

```
if(form.select1[3].selected){
  top.location.assign('
http://www.speedtrap.com/~aww/')}
if(form.select1[4].selected){
  top.location.assign('
http://www.speedtrap.com/speedtrap/thanks.html')}
if(form.select1[5].selected){
  top.location.assign('
http://www.speedtrap.com/speedtrap/publicity.html')}
}<!-- Done hiding JavaScript -->

</SCRIPT> <BR>

<CENTER>
<FORM>
<SELECT NAME="select1">
<OPTION SELECTED>United State A-M
<OPTION>United States N-Z
<OPTION>Foreign
<OPTION>Submit Traps
<OPTION>Credits
<OPTION>Publicity
</SELECT>
<INPUT TYPE=BUTTON VALUE="Select" onClick=" update(this.form)">
</H6>
<P>
</FORM>
```

Syntax Example

```
<FORM>
<SELECT name="list" MULTIPLE onChange='alert("You must like " +
this.form.list.options[this.form.list.selectedIndex].value)'>
<OPTION SELECTED value="apples."> apples
<OPTION value="oranges."> oranges
<OPTION value="bananas."> bananas
</SELECT>
</FORM>
```

Comments

A select object can be used to create either scrolling lists or pop-up menus. An event handler reacts to the user's selection within the object, or elsewhere via a button object, for example. The menus contain strings that are seen on the list and can have variables associated with them. You can associate numbers, strings, or any other values to the options to be used in the JavaScript.

Online Example

"The WWW Speedtrap Registry," by Andrew Warner, email: **andy@andy.net**

URL: **http://www.speedtrap.com/speedtrap/java-index.html**

Description

When you press the button on this page, a new page will be loaded according to the current value of the select object. Depending on the option selected in the object, a series of *if* statements determines what page is to be loaded.

Step-by-Step

The select object is in the form of:

```
<SELECT NAME="selectName" [SIZE="integer"] [MULTIPLE]
 [onBlur="handlerText"]
 [onChange="handlerText"]
 [onFocus="handlerText"]>
<OPTION VALUE="optionValue" [SELECTED]> textToDisplay
[ ... <OPTION> textToDisplay]
</SELECT>
```

<NAME> will give the select object a name such that it can be referred to in the JavaScript.

<SIZE> specifies the number options shown in the list. With *SIZE* > 1, the list will automatically be *<MULTIPLE>*.

<MULTIPLE> will make the list a scrolling list.

The rest of the parameters are event handlers that can be used to execute JavaScripts.

Following the select tag are option tags that list the text in the list. If *<SELECTED>* is in the option, it will be selected when the page first loads. The options can be given *<VALUE>* parameters that can be accessed by the JavaScript.

The properties of the select object are:

length	This represents the number of options in the select object.
name	This is the name of the object.
option	This refers to the options in the object.
selectedIndex	This is the number of the option selected.

The methods of the select object are:

blur()	This removes focus from the object.
focus()	This gives focus to the object.

In this page there is a selection object named *"select1"* that refers to different pages on the site. When the button object is pressed, the *update()* function is called to pass *this.form*. In the *update()* function, *if* statements are used to check which options were selected, and the *location.assign* property is used to link to a new page.

Related Techniques

Displaying an Image via a Selection List

Automatically Moving to an Updated Page

Sending Mail to Multiple Addresses

Sending Mail Within JavaScript

Type: JavaScript

Used in: Location objects

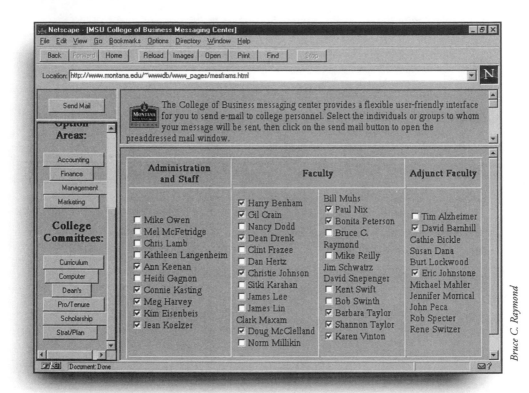

Bruce C. Raymond

File: mesframs.html

```
<frameset COLS="150,*">

<frameset ROWS="60,*">
<frame SRC="mesfram0.html" SCROLLING=no NAME="frame0">
<frame SRC="mesfram2.html" NAME="frame2">
</frameset>
```

```
<frameset ROWS="100,*">
<frame SRC="mesfram1.html" NAME="frame1">
<frame SRC="mesfram3.html" NAME="frame3">
</frameset>

</frameset>
```

File: mesfram0.html

```
function sendMail()
{var mailAddresses="";
for (n=0;n<parent.frame3.document.entryForm.elements.length; n++)
  if(parent.frame3.document.entryForm.elements[n].checked==true)
mailAddresses+=parent.frame3.document.entryForm.elements[n].value
+"\n"
 this.location.href="mailto:"+mailAddresses
 for (n=0;n<parent.frame3.document.entryForm.elements.length; n++)
   parent.frame3.document.entryForm.elements[n].checked=false
}



<form name="sendMailForm">
<center><input type="button" name="sendmail" value="Send Mail"
onClick=sendMail()></center>
</form>
```

File: mesfram2.html

```
function financeSelect()
    {if (parent.frame3.document.entryForm.jlin.checked==false)
{parent.frame3.document.entryForm.jlin.checked=true;
 parent.frame3.document.entryForm.ddren.checked=true;
parent.frame3.document.entryForm.talzh.checked=true;  }
      else
          {parent.frame3.document.entryForm.jlin.checked=false;
parent.frame3.document.entryForm.ddren.checked=false;
parent.frame3.document.entryForm.talzh.checked=false; }
    }
<input type="button" name="finance" value="Finance"
onClick=financeSelect()><br>
```

File: mesfram3.html

```
<input type="checkbox" name="ddren"
 value="ubbdd@msu.oscs.montana.edu">Dean Drenk<br>
 <input type="checkbox" name="cfraz"
 value="zdb7019@maia.oscs.montana.edu">Clint Frazee<br>
 <input type="checkbox" name="dhert"
 value="zdb7014@maia.oscs.montana.edu">Dan Hertz<br>
```

Syntax Example

```
location.href="mailto:user@xyz.com"
```

Comments

Because files cannot be opened, closed, or sent in any manner in JavaScript, other techniques must be used to save or convey information. One method is using cookie functions, whereas another option is through email. These are currently the only ways to work with files in JavaScript.

Online Example

"MSU College of Business Messaging Center," by Bruce C. Raymond, email: **ibmbr@msu.oscs.montana.edu**

URL: **http://www.montana.edu/~wwwdb/www_pages/mesframs.html**

Description

This page sets up a mailing command to mail to various people using checkbox objects. This is a convenient graphical method to select people in a group to send mail to. You wouldn't need to copy down addresses, or mail a group of people individually using this technique.

Step-by-Step

The large frame in this page (*frame3*) contains all the names that can be sent mail. Each name is associated with a checkbox object and the value of each object is the email address of the person.

The buttons in the lower-left frame (*frame2*) enable you to select a multiple section of buttons in *frame3* by using the *checked* property of the checkbox object. The *onClick* event handler of the button in the upper-left frame (*frame0*) executes the *sendMail()* function. This function uses a *for* loop to see if each checkbox in *frame3* is checked. If so, the value of the checkbox is assigned to a string. The *location.href* command is used to send mail to these addresses. Then, another *for* loop is used to set all the checkbox objects back to the unchecked state.

Related Techniques

Page Navigation via Frames

Implementing a Multiple Choice Worksheet

JavaScript Question Examples

Using the Form Object

Type: JavaScript object

Used in: Document object

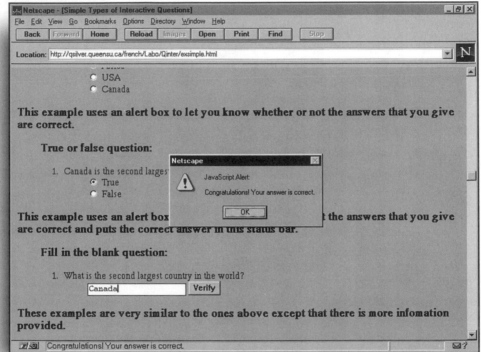

```
<P><P><H3>This example uses the status bar (at the bottom of the
page) to let you know whether or not the answers that you give
are correct.</H3>

<FORM NAME=QUESTIONS1>
<UL><H3>Multiple Choice Question:</H3>
<OL><LI>Which country is the second largest in the world?
<UL><INPUT TYPE="RADIO" NAME="Q1" VALUE="Australia"
ONCLICK="(window.status='Unfortunately, your answer is incorrect.')">
Australia<BR>
<INPUT TYPE="RADIO" NAME="Q1" VALUE="Africa"
ONCLICK="(window.status='Unfortunately, your answer is incorrect.')">
Africa<BR>
<INPUT TYPE="RADIO" NAME="Q1" VALUE="USA"
```

```
ONCLICK="(window.status='Unfortunately, your answer is incorrect.')">
USA<BR>
<INPUT TYPE="RADIO" NAME="Q1" VALUE="Canada"
ONCLICK="(window.status='Congratulations! Your answer is correct.')">
Canada
</UL>
</OL>
</UL>

<P><P><H3>This example uses an alert box to let you know whether or
not the answers that you give are correct.</H3>

<UL><H3>True or false question:</H3>
<OL><LI>Canada is the second largest country in the world.
<UL><INPUT TYPE="RADIO" NAME="Q1" VALUE="TRUE"
ONCLICK="alert('\nCongratulations! Your answer is correct.')">
<! The \n inserts a line feed.>
True<BR>
<INPUT TYPE="RADIO" NAME="Q1" VALUE="FALSE"
ONCLICK="alert('\nUnfortunately, your answer is incorrect.')">
False
</UL>
</OL>
</UL>

<P><P><H3>This example uses an alert box to let you know whether or
not the answers that you give are correct and puts the correct answer
in this status bar.</H3>
<UL><H3>Fill in the blank question:</H3>
<OL><LI>What is the second largest country in the world?
<UL><INPUT TYPE="TEXT" NAME="FB1" VALUE="" SIZE=20
onBlur="if (this.value == 'Canada') {
alert('\nCongratulations! Your answer is correct.')
}
else {
window.status = ('The correct answer is: Canada')
alert('\nUnfortunately, your answer is incorrect.')
}">
<INPUT TYPE="BUTTON" NAME="RESULTS" VALUE="Verify"
onClick="if (this.value == 'Canada') {
alert('Congratulations! Your answer is correct.')
}
else {
window.status = ('The correct answer is: Canada')
alert('\nUnfortunately, your answer is incorrect.')
}">
<! This 'Verify' button was added to make the question easier to
answer. Now the user can click elsewhere on the page to trigger
the onBlur even or can click on this button to trigger the
onClick event. Notice that except for these two event handlers
the code is identical.>
</UL>
</OL>
</UL>
```

Syntax Example

```
<INPUT TYPE="RADIO" NAME="Q1" VALUE="USA"
ONCLICK="(window.status='Unfortunately, your answer is incorrect.')">
```

Comments

The main benefit of JavaScript is its interactivity. Various form data can be used to communicate with the user. This page uses radio button objects and text objects to enable the user to respond to questions. The event handlers of *onClick* and *onBlur* are used to execute JavaScript commands to react to the user's choices.

Online Example

"Simple Types of Interactive Questions," by Queen's University at Kingston French Department, email: **web.fren@qsilver.queensu.ca**

URL: **http://qsilver.queensu.ca/french/Labo/Qinter/exsimple.html**

Description

This page shows various examples of how a question can be presented to a user. It also examines how JavaScript can be used to respond. Multiple choice, true/false, and fill-in-the-blank questions are displayed. The status bar and alert dialog boxes are used to respond to the user's answer.

Step-by-Step

1. The first question is a multiple choice question that uses radio buttons for the options, and responds with text on the browser's status bar. An answer to the question is in the form of:

```
<INPUT TYPE="RADIO" NAME="Q1" VALUE="Canada"
ONCLICK="(window.status='Congratulations! Your answer is correct.')">
Canada
```

This form is defined as the type *radio*, so that the radio button is displayed. The name *Q1* is the same as the other radio buttons for this question so that they are defined as a set. For the set of radio buttons, only one can be selected at a time.

The value gives it a name that the JavaScript can use to access the object's properties. The *OnClick* event handler is used to execute a JavaScript statement if this button is clicked. The statement assigns a string to the *window.status* property, which will display the string on the browser's status bar.

2. The second question is a true or false question that uses radio buttons for the options, and responds with an alert dialog box. The false option is in the form of:

```
<INPUT TYPE="RADIO" NAME="Q1" VALUE="FALSE"
ONCLICK="alert('\nUnfortunately, your answer is incorrect.')">
False
```

This form is very similar to the previous radio button example. The only change is the statement that the *OnClick* event handler executes. The *alert* method is used to display the string contained in the parentheses in a dialog box. A disadvantage to using this is that when the dialog box is created nothing else on the page can continue until the user presses OK and the box is cleared from the browser.

3. The third question is a fill-in-the-blank style of question. The answer blank to this question is in the form of:

```
<UL><INPUT TYPE="TEXT" NAME="FB1" VALUE="" SIZE=20
onBlur="if (this.value == 'Canada') {
alert('\nCongratulations! Your answer is correct.')
}
```

This form is defined as the type *text* with *<SIZE=20>*, so a text box 20 characters long is displayed. The name *FB1* gives it a name that the JavaScript can use to access the object's properties. The value is a null string so that no default value will be displayed to the text object. The *OnBlur* event handler is used to execute a JavaScript statement if the text object is selected and then the object loses focus by selecting something else. The statement uses the *alert* method to display a dialog box with a given string.

4. The third question also uses a button to check the answer. The button is in the form of:

```
<INPUT TYPE="BUTTON" NAME="RESULTS" VALUE="Verify"
onClick="if (this.value == 'Canada') {
alert('Congratulations! Your answer is correct.')
}
```

This form object is defined as a button using the type *button*. The *OnClick* event hander is used in the same way as the radio buttons.

Related Techniques

Creating a Multiple Choice Test

Implementing a Multiple Choice Worksheet

Displaying MouseOver Information to a Form

Calculating an Income Tax

Using if-else Nesting

Type: JavaScript statement

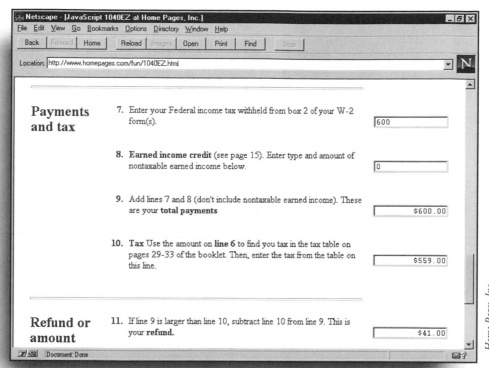

Home Pages, Inc.

```
function calculateTax(income, single)
{
        if (income < 1000) {
                step = 5;
        } else if (income < 3000) {
                step = 25;
        } else {
                step = 50;
        }
```

continues

```
        if (!single) {
                if (income < 23350) {
                        base = 0;
                        value = 0;
                        rate = .15;
                } else if (income < 56500) {
                        base = 3502.50;
                        value = 23350;
                        rate = .28;
                } else if (income < 117950) {
                        base = 12798.50;
                        value = 56500;
                        rate = .31;
                } else if (income < 256500) {
                        base = 31832.50;
                        value = 117950;
                        rate = .36;
                } else {
                        base = 81710.50;
                        value = 256500;
                        rate = .396;
                }
        } else {
                if (income < 39000) {
                        base = 0;
                        value = 0;
                        rate = .15;
                } else if (income < 94250) {
                        base = 5850;
                        value = 39000;
                        rate = .28;
                } else if (income < 143600) {
                        base = 21320;
                        value = 94250;
                        rate = .31;
                } else if (income < 256500) {
                        base = 3618.50;
                        value = 143600;
                        rate = .36;
                } else {
                        base = 77262.50;
                        value = 256500;
                        rate = .396;
                }
        }

        ival = income - (income % step) + step / 2;

        return Math.round((ival - value) * rate + base);
}
```

Syntax Example

```
if ( i < 0 )
        j = 0
else if ( i < 100 )
        j = i
else
        j = 100
```

Comments

If statements can be nested together to create a large decision-making block in JavaScript. To create the block an *if* statement is contained in the *else* block of a previous *if* statement. This can continue indefinitely to provide a group of decisions in one block. The block can be used to differentiate ranges of values, or act upon certain values of a string.

Online Example

"JavaScript 1040EZ at HomePages, Inc.," by HomePages, Inc., email: **feedback@homepages.com**

URL: **http://www.homepages.com/fun/1040EZ.html**

Description

This pages creates a spreadsheet-type format of the 1040EZ tax form using JavaScript. *If-else* statements are used to calculate the tax. The *if-else* blocks are used to determine what ranges the income is in.

Step-by-Step

If-else nesting statements are in the form of:

```
if (condition1)
   statements1
else if (condition2)
   statements2
else if (condition3)
   statements3
   .
   .
   .
else
   defaultstatements
```

If any of the Boolean variable or expression conditions are true, the statements following the *if* statement will execute. Then the JavaScript interpreter will exit from the *if-else* group. The statements are executed in turn, so if a case occurs that would satisfy both *condition2* and *condition3*, only *statments2* would be executed. If none of the conditions results in true, default statements would be executed.

The function *calculateTax()* in this page is used to calculate the tax as it would be in a tax table. Two variables are tested in the *if* statements, the number *income* and the Boolean variable *single*. The first *if-else* nest is used to determine the step in the tax table. If *income* is less than 1,000 it sets *step* to 5. The next statement tests if *income* is less that 3,000. If the JavaScript interpreter got as far as this statement, *income* must be 1,000 or more due to the first *if* statement. Therefore, if *income* is between 1,000 and 3,000 *step* will be set to 25. The default case will execute if *income* is 3,000 or greater, setting *step* to 50.

The next section has one *if-else* statement using *single*. It determines whether to set the parameters for the tax table for a married or single tax filer. One *if-else* nest follows the *if* for the married case. Another *if-else* nest follows the *else* for the single case. Each *if-else* nest is similar to the first *if-else* nest in the function. It sets the *base*, *value*, and *rate* variables for the tax. At the end of the function are statements to evaluate the tax and that value is returned to function caller.

Related Techniques

Drawing with a Pixel Sized Graphic

Using Time-Dependent Web Page Properties

Creating a Memory Game

Submitting a Form

Submit Object

Type: JavaScript object

Used in: Form objects

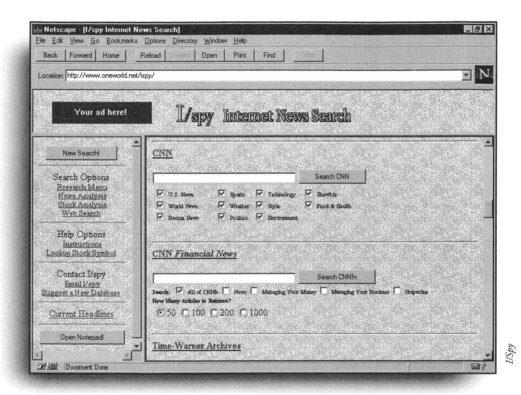

```
<b><a href="http://www.cnnfn.com">CNN <i>Financial News</i></a></b>
<form name="search3" method="post"
action="http://www.cnnfn.com/cgi-bin/searcher">
<font size=-3>
<INPUT TYPE="text" NAME="terms" SIZE="30" MAXLENGTH="100" >
<input type="submit" Value="Search CNNfn">
<br>
<b>Search:</b> 
<INPUT TYPE=checkbox NAME=all checked> All of CNNfn
<INPUT TYPE=checkbox NAME=news> News
<INPUT TYPE=checkbox NAME=mymoney> Managing Your Money
```

continues

```
<INPUT TYPE=checkbox NAME=mybusiness> Managing Your Business
<INPUT TYPE=checkbox NAME=grapevine> Grapevine<BR>

<b>How Many Articles to Retrieve?</b>
<table>
<TR>
<TD><INPUT TYPE=radio NAME=number value=50 CHECKED>50</TD>
<TD><INPUT TYPE=radio NAME=number value=100>100</TD>
<TD><INPUT TYPE=radio NAME=number value=200>200</TD>
<TD><INPUT TYPE=radio NAME=number value=1000>1000</TD>
</TR>
</table>
</form>
</font>
```

Syntax Example

```
<FORM method="get" action="http://search.yahoo.com/bin/search">
<input type="submit" name="yahoo" value="search" >
</FORM>
```

Comments

A submit object is similar to a button object. You can use *onClick* or *OnSubmit* event handlers with the object. It is used to submit a form. You can submit a CGI script of your own, or another script available on the Web.

Online Example

"I/Spy Internet News Search," by I/Spy, email: **ispy@www.oneworld.net**

URL: **http://www.oneworld.net/ispy/**

Description

This example accesses various search engines from one page. It uses forms and submit objects to transfer data to various CGI scripts on the web. This allows users of the page an easy method for accessing the search engines. The user doesn't have to go directly to the page containing the search engine.

Step-by-Step

A submit object is in the form of:

```
<INPUT TYPE="submit" NAME="submitName" VALUE="buttonText"
[onClick="handlerText"] [onSubmit="handlerText"]>
```

NAME will give the text object a name such that it can be referred to in the JavaScript.

VALUE is the text that will be displayed on the button.

OnClick and *OnSubmit* are event handlers that can execute a function or statement when the button is pressed or the form is submitted.

The properties of the submit object are

name	This is the name of the object.
value	This can be used to access the value of the object.

The method of the text object is:

click()	This can be used to simulate clicking the submit button.

One section of the page is used to access the CNN Financial News search engine. All of the data to be submitted to this search is enclosed in one set of form tags named *search3*. Within the form tags is a *method* parameter and an *action* parameter. The *method* parameter can be *get*, which submits the form data with the URL, or *post*, which submits the form data in a data body to the URL.

The *action* parameter specifies the URL to which the form data is submitted. A *mailto:* protocol can be used in the URL to send form information over email. Also, an *OnSubmit* event handler can be included in the form tags that execute JavaScript before the form is submitted. You can use this to check the form for errors. If the form is incorrect you can give a *return false;* command in the error checking function. This command will abort the submission process.

Related Techniques

Creating a Remote in a Separate Window

Examining Form Data

Performing Calculations in a Form via a Hidden Object

Hidden Objects

Type: JavaScript object

Used in: Form objects

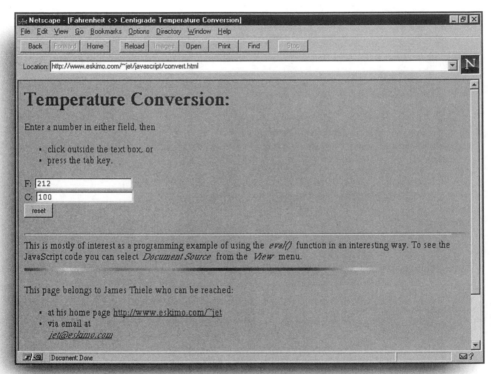

James Thiele

```
<form>
F: <input type="text" name="F" value="32"
    onChange="eval('C.value = ' + this.form.C_expr.value)">
    <input type="hidden" name="F_expr"
    value="(212-32)/100 * C.value + 32 ">
    <br>
C: <input type="text" name="C" value="0"
    onChange="eval('F.value = ' + this.form.F_expr.value)">
```

```
   <input type="hidden" name="C_expr"
   value="100/(212-32) * (F.value - 32 )">
    <br>
   <input type=reset name=reset value=reset>
</form>
```

Syntax Example

```
<FORM>
<input type="hidden" name="pi" value="3.14159" >
</FORM>
```

Comments

A hidden object is an object not visible to the user that can hold data. It could be used to hold formulas or store user information in the background. It is often used in CGI scripts or JavaScripts to send information not needed to be seen by a user (a product code) when a form is submitted.

Online Example

"Fahrenheit <-> Centigrade Temperature Conversion," by James Thiele, email: **jet@eskimo.com**

URL: **http://www.eskimo.com/~jet/javascript/convert.html**

Description

This page converts Celsius and Fahrenheit temperature values using *OnChange* event handlers in text objects. Hidden objects contain the conversion formulas so that they can be easily accessed by the text objects on the page to evaluate the temperature.

Step-by-Step

A hidden object is in the form of:

```
<INPUT TYPE="hidden" [NAME="textName"] [VALUE="textValue"] >
```

NAME will give the text object a name such that it can be referred to in the JavaScript.

VALUE will give an initial value to the text object. This is the data that you wish to store in the object.

The properties of the text object follow:

defaultValue	This represents the initial value of the object. Setting this value will not update the value of the object.
name	This is the name of the object.
value	This is the current value of the object and can be modified by JavaScript.

The hidden object has no methods and uses no event handlers.

For each temperature there are two forms:

- One is a hidden object whose value is a string of the formula used for conversion.

- The other is a text object with an *OnChange* event handler. The event handler will execute an *eval* function. The *eval* function takes a string and evaluates it as though it was an normal JavaScript expression. In this case it evaluates the string stored in the hidden object and stores it in the other temperature's text object's value.

Related Techniques

Displaying MouseOver Information to a Form

Performing Calculations in Forms

Submitting Forms with JavaScript

Using the Submit Button and the onSubmit Event Handler

Type: Form element, JavaScript

Used in: Text field, text area, or select objects

Zoegas Gourmet Coffee

```
<html>
<head><title> Sweden ZOEGAS ON-LINE ORDER USA</title>
<script>
<!--


function checkList(){
var msg = " . . . Please check item and then resubmit.";
doUpdate();
```

continues

```
    if( !(document.f1.NAME.value.length > 3 || document.f1.CCNA.value.length > 3)){
      alert("Name?" + msg);
      return false;}
  if( document.f1.ADDR.value.length < 6){
      alert("Address?" + msg);
      return false;}
   if( document.f1.CITY.value.length < 3){
      alert("City?" + msg);
      return false;}
   if( document.f1.STAT.value.length < 2){
      alert("State?" + msg);
      return false;}
   if( document.f1._ZIP.value.length < 5){
      alert("ZipCode?" + msg);
      return false;}
   if( document.f1._CCN.value.length < 12){
      alert("Credit Card Number?" + msg);
      return false;}
   if( document.f1.ExDT.value.length < 4){
      alert("Credit Card Expiration Date?" + msg);
      return false;}
   return true;
}
//-->
</script>
</head>
<body  background = "gfx/stripe2.GIF">

<center><B>ZOEGA ON-LINE ORDER FORM!<br>

<FORM NAME="f1" onSubmit="return checkList()" ACTION =
 "http://forms.mcn.org/MCNForms/GFP/GFP.acgi"
METHOD = POST>
<INPUT TYPE = "hidden" NAME="email" VALUE=
"zoegas@mail.mcn.org">

<INPUT TYPE="text" NAME="QUA1" SIZE="4" MAXLENGTH="2"
onChange="doSum(this,9.95,document.f1.MELA)"> @ $9.95
<INPUT TYPE="text" NAME="MELA" SIZE="8"
onChange="doSum(document.f1.QUA1,9.95,this)">
MELLANROST - Medium Roast - 1/2 Kilo (17.6 oz.)<br>


</form></body></html>
```

Syntax Example

```
<FORM NAME="f1" onSubmit="return checkList()" ACTION
= "http://forms.mcn.org/MCNForms/GFP/GFP.acgi"
METHOD = POST>
```

Comments

One of the most mundane, and yet most useful applications of JavaScript, is forms validation. The example takes this application to its logical extreme: it will not let you submit your order unless you enter information of the correct length into each of the fields.

Online Example

"Zoega On-line Order Form," by Zoegas Gourmet Coffee, email: **Ron@mcn.org**

URL: **http://www.mcn.org/A/Zoegas/OrderForm.html**

Description

At first glance this order form does not look at all remarkable. Pick your coffee and your quantity; fill in your name and payment information; hit Submit; and that's it, right? Not so fast!

If you click submit with an empty form, it asks for your name. Enter your name. Now, if you click submit, it asks for your address. Picky, isn't it! Fine, enter something in all of the address fields. Now my credit card number isn't long enough!

If you enter a valid order, it calculates a running total, including shipping. If you enter a letter where a number goes, it changes the letter to zero. If you enter anything but two letters in the state field, it prompts you to enter your two-letter state code.

Step-by-Step

The key to the error detection begins in the <FORM> tag:

```
<FORM NAME="f1" onSubmit="return checkList()" ACTION =
 "http://forms.mcn.org/MCNForms/GFP/GFP.acgi"
METHOD = POST>
```

The syntax of the *onSubmit* event handler is *onSubmit="return checkList()"*. This syntax means that this event handler will execute the function *checkList()*, which must return a boolean (true or false) value. If it returns true, the form is submitted; if not, nothing happens.

If nothing happens, why does the script alert you to your error? Let's take a look at the *checkList* function:

```
// Functions to create the board

function makeboard() {
for (var i=1; i<= 10; i++)
this[i] = new makeRow();
return this;
}

function makeRow() {
for (var i=1; i<= 10; i++)
this[i]=blank;
return this;
}

// Functions to fill & clear the board.

function clearBoard (form) {
// Clears & resets the board
x = 0;
y = 0;
form.xval.value = 1;
form.yval.value = 1;
for (var i=1; i<= 10; i++)
for (var j=1; j<= 10; j++)
theBoard[i][j]=blank;
drawMaze();
fillBoard(form);
return;
}

function fillBoard (form) {
     // Clear board buffer
line = "";
form.grid.value = "";
     // Fill board buffer
for (var i=1; i<= 10; i++)
for (var j=1; j<= 10; j++)
line += theBoard[i][j];
     // Move buffer contents to board
form.grid.value=line;
}

function plot (v, h) {
     theBoard[v][h] = fill;
}

function drawMaze() {
// Plots the walls of the maze
//
// Ideally, a function should do this automatically,
// or maybe I should write a maze generating function in JS!
```

```
// Note: This program operates in Y,X co-ordinates
// (not standard X,Y).

theBoard[10][10] = goal;
theBoard[1][2] = wall;
theBoard[2][2] = wall;


     .
     .
     .

theBoard[5][9] = wall;
theBoard[4][9] = wall;
}

function update(form) {
var horiz = eval(form.xval.value);
var vert = eval(form.yval.value);
      plot(vert,horiz);
fillBoard(form);
return;
}

function initBoard() {
      theBoard = new makeboard();
      fill = full;
      clearBoard(document.board);
      update(document.board);
}

// Functions to handle the player piece
//
// I suppose I could have written one function to handle this,
// but it was getting too complex.  Feel free to try. :)
//

function decx(form) {
fill = blank;
update(form);
checkx = eval(form.xval.value - 1);
checky = form.yval.value;
if (form.xval.value > 1) {
if (theBoard[checky][checkx] != wall) {
form.xval.value=eval(form.xval.value - 1);
}
else {
alert("THUD!\nYou hit a wall.");
}
```

continues

```
if (theBoard[checky][checkx] == goal) {
alert("YOU WIN!");
location.href="http://www.tisny.com/js_demo.html";
}
}
fill = full;
update(form);
}
```

Functions *incx()*, *decy()* and *incy()* are very similar to *decx()*:

```
function incx(form) {
}
function decy(form) {
}
function incy(form) {
}

// Various Functions

function cheater (form) {
// Refuse to change values manually, and start over. CHEATER!
alert("You can't change this value manually.\n
Please use the buttons.");
clearBoard(form);
update(form);
}

<form method="post" name="board">
<input type='button' value='Reset'
onClick='clearBoard(this.form);update(document.board);'>
<br>
<textarea name="grid" rows="9" cols="10" wrap=virtual></textarea>
<br>
<!-- virtual-wrap is the key! Now one text line becomes a grid! -->
<table>
<tr>
<td><input type='button' value='UP' onClick='decy(this.form)'>
</td>
<td><input type='text' value='1' size=5 name='yval'
onChange='cheater(this.form);'></td>
<td><input type='button' value='DOWN' onClick='incy(this.form)'>
</td>
<tr>
<td><input type='button' value='LEFT' onClick='decx(this.form)'>
</td>
<td><input type='text' value='1' size=5 name='xval'
onChange='cheater(this.form);'></td>
<td><input type='button' value='RIGHT' onClick='incx(this.form)'>
</td>
</table>
</form>
```

Syntax Example

```
if (theBoard[checky][checkx] == goal)
```

Comments

A two-dimensional array is similar to a one-dimensional array, although two indices are used instead of one to refer to the value of the variable. You can visualize the array as a table of numbers. The row and column numbers in the table represent the indices of the array. The number at the specified row and column represents the value of the array at the specified indices.

Online Example

"The Amazing JavaScript Maze," by Steven J. Weinberger, email: **steve@garcia.tisny.com**

URL: **http://www.tisny.com/js_maze.html**

Description

This page forms a maze using a textarea object. The symbols of the maze are stored in a two-dimensional array and displayed to that object. Buttons on the page control your character through the maze. Pressing a button will update the array and redisplay the array to the textarea object. Using a textarea object and a two-dimensional array this way gives you a way to display specifically placed ASCII characters. A possible use might be an ASCII map that can be updated.

Step-by-Step

An *OnLoad* event handler executes the *initBoard()* function when the page first loads. The first statement in the function creates the two-dimensional array called *theBoard*. This is done by initializing all the values in the array using the functions *makeboard()* and *makeRow()*. The *makeboard()* function uses a *for* loop to create 10 columns of rows. The rows are created by the *makeRow()* function, which uses a *for* loop to create 10 slots in the row (essentially just a 10 item one-dimensional array). This group of nested functions creates the two-dimensional array.

311

Next, the *clearBoard()* function is called. This function sets the *xval* and *yval* text object values to 1. These values represent the coordinates. Two nested *for* loops are used to clear all the values of the array:

```
for (var i=1; i<= 10; i++)
for (var j=1; j<= 10; j++)
theBoard[i][j]=blank;
```

Note how these *for* loops will go through every combination of array indices so that the array can be set to the blank value. The *drawMaze()* function is then called. This function assigns the wall and goal characters to specific locations in the array. Then the *fillBoard()* function is called. This function uses nested *for* loops to append all the characters in the array to a string called *line*. A textarea object named *grid* is used to display the array. A *wrap=virtual* parameter is added to the textarea tag; it enables the characters in the array to wrap around the textarea. Assigning *line* to the textarea *grip* will display the array.

Buttons on the page guide you through the maze. These buttons enable you to move up, down, left, and right. Event handlers associated with these buttons are used to execute functions such as *decx()*. This function checks to see if your movement has directed you into a wall or the goal and then displays a message. If not, the array is changed appropriately and the *update()* function is called to redraw the grid.

Related Techniques

Grouping Variables Together

Displaying a Calendar Month

Using Multiple Functions on a Page

Using the String Object to Correct Form Entries

Using the String Object and Its Properties

Type: JavaScript

Used in: Objects

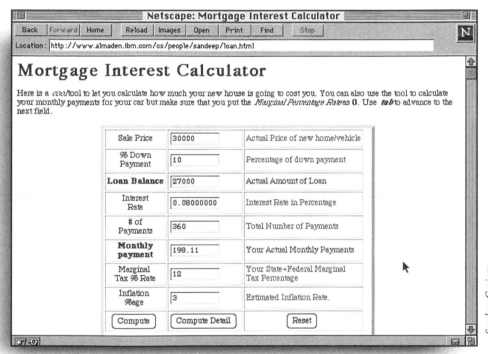

Sandeep Gopisetty

```
<HTML><HEAD><TITLE>Mortgage Interest Calculator</TITLE>
<SCRIPT LANGUAGE="JavaScript">

// JavaScript handling of the floats is poor - Fix it
function fixFloatFormat(input)
{
    var str = input.value;
    var index = 0;
    var newstr = 0;
```

continues

```
    for (var i = 0; i < str.length; i++) {
        var ch = str.substring(i, i + 1)
        if (ch == '.') {
            index = i;
        }
    }
    newstr = str.substring(0, index);
     input.value = newstr + "." + str.substring
(index+1, index+3);
    return true;
}

// Check for the validity of the input String
function checkNumber(input, min, max, msg)
{
    msg = msg + " Field has Invalid Data: " + input.value;
    var str = input.value;
    for (var i = 0; i < str.length; i++) {
        var ch = str.substring(i, i + 1)
        if ((ch < "0" || "9" < ch) && ch != '.') {
            alert(msg);
            return false;
        }
    }
    return true;
}

/<!-- done hiding from old browsers -->
</SCRIPT>

</HEAD>
```

Syntax Example

```
for (var i = 0; i < str.length; i++) {
    var ch = str.substring(i, i + 1)
    if (ch == '.') {
        index = i;
    }
}
```

Comments

It is obvious that this code is written by a professional computer scientist; it is tight, accurate, and complete. This calculator is a fine example of how to work with numeric data in text fields.

Online Example

"Mortgage Interest Calculator," by DSandeep Gopisetty, email: **sandeep@almaden.ibm.com**

URL: **http://www.almaden.ibm.com/cs/people/sandeep/loan.html**

Description

The Mortgage Interest Calculator takes the sale price, down payment, interest rate, and number of payments, and calculates the monthly payment on the loan. Furthermore, if you enter the tax and inflation rates, it will calculate tax adjusted and inflation adjusted numbers.

Step-by-Step

When you enter your figures, the monthly payment always is in the form of dollars and cents; it looks like "155.26," but never like "155.25465456345." In order to assure that the number looks right, it works with strings, because the text fields have string values.

First, the variables are initialized:

```
var str = input.value;
var index = 0;
var newstr = 0;
```

Next, it figures out where the decimal point is.

```
for (var i = 0; i < str.length; i++) {
        var ch = str.substring(i, i + 1)
        if (ch == '.') {
            index = i;
        }
    }
```

This *for* loop goes through the string *str* from beginning (i=0) to end (i=str.length), finding a one-character substring, and seeing if it is a period. If it is, the variable *index* is set to the character in the string that was the period. This example uses the length property and the substring method of strings.

Next, the input string must be broken into three pieces: the part to the left of the decimal point, the decimal point itself, and the two digits to the right of the decimal point.

```
newstr = str.substring(0, index);
        input.value = newstr + "." + str.substring
(index+1, index+3);
    return true;
```

newstr is the part of the number to the left of the decimal point; *str.substring(index+1, index+3)* is an expression that yields the two digits to the right of the decimal point, because index was the position of the period (decimal point) in the initial string.

Notes

This example works with strings because it got its value out of a text field. By starting with a number (*longNumber*), it could have truncated it with the following expression:

```
dollarValue = Math.floor(100 * longNumber) /100
```

This expression takes a number like 12.34567, multiplies by 100 (1234.567), truncates it (1234), and then divides by 100 (12.34).

Related Techniques

Performing Calculations in Forms

Implementing a Game Using Form Objects

Implementing a Multiple Choice Worksheet

Form Object

Type: JavaScript object

Used in: Document object

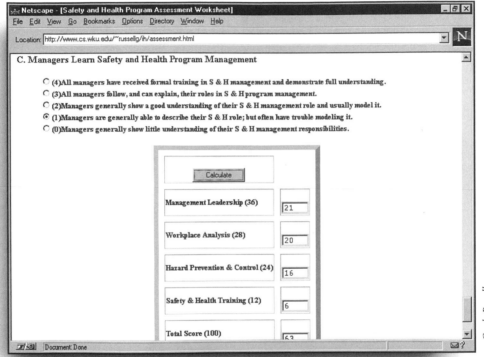

```
function managersexcellent(form){
    form.managers.value=4
    }
function managersgood(form){
    form.managers.value=3
    }
function managersaverage(form){
    form.managers.value=2
    }
```

continues

```
function managersbad(form){
    form.managers.value=1
    }
function managerspoor(form){
    form.managers.value=0
    }


function calculate(form){
    form.management.value=form.policy.value + form.goals.value +
form.leadership.value + form.examples.value + form.involvement.value +
form.responsibilities.value + form.resources.value +
 form.accountability.value + form.review.value
form.analysis.value=form.indentification.value +
form.indentification2.value + form.indentification3.value +
form.indentification4.value + form.report.value +
form.investigation.value + form.iianalysis.value
form.prevention.value=form.control.value + form.maintenance.value +
form.planning.value + form.equipment.value + form.health.value +
form.medical.value
form.training.value=form.employees.value + form.supervisors.value +
form.managers.value
form.total.value=(form.management.value *1) + (form.analysis.value*1) +
 (form.prevention.value * 1) + (form.training.value * 1)
}


<h4>C. Managers Learn Safety and Health Program Management</h4>
<blockquote><h5><input name="managers" type=radio value=radio
onclick="managersexcellent(form)">(4)All managers have received
formal training in S & H management and demonstrate full
understanding.<br>
<input name="managers" type=radio value=radio
onclick="managersgood(form)">(3)All managers follow,
and can explain, their roles in S & H program management.<br>
<input name="managers" type=radio value=radio
onclick="managersaverage(form)">(2)Managers generally show a good
understanding of their S & H management role and usually model it.<br>
<input name="managers" type=radio value=radio
onclick="managersbad(form)">(1)Managers are generally able to
describe their S & H role; but often have trouble modeling it.<br>
<input name="managers" type=radio value=radio
onclick="managerspoor(form)">(0)Managers generally show little
understanding of their S & H management responsibilities.<br>
</h5></blockquote>
<TABLE border=8 cellspacing=10>
<TR>
```

```
<TD BGCOLOR=#CBCBCB><DIV ALIGN=CENTER><br><input name="name"
type="button" value="Calculate" onClick="calculate(form)">
<br></DIV></TD></TR>
<TD BGCOLOR=#CBCBCB><DIV ALIGN=Left><h5>Management Leadership
(36)</DIV></TD><TD><DIV ALIGN=Center><br><input name="management"
type=text value="0" size=5><br></DIV></TD></TR>
<TD BGCOLOR=#CBCBCB><DIV ALIGN=Left><h5>Workplace Analysis (28)
</DIV></TD><TD><DIV ALIGN=Center><br><input name="analysis"
type=text value="0" size=5><br></DIV></TD></TR>
<TD BGCOLOR=#CBCBCB><DIV ALIGN=Left><h5>Hazard Prevention & Control
(24)</DIV></TD><TD><DIV ALIGN=Center><br><input name="prevention"
type=text value="0" size=5><br></DIV></TD></TR>
<TD BGCOLOR=#CBCBCB><DIV ALIGN=Left><h5>Safety & Health Training
(12)</DIV></TD><TD><DIV ALIGN=Center><br><input name="training"
type=text value="0" size=5><br></DIV></TD></TR>
<TD BGCOLOR=#CBCBCB><DIV ALIGN=Left><h5>Total Score (100)
</DIV></TD><TD><DIV ALIGN=Center><br><input name="total"
type=text value="0" size=5><br></DIV></TD></TR>
</h5>
</table>
```

Syntax Example

```
form.question7.value=5
```

Comments

Form objects are the main way in JavaScript to send and receive information to the user. This page uses radio button, text, and button objects. Also available are textarea, password, reset, submit, checkbox, and select objects. All of these objects have event handlers that accept data from the user. The text and textarea objects allow their values to be changed to display data to the user.

Online Example

"Safety and Health Program Assessment Worksheet," by Grady Russell, email: **russellg@pulsar.cs.wku.edu**

URL: **http://www.cs.wku.edu/~russellg/ih/assessment.html**

Description

This page implements a multiple choice worksheet using radio buttons. The values of the questions are calculated and displayed using a button at the end of the page.

Step-by-Step

All of the objects on this page are enclosed within one set of form tags. Therefore, the objects can be accessed through the same form object. Each question on the page has a series of radio buttons used as the answers.

The series of radio buttons are defined as a set by giving them the same name. The *onClick* event handler is used with each radio button to call a separate function passing the form object. The function that it calls sets the value of the named radio button. Here is an example of the function called from the middle radio button form the set named *managers*:

```
function managersaverage(form){
    form.managers.value=2
    }
```

At the end of the page is a table that contains a button and five text objects. The text objects display the scores of the worksheet. Each text object is named so it can be accessed in the *calculate()* function. The button has an *OnClick* event handler that executes the *calculate()* function passing the form object.

This function uses all the values set from the functions called from the radio buttons to calculate the desired values. These values are assigned to the value properties of the text objects to display the data. For example,

```
form.training.value=form.employees.value + form.supervisors.value +
form.managers.value
```

In this case, *training* is the name of the text object. *Employees, supervisors,* and *managers* are the names of the radio button object sets.

Related Techniques

Blinking Radio Buttons

Displaying MouseOver Information to a Form

Performing Calulations in Forms

Performing Calculations in Forms

Form Object

Type: JavaScript object

Used in: Document object

Matthew J. Graci

```
<SCRIPT>
<!-- hide this script tag's contents from old browsers
//Copyright 2/01/96 to Matthew J Graci
//This code and intellectual property is not to be used
//by any individual without the express written consent
//of its owner
```

continues

```
function checkNumber(input,form1,form2)
{
if(input.value=='')
     {input.value=input.defaultValue}
status=''
msg ="This field requires numeric data: " + input.value;

var str = input.value;
for (var i = 0; i < str.length; i++)
           {var ch = str.substring(i, i + 1)
     if ((ch < "0" || "9" < ch) && ch != '.') {
                     input.focus()
                     input.value=input.defaultValue;
                     input.select()
                     status=msg;}
}
add_input(form1,form2)
}
function add_input(form1,form2)
{    var total1,total2,total3,total4,total5,total6;

     total1=(form1.cost1.value*1+form1.cost2.value*1+
form1.cost3.value*1+form1.cost4.value*1+form1.cost5.value*1)
     total2=(total1*1+form1.cost6.value*1+form1.cost7.value*1+
form1.cost8.value*1+form1.cost9.value*1+form1.cost10.value*1)
     total3=(total2-form2.incentives.value*1)
     total4=(total3*1 + (('.01' * form2.above_invoice.value)* total3))
     total5=(total4*1+form2.destination.value*1)
     total6=(total5*1 + (('.01' * form2.state_tax.value)* total5))
     form2.total_cost.value=(total6*1 -form2.down_payment.value)
     compute_payments(form2)
}
function compute_payments(form2)
{
var i = form2.interest_rate.value;
if (i > 1.0) {
i = i / 100.0;
}
i /= 12;

var pow = 1;
for (var j = 0; j < form2.no_of_payments.value; j++)
pow = pow * (1 + i);
form2.monthly_payments.value = (form2.total_cost.value * pow * i)
 / (pow - 1)
}
function selectField(field)
{
```

```
     field.select()
}
function clearForm(form1,form2)
{
     form1.cost1.value = "0"
     form1.cost2.value = "0"
     form1.cost3.value = "0"
     form1.cost4.value = "0"
     form1.cost5.value = "0"
     form1.cost6.value = "0"
     form1.cost7.value = "0"
     form1.cost8.value = "0"
     form1.cost9.value = "0"
     form1.cost10.value = "0"
     form2.incentives.value = "0"
     form2.above_invoice.value="3"
     form2.destination.value="0"
     form2.down_payment.value = "0"
     form2.total_cost.value="0"
     form2.interest_rate.value="8"
     form2.no_of_payments.value="60"
     form2.monthly_payments.value="0"
}
<!-- done hiding from old browsers -->
</SCRIPT>


<FORM NAME="form1">
     <TABLE>
     <TR>
     <TH></TH><TH>Invoice Cost</TH>
     </TR>
     <TR>
     <TD><A HREF="#Base">Base Vehicle</A></TD>
     <TD>$<INPUT TYPE=TEXT NAME=cost1 VALUE=0 SIZE=9
onFocus="selectField(this)"
onChange="checkNumber(this,form1,form2)"> </TD>
     </TR>
     <TR>
     <TD><A HREF="#Options">Options</A></TD>
     <TD>$<INPUT TYPE=TEXT NAME=cost2 VALUE=0 SIZE=9
onFocus="selectField(this)"
onChange="checkNumber(this,form1,form2)"> </TD>
```

Syntax Example

```
form2.total_cost.value=(total6*1 -form2.down_payment.value)
```

Comments

Form objects can be used with *onChange* event handlers to create spreadsheet-like tables in JavaScript. This way users can perform quick calculations on a Web page. Tables like these are a great way to make order forms. The users can see the taxes, total cost, shipping costs, and so on, before they submit the form.

Online Example

"Car Cost Calculator," by Matthew J. Graci, email: **incomputnt@aol.com**

URL: **http://www.ems.psu.edu/~fraser/Bozo/Bozo.html**

Description

This example enables you to enter various information pertaining to the purchase of a car. The data is entered into text object. JavaScript uses the values from the text objects, whenever any value is changed, to calculate the finance amount and monthly payment.

Step-by-Step

All the text object forms on this page have an *OnChange* event handler executing the *checkNumber()* function.

```
<TD>$<INPUT TYPE=TEXT NAME=cost2 VALUE=0 SIZE=9
onFocus="selectField(this)"
onChange="checkNumber(this,form1,form2)"> </TD>
```

This function is passed to the current text object and the two forms in the page.

```
function checkNumber(input,form1,form2)
{
if(input.value=='')
        {input.value=input.defaultValue}
status=''
msg ="This field requires numeric data: " + input.value;

var str = input.value;
for (var i = 0; i < str.length; i++)
                {var ch = str.substring(i, i + 1)
```

```
            if ((ch < "0" ¦¦ "9" < ch) && ch != '.') {
                            input.focus()
                            input.value=input.defaultValue;
                            input.select()
                            status=msg;}
}
add_input(form1,form2)
}
```

checkNumber() treats the value of the text object (which the function calls *input*) as a string. A *for* loop is used to verify that every character in *input.value* is a number or a decimal point. If a character is invalid, the function will reset the *input.value* to its default and display a warning message on the status bar. The function will then call the *add_input()* function passing the two forms it was passed earlier.

The *add_input()* function uses the values from both forms to calculate the finance amount.

```
function add_input(form1,form2)
{    var total1,total2,total3,total4,total5,total6;
     total1=(form1.cost1.value*1+form1.cost2.value*1+
form1.cost3.value*1+form1.cost4.value*1+form1.cost5.value*1)
```

The values are accessed by using a command like *form1.cost1.value*. Because many values are needed to calculate the finance amount, temporary values like *total1* are used. This way the statements are shortened and are easier to read. The final calculation is stored on *form2.total_cost.value*. Then the *compute_payments()* function is called passing *form2*.

The *compute_payments()* function calculates the monthly payment from the previously calculated information. The *interest_rate*, *no_of_payments*, and *total_cost* text object values are used. The final result is stored in the *monthly_payments* text object.

Whenever a value is changed in this page, all of these functions will be executed. The values will be updated as if they are in a spreadsheet.

Related Techniques

Calculating an Income Tax

Calculating a Formula

Implementing a Game Using Form Objects

Using the Form Object

Type: JavaScript object

Used in: Document object

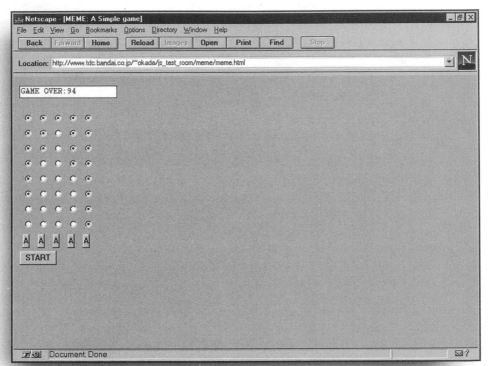

Hiroshi Okada

```
<SCRIPT LANGUAGE="JavaScript">

// ---- Make array
function MakeArray( n){
this.length = n;
for (var i = 1; i <= n; i++) {
this[i] = 0
}
```

```
return this
}

// ----- poor man's random number
var d0 = new Date();
var r0 = d0.getSeconds();
function poor_rand(){
d1 = new Date();
r0 = (r0 * r0 + r0 + d1.getSeconds()) % 3721 ;
return r0 % width_n;
}

// ---- Parameters of game
var height_n = 8;
var width_n =5;

// ---- state of game
var enemy = new MakeArray( width_n); // enemy positions
var wtime; // wait time
var score; // points
var gameover; // in case of gameover set to true

// ----- Make the battlefield.
document.write( "<FORM NAME='fm1'>");
document.write( "<INPUT TYPE='text' NAME='message' SIZE=20>");
document.write( "</FORM>");
document.write( "<FORM NAME='fm2'><TABLE>");
for( var i=0; i<height_n; i++){
document.write( "<TR>");
for( var j=0;j<width_n; j++){
document.write( "<TD><CENTER><INPUT TYPE='radio'></CENTER></TD>");
}
document.write( "</TR>");
}
document.write( "<TR>");
for( var j=0;j<width_n; j++){
document.write( "<TD><INPUT TYPE='button' VALUE='A' onClick='fire("
+ j + ")'></TD>");
}
document.write( "</TR>");
document.write( "</TABLE>");
document.write( "<INPUT TYPE='button' VALUE='START'
     onClick='game_start()'>");
document.write( "</FORM>");

// ----- game main timer event
// -----      enemy come one step
```

continues

327

```
function come(){
var n = poor_rand();
document.fm2.elements[ width_n * enemy[n+1] + n].checked = true;
enemy[n+1]++;
if( enemy[n+1] < height_n){
setTimeout("come()", wtime);
}else{
gameover = true;
document.fm1.message.value =  "GAME OVER:" + score ;
}
}

// ----- Fire the n th beam
function fire( n){
if( gameover ) return;
for( var i=0; i<enemy[n+1]; i++){ // clear enemy
document.fm2.elements[ width_n * i + n].checked = false;
}
score += enemy[ n+1];
document.fm1.message.value = "Points:" + score;
enemy[ n+1] = 0;
if( wtime > 100){ wtime -= 10};
}

// ---- initialize & start game
function game_start(){
for( var n=0; n<width_n; n++){
for( var i=0; i<enemy[n+1]; i++){
document.fm2.elements[ width_n * i + n].checked = false;
}
enemy[n+1] = 0;
}
wtime = 400;
score = 0;
gameover = false;
document.fm1.message.value = "Points:" + score;
setTimeout("come()", wtime);
}

// -->
</SCRIPT>
```

Syntax Example

```
<INPUT TYPE='button' VALUE='A' onClick='fire(" + j + ")'>
```

Comments

Without any sophisticated interactive graphic capabilities in JavaScript, you may need to resort to what JavaScript can offer. Form objects such as radio buttons and checkboxes can be used in a creative fashion to achieve various effects.

Online Example

"MEME: A Simple game," by Hiroshi Okada, email: **okada@tdc.bandai.co.jp**

URL: **http://www.tdc.bandai.co.jp/~okada/js_test_room/meme/meme.html**

Description

This page implements a game using radio buttons and normal buttons. The radio buttons are filled in vertical line from the top. The user must press the buttons underneath the line before the line is fully filled in. Pushing a button clears all of the filled in dots, and adds the number of dots in the line to the user's score. If a line is filled, the game is over.

Step-by-Step

1. The "battlefield" of this game is created using *document.write* methods to display the forms to the page. A form named *fm1* containing a text object named *message* is displayed. This text object is used to display the user's score in the game. All of the other objects are contained in a form called *fm2*. A table is used within the form so that the elements can be positioned properly.

   To display the radio buttons in a five by eight grid, two *for* loops are used. The *for* loops are nested such that the inner loop displays a row of five radio button objects using the *<TD>* tag. The outer loop uses the *<TR>* tag with the inner loop to display the eight rows. After the radio buttons, another *for* loop is used to display a row of five standard button objects. An *OnClick* event handler is used in each button object to call the *fire()* function. The parameter of each function is given the index of the *for* loop. This is to distinguish which button was pressed. For example, the first button will call *fire(0)*, the second button will call *fire(1)*, and so on. Finally, a single button object labeled *START* has an *OnClick* event handler to execute a function starting the game.

2. The *game_start()* function is used to start the game. First you clear the radio buttons if necessary. There is an array of length five called *enemy* that keeps track of the number of radio buttons checked in each column. A set of nested *for* loops clears the radio buttons up to the value in the *enemy* array for each column. Because the radio button objects were not given names, they are accessed from the elements property of the form object such as:

```
document.fm2.elements[ width_n * i + n].checked
```

The elements property is an array. Each element in the form can be accessed from the array. The first object in *fm2* would be the text object. It could be accessed by *document.fm2.elements[0]*. The radio buttons are elements 1 through 48 in the array. The *for* loops set the checked property of the radio button objects to false. Also, various variables are initialized including a global variable *wtime* that sets the speed of the game to 400 milliseconds. Then the *come()* function is called after *wtime* number of milliseconds using the *setTimeout* method.

3. The *come()* function is the function that continuously runs during the game. A random number representing a column is generated using the *poor_rand()* function. Based on this number, the next radio button in the column using the elements property of *fm2* is checked and the *enemy* array is updated. The value in *enemy* is tested to see if the line is full and the game is over. Otherwise *come()* is called again after *wtime* milliseconds.

4. As stated previously, the buttons underneath the radio button execute the *fire()* function. Based on the parameter passed to it, the function will clear that column of radio buttons. The score will be added to by the value in the *enemy* array. The value of that column in the *enemy* array will be reset to zero. The score will be displayed in the *message* text object. Finally, to increase the speed of the game, *wtime* is decreased so that the *come()* function will be called more frequently.

Related Techniques

Creating Random Phrases

Grouping Variables Together

Displaying Repeating Information on a Page

Using Complex Numbers

Using Numerical Variables

Type: JavaScript data type

K. Selvakumar

```
<SCRIPT LANGUAGE="JavaScript">
function tonum(obj)
{
 return parseFloat(obj);
}
function inputtest(form, button)
{
 solve_quad(form);
 return;

}
```

continues

```
function solve_quad(form)
{
if(form.inputbox1.value=="" || form.inputbox1.value==" " ||
form.inputbox1.value=="0")
{
alert("It is not an Quadratic Equation");
return;
}
var a=tonum(form.inputbox1.value);
var b=tonum(form.inputbox2.value);
var c=tonum(form.inputbox3.value);
var d=b*b-(4*a*c);
if(d<0)
{
var e=Math.sqrt(-d);
var neg=true;
}
else
{
var e=Math.sqrt(d);
var neg=false;
}
var f=-b/(2*a);
var g=e/(2*a);
if(neg)
{
form.outputbox1.value=f+"+"+g+"i";
form.outputbox2.value=f+"-"+g+"i";
}
else
{
form.outputbox1.value=f+g;
form.outputbox2.value=f-g;
}
return;
}
</SCRIPT>


Enter the Coefficient of X^2 here----->
<INPUT TYPE=text NAME=inputbox1><P>
Enter the Coefficient of X here------->
<INPUT TYPE=text NAME=inputbox2><P>
Enter the Constant here --------->
<INPUT TYPE=text NAME=inputbox3><P>
<HR>
<CENTER>
<INPUT TYPE=button NAME=C2F VALUE="SOLVE"
        onclick=inputtest(this.form,this)><P>
```

```
</CENTER>
<HR>
Root1
<INPUT TYPE="text" SIZE=50 NAME="outputbox1">
<P>
Root2
<INPUT TYPE="text" SIZE=50 NAME="outputbox2">
```

Syntax Example

```
form.outputbox1.value=f+"+"+g+"i";
```

Comments

There is no specific way in JavaScript to keep track of complex or *imaginary numbers* (numbers involving the square root of a negative number). To use a complex number, you have to use two numerical variables to account for the real and imaginary parts of the number.

Online Example

"Solving Quadratic Equations," by K. Selvakumar, email: **selvakum@tech.iupui.edu**

URL: **http://www.engr.iupui.edu/~selvakum/quad.html**

Description

This page enables you to enter the coefficients of a quadratic equation. The JavaScript function in this page will calculate the roots of that equation, taking care of any complex value. The roots are then displayed to the page.

Step-by-Step

On the page are three text forms named *inputbox1*, *inputbox2*, and *inputbox3*. These forms are used to contain the coefficients of the quadratic equation. Two additional forms named *outputbox1* and *outputbox2* store the roots of the solved equation.

A button on the page is used to start the calculation of the roots. The button uses an *onClick* event handler to call the *inputtest()* function passing *this.form*.

The *inputtest()* function calculates the roots using the *solve_quad()* function. First, the value in *inputbox1* is tested to make sure it is not 0. If it is 0, the equation is not quadratic and the root cannot be calculated from this method:

```
var a=tonum(form.inputbox1.value);
var b=tonum(form.inputbox2.value);
var c=tonum(form.inputbox3.value);
```

The coefficients are stored the variables *a*, *b*, and *c*. The key to this equation is the discriminant, stored in variable *d*.

```
var d=b*b-(4*a*c);
if(d<0)
{
var e=Math.sqrt(-d);
var neg=true;
}
else
{
var e=Math.sqrt(d);
var neg=false;
}
```

The equation needs to take the square root of *d*. However, if *d* is negative, the result is an imaginary number, which results in a JavaScript error. Therefore, the value of *d* is tested in an *if* statement to see if it is negative. The positive square root of *d* is stored in *e* and a Boolean variable *neg* is set to indicate if the value was negative.

```
var f=-b/(2*a);
var g=e/(2*a);
if(neg)
{
form.outputbox1.value=f+"+"+g+"i";
form.outputbox2.value=f+"-"+g+"i";
}
else
{
form.outputbox1.value=f+g;
form.outputbox2.value=f-g;
}
```

The variables *f* and *g*, parts of the quadratic formula, are then calculated. The *neg* value will determine if the roots are complex. If *neg* is true, *f* and *g* are displayed to the *outbox* forms as a complex value. If *neg* is false, the roots will be real and *f* and *g* are added and subtracted together to get the result displayed to the *outbox* forms.

Related Techniques

Calculating a Formula

Performing Calculations in Forms

Creating a Quiz

Form Object

Type: JavaScript object

Used in: Document objects

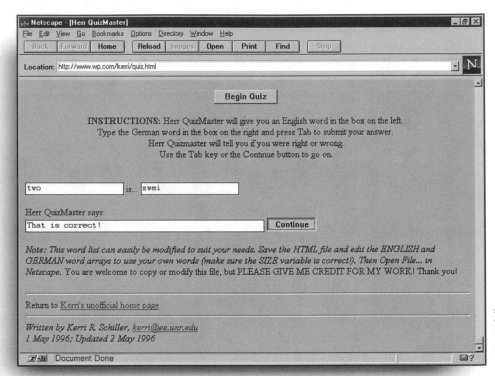

Kerri Schiller

```
<SCRIPT>
<!--
function makeArray(size)
        {
        this.length = size;
        for (var i=1;i<=size;i++)
                {
                this[i] = 0;
                }
        }
```

```
/*      Define global variables, including the word list.
        You can change the test word list by modifying the
        ENGLISH and GERMAN arrays.                          */

        SIZE = 10;
        ENGLISH = new makeArray(SIZE);
        GERMAN = new makeArray(SIZE);
        ENGLISH[1] = 'one';
        GERMAN[1] = 'eins';
        ENGLISH[2] = 'two';
        GERMAN[2] = 'zwei';
        ENGLISH[3] = 'three';
        GERMAN[3] = 'drei';
        ENGLISH[4] = 'four';
        GERMAN[4] = 'vier';
        ENGLISH[5] = 'five';
        GERMAN[5] = 'funf';
        ENGLISH[6] = 'six';
        GERMAN[6] = 'sechs';
        ENGLISH[7] = 'seven';
        GERMAN[7] = 'sieben';
        ENGLISH[8] = 'eight';
        GERMAN[8] = 'acht';
        ENGLISH[9] = 'nine';
        GERMAN[9] = 'neun';
        ENGLISH[10] = 'ten';
        GERMAN[10] = 'zehn';

        available = new makeArray(SIZE);
        //available[] keeps a list of words that haven't been asked yet
        wrong = new makeArray(SIZE);
            //wrong[] keeps track of the words missed
        availSize = SIZE;
                    //holds current size of available array
        wrongSize = 0;
                    //holds the current size of the wrong array
        currentElement=SIZE;
                    //current index into the available array
        inReplay = false;
                    //Are we in replay (redo wrong answers) mode?
        done = true;
                    //Have we completed the test?
                      // Wait for test to begin
                      // before resetting
        justContinue = false;

/*      initAvail() is called at the beginning of each test to
        initialize variables, clear the input areas, and get
        the first word                                        */
```

continues

```
function initAvail()
        {
        for (var i=1;i<=SIZE;i++)
                {
                available[i] = i;
                }
        availSize = SIZE;
        wrongSize = 0;
        currentElement = SIZE;
        inReplay = false;
        done = false;

        document.forms[0].question.value = "";
        document.forms[0].answer.value = "";
        document.forms[0].response.value = "";

        getWord();        //get first word
        }

/*      random() generates a pseudo-random number in the range of
        (1 - max) using the Date object                         */

function random(max)
        {
        var now = new Date();
        var hour = now.getHours();
        var min = now.getMinutes();
        var sec = now.getSeconds();
        return ((((hour +1)*(min +1)*(sec))%max) + 1);
        }

/*      getWord() uses the random function to choose the next element
           out of the proper array (the wrong[] array
        if we are in replay, otherwise the available[] array)       */


function getWord()
        {
        if (!inReplay) //if not in replay mode, choose
                       // the next element from the
                       // available array and output
                {
                currentElement = random(availSize);
                document.forms[0].question.value =
                ENGLISH[(available[currentElement])];
                }
        else    {       //else if in replay mode, choose
                        // next element from wrong array
                currentElement = random(wrongSize);
                document.forms[0].question.value =
                ENGLISH[(wrong[currentElement])];
                }
        }
```

```
/*      checkWord() checks the user input (answer).It is called when
        the Submit button is clicked.  If the answer is wrong, the
        correct answer is displayed and the missed word is added to
        the wrong[] array for use in replay.  In either case, the
        available[] array is adjusted to "delete" the word entry that
        was just asked (therefore listing only the word entries that
        have NOT been asked)                                         */

function checkWord(input)
      {
      if (done); //Do nothing if test is over
      else if (!inReplay)
            {
            if (input == GERMAN[(available[currentElement])])
                  document.forms[0].response.value =
                   "That is correct!";
            else
                  {
                  document.forms[0].response.value =
                   "No, it should be "
                   + GERMAN[(available[currentElement])];
                  wrong[wrongSize + 1] =
                   available[currentElement];
                  wrongSize++;
                  }
            for (var i=currentElement;i<availSize;i++)
                  available[i] = available[i+1];
                  //get rid of "used" array element
            availSize--;
            }
      else if (inReplay && justContinue);

      else
            { available[]
            if (input == GERMAN[(wrong[currentElement])])
                  document.forms[0].response.value =
                   "That is correct!";
            else
                  document.forms[0].response.value
                   "No, it should be "
                   + GERMAN[(wrong[currentElement])];
            for (var i=currentElement;i<wrongSize;i++)
                  wrong[i] = wrong[i+1];
            wrongSize--;
            }
      }
```

continues

339

```
/*      moreQuiz() clears the input and output fields and checks
        to see if you're done with the quiz (or if you are ready
        to start replay mode).  It is called when the Continue
        button is clicked.  If you are just starting replay it
        sets the inReplay flag. */

function moreQuiz()
        {
        document.forms[0].question.value = "";
        document.forms[0].answer.value = "";
        document.forms[0].response.value = "";
        if (done)
                document.forms[0].response.value =
                "Click Begin Quiz to start again";
        else if (availSize == 0 && wrongSize == 0)
                {
                document.forms[0].response.value =
                "You're done - sehr gut!";
                done = true;
                }
        else if (availSize == 0 && wrongSize != 0 && (!inReplay))
                {
                inReplay = true;
                document.forms[0].response.value =
                "Now to redo the tough ones - click Continue";
                justContinue = true;
                }
        else    {
                justContinue = false;
                getWord();
                }
        }

// -->
</SCRIPT>


<INPUT TYPE="BUTTON" VALUE="Begin Quiz" onClick="initAvail()"></A>

<INPUT TYPE="TEXT" NAME="question" VALUE="" SIZE=20> is...
<INPUT TYPE="TEXT" NAME="answer" VALUE="" SIZE=20
onBlur="checkWord(document.forms[0].answer.value)">
<BR>
<BR>
Herr QuizMaster says:
<BR><INPUT TYPE="TEXT" NAME="response" VALUE=
"Press 'Begin Quiz' to begin" SIZE=50 onBlur="moreQuiz()">
<INPUT TYPE="BUTTON" NAME="continue" VALUE="Continue"
onClick="moreQuiz()")
```

Syntax Example

```
document.forms[0].response.value = "No, it should be "
 + GERMAN[(wrong[currentElement])];
```

Comments

A quiz a of this type is easily done in JavaScript. Because you want a quick response in a quiz, a server-side quiz would not work. The server would have to be accessed to get each question and answer. With JavaScript, all the questions and answers are loaded with the page.

Online Example

"Herr QuizMaster," by Kerri Schiller, email: **Kerri@ee.unr.edu**

URL: **http://www.wp.com/kerri/quiz.html**

Description

This page gives a quiz where the script will display a number in English. You have to give the translation in German, and the script will tell you if you are correct. You can customize this quiz to suit your needs by simply changing the word list arrays.

Step-by-Step

In this page the word lists are stored in global arrays. They can be used in all of the functions without having passed to the functions. The English words are stored in a array named ENGLISH[], whereas the German words are stored in array named GERMAN[]. Because these arrays are global variables, they are created before the quiz can begin.

To begin the quiz, a button on the page uses the *onClick* event handler to call the *initAvail()* function. This function clears all the variables that keep track of the quiz. The text objects containing the quiz are cleared, and the *getWord()* function is called to get the first word of the quiz.

The *getWord()* function is used to display a word from the ENGLISH[] array. A random number is obtained to pick a word from the remaining words.

The user can then enter guesses in the answer text object. An *onBlur* event handler is used to call the *checkWord()* function when the focus is lost on this object. The function will determine whether the answer is correct and display an appropriate message. The word will be deleted from the list of available words. If incorrect, it will be added to a list of incorrect words. This list will be tested again after all of the original words are displayed.

To get the next word, a continue button on the page has an *onClick* event handler to call the *moreQuiz()* function. This function will test if the quiz is over and other various variables concerning the status of the quiz. If the quiz is not over, the *getWord()* function is called to display the next word.

Related Techniques

JavaScript Question Examples

Creating a Multiple Choice Test

Creating Time and Date Updates and Status Line Scrollers

Using the *OnLoad* Event Handler

Type: JavaScript event handler

Used in: Window objects, frame objects

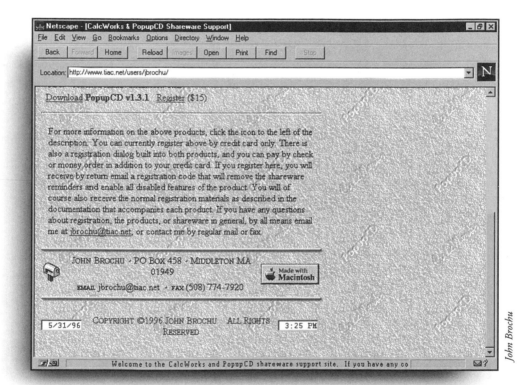

John Brochu

```
<SCRIPT LANGUAGE="JavaScript"><!--

var clkUpdateRate = 15; // Clock update rate in seconds
var timerID = null, msgTimer = null;
var timerRunning = false;
var gMonth=0, gDate=0, gYear=0, gHour=0, gMinute=0;
```

continues

```
var m1 = "W e l c o m e   t o   t h e   C a l c W o r k s   a n d
  P o p u p C D   s h a r e w a r e   s u p p o r t   s i t e . ";
var m2 = "I f   y o u   h a v e   a n y   c o m m e n t s   o n
t h i s   s i t e   o r   m y   p r o d u c t s ,   p l e a s e
l e t   m e   k n o w .       ";
var m3 = "J u s t   c l i c k   m y   e m a i l   a d d r e s s
a t   t h e   b o t t o m   o f   t h e   p a g e .       T h a n k s
  f o r   v i s i t i n g !       ";
var msg = m1+m2+m3;


var pad25 = "                         ";
var pad = pad25+pad25+pad25+pad25+pad25+pad25;
// The following are expressed in milliseconds
// (thousandths of a second)
var scrollDelay = 100; // Controls the scrolling speed.
var initialDelay = 1000; // Delay before beginning scroll
var repeatDelay = 100; // Delay before repeating message.

var repeatCount = 0; // Times to repeat.
              //(0 for one pass, -1 for continuous)

var scrollOffset = pad.length;
var offset;
var msgTimer = null;

function startMessage()
{
 offset = scrollOffset;
msgTimer = window.setTimeout("scrollMessage()", initialDelay);
}

function scrollMessage()
{
 if ((offset <= scrollOffset) && (offset > 0)) {
  window.status = pad.substring(0, offset) + msg;
  offset--;
msgTimer = window.setTimeout("scrollMessage()", scrollDelay);
 }
 else if (offset <= 0) {
  if (-offset < msg.length) {
window.status = msg.substring(-offset, msg.length);
   offset--;
   msgTimer = window.setTimeout("scrollMessage()", scrollDelay);
  }
  else {
   window.status = "";
   if (repeatCount) {
    offset = scrollOffset;
msgTimer = window.setTimeout("scrollMessage()", repeatDelay);
```

```
    if (repeatCount > 0)
      repeatCount--;
    }
   }
  }
 }


function stopClock() {
 if (timerRunning)
  window.clearTimeout(timerID);
 timerRunning = false;
}

function startClock() {
 update(true);
}

function showDate(theDate, forceUpdate) {
 var month = theDate.getMonth() + 1;
 var date = theDate.getDate();
 var year = theDate.getYear();

 if (year >= 100)
  year -= 100;
if ((forceUpdate) ¦¦ (month != gMonth) ¦¦ (date != gDate) ¦¦
 (year != gYear)) {
  document.clock.date.value = (month<10 ? " " : "")
+ (date<10 ? " " : "") + month + "/" + date + "/" + year;
  gMonth = month;
  gDate = date;
  gYear = year;
 }
}

function showTime(theDate, forceUpdate) {
 var hours = theDate.getHours();
var clkHours = ((hours >12) ? hours-12 : (hours==0 ? 12 : hours));
 var minutes = theDate.getMinutes();

 if ((forceUpdate) ¦¦ (clkHours != gHour) ¦¦ (minutes != gMinute)) {
  document.clock.time.value = (clkHours < 10 ? " " : "")
+ clkHours + ((minutes < 10) ? ":0" : ":") + minutes
+ ((hours >= 12) ? " PM" : " AM");
  gHour = clkHours;
```

continues

345

```
  gMinute = minutes;
 }
}

function update(forceUpdate) {
 var theDate = new Date();
 showDate(theDate, forceUpdate);
 showTime(theDate, forceUpdate);
 if (forceUpdate)
  stopClock();
timerID = window.setTimeout("update(false)", clkUpdateRate*1000);
 timerRunning = true;
}

// end of script --></SCRIPT>

</HEAD>

<BODY BACKGROUND="img/Background.gif"
ONLOAD="startMessage(); startClock()">
```

Syntax Example

```
<FRAMESET COLS="30%,70%" onLoad="startfunction()"
```

Comments

OnLoad is an event handler that executes JavaScript when the page first loads. You can use this event handler for any function that you want to activate as soon as possible. Such functions include clocks, scrollers, or random backgrounds.

Online Example

"CalcWorks & PopupCD shareware support," by John Brochu, email: **jbrochu@tiac.net**

URL: **http://www.tiac.net/users/jbrouchu/**

Description

This page implements time and date updates and a status line scroller. The *onLoad* event handler is used to begin both functions. This causes the functions to start operating as soon as the page has loaded and allows the functions to run in the background with no need for user interaction.

Step-by-Step

The *onLoad* event handler is activated when the page is completely loaded, including all images and additional items. Then, the function or statements enclosed in the quotes are executed:

```
<BODY BACKGROUND="img/Background.gif"
ONLOAD="startMessage(); startClock()">
```

These functions are executed using the *onLoad* event handler in the *<BODY>* tag of this page. The *startMessage()* function will start the scrolling text in the status bar. The *startClock()* function will start time and date updates.

Notes

The *onLoad* event handler can be included in a *<BODY>* tag. For a framed page it can be included in the *<FRAMESET>* tag.

Related Techniques

Creating a Real-Time Clock

Scrolling Text Field Banner

Fade In/Fade Out Technique

Drawing with a Pixel Sized Graphic

Using JavaScript If Statements

Type: JavaScript statement

Used in: JavaScript syntax

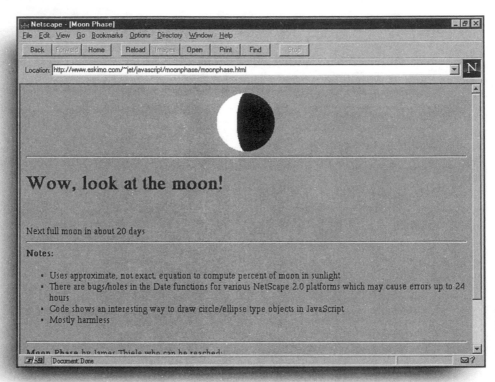

James Thiele

```
<script language=JavaScript>
<!--hide
function showMoon() {
var height=1
var size = 50
var i

// var currentDate  = new Date(96, 1, 22, 16, 15, 0)
var currentDate  = new Date()
var x = currentDate
// alert("date = "+(x.getMonth()+1)+"/"+x.getDate()+"/"+x.getYear())
```

```
// Convert it to GMT
  currentDate.setTime(currentDate.getTime() +
(currentDate.getTimezoneOffset()*60000))

// Get Date (GMT) for recent full moon
// NOTE: months, hours, and minutes are 0 based
var blueMoonDate = new Date(96, 1, 3, 16, 15, 0)

// Compute length of lunar period — source: World Almanac
var lunarPeriod  = 29*(24*3600*1000) + 12*(3600*1000) + 44.05*(60*1000)

var moonPhaseTime = (currentDate.getTime() - blueMoonDate.getTime())
           % lunarPeriod
// alert("Moon phase in days = "+moonPhaseTime/(24*3600*1000))

// Compute various percentages of lunar cycle
var percentRaw = (moonPhaseTime / lunarPeriod)
  // alert("% = "+percentRaw)
var percent     = Math.round(100*percentRaw) / 100
  // alert("% = "+percent)
var percentBy2 = Math.round(200*percentRaw)

var left  = (percentRaw >= 0.5) ? "singleblack.gif" : "singlewhite.gif"
var right = (percentRaw >= 0.5) ? "singlewhite.gif" : "singleblack.gif"

document.write("<center>")

  if (percentBy2 > 100) {
    percentBy2 = percentBy2 - 100
    }

  for (i = -(size-1); i < size; ++i) {
    var wid=2*parseFloat(Math.sqrt((size*size)-(i*i)));
    if (percentBy2 != 100)
      document.write ("<img src="+left +"
           height=1 width="+(wid*((100-percentBy2)/100))+">")
    if (percentBy2 != 0)
      document.write ("<img src="+right+" height=1 width="+(wid*((percentBy2)/
100))+">")
    document.write ("<br>")
  } // for

document.write(  "</center>",
  "<HR>",
  "<h1>Wow, look at the moon!</h1>",
  "<BR>",
  "Next full moon in about ",
  Math.round((lunarPeriod-moonPhaseTime)/(24*3600*1000)),
  " day",
```

continues

349

```
  Math.round((lunarPeriod-moonPhaseTime)/(24*3600*1000))
          != 1 ? "s" : "",
  "")
}
// -->
</script>
<script>
showMoon()
</script>
```

Syntax Example

```
if ( i < 0 )
   return(i);
```

Comments

An *if* statement is the main decision making statement in JavaScript.

Online Example

"Moon Phase," by James Thiele, email: **jet@eskimo.com**

URL: **http://www.eskimo.net/~jet/javascript/moonphase/moonphase.html**

Description

This pages uses JavaScript to "draw" an image. It uses two images, a single black pixel and a single white pixel to display the current phase of the moon.

Step-by-Step

1. An *if* statement is in the form of:

```
if (condition) {
   statements1
} [else {
   statements2
}]
```

If the Boolean variable or expression *condition* is true, *statements1* will be executed. If the optional *else* parameter is included and *condition* is false, *statements2* will be executed.

350

2. To find the portion of the moon displayed, first the current date is obtained and changed into the GMT format by using the *getTimezoneOffeset()* method. The number of milliseconds of the current date is subtracted from the number of milliseconds of a recent full moon.

   Then the remainder operator (%) is used to get the remainder value of this value divided by the milliseconds in the lunar period. This value (*moonPhaseTime*) will be the number of milliseconds since the last full moon.

   By dividing this value by the lunar period, the fractional value of the lunar period is known (*percentRaw*). What *percentRaw* indicates is that 0 represents a full moon up to .5, which indicates no moon visible up to .99 which approaches a full moon again.

3. Two variables, *left* and *right,* are set to the names of the white and black pixel images, dependent on whether *percentRaw* is more or less than .5. The value *percentBy2* is the integer of *percentRaw* times 200. Using an *if* statement, if *percentBy2* is greater than 100, 100 is subtracted from it. The moon graphic is displayed line by line using a *for* loop. The width of each line is calculated (*wid*).

   The *left* and *right* images are displayed with a width size calculated using *wid* and *percentBy2*, except for 2 cases. If *percentBy2* equals 100 (no moon to display), the *left* image is not displayed. If *percentBy2* equals 0 (full moon), the *right* image is not displayed.

4. To complete the *for* loop, a break is displayed after each line.

Notes

There are many commented statements in this JavaScript. Most of these statements were included for debugging purposes. *alert()* statements strategically used throughout the script are a useful debugging tool.

Related Techniques

Using Time-Dependent Web Page Properties

Displaying a Calendar Month

Creating a Memory Game

Using Time-Dependent Web Page Properties

Date Object

Type: JavaScript object

Used in: Methods concerning the date and time

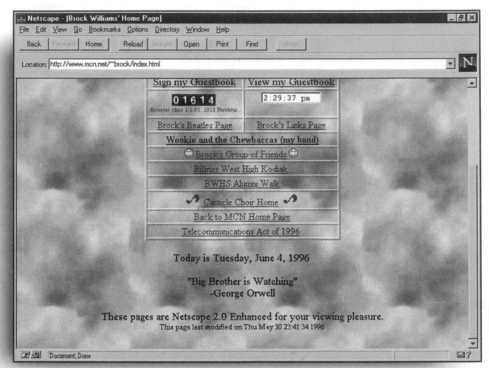

Brock Williams

```
<script>
<!--
today=new Date()
hour=today.getHours()
if (hour<11) {
    document.write("<body background=java.jpg text=white
 link=blue vlink=red nLoad='startclock()'>");
    document.write("<a href=http://www.eff.org/blueribbon.html>
<img rc='blueicons.gif' align=right></a>")
```

```
     document.write("<a href=http://www.eff.org/blueribbon.html>
<img rc='blueicons.gif' align=left></a>")
}
if ((hour<18)&&(hour>10)) {
     document.write("<body background=bluesky.jpg text=black
 link=darkred link=forestgreen onLoad='startclock()'>");
document.write("<a href=http://www.eff.org/blueribbon.html>
<img rc='ribbon.gif' align=right></a>");
document.write("<a href=http://www.eff.org/blueribbon.html>
<img rc='ribbon.gif' align=left></a>");
}
if (hour>17) {
     document.write("<body background=night.jpg text=white
 link=mintcream link=lightyellow onLoad='startclock()'>");
     document.write("<a href=http://www.eff.org/blueribbon.html>
<img rc='blueicons.gif' align=right></a>")
     document.write("<a href=http://www.eff.org/blueribbon.html>
<img rc='blueicons.gif' align=left></a>")
}
// end  -->
</script>


<script>
<!--
today = new Date()
curmonth=today.getMonth()
curday=today.getDay()
curdate=today.getDate()
curyear=today.getYear()

if (curday==1) {
     dayname="Monday";
     } else {
     if (curday==2){
     dayname="Tuesday";
     } else{
     if (curday==3){
     dayname="Wednesday";
     } else{
     if (curday==4){
     dayname="Thursday";
     } else{
     if (curday==5){
     dayname="Friday";
     } else{
     if (curday==6){
     dayname="Saturday";
     } else{
```

continues

```
        if (curday==0){
        dayname="Sunday";
        }}}}}}}

if (curmonth ==0){
        monthname="January";
        } else {
        if (curmonth==1){
        monthname="February";
        } else {
        if (curmonth==2){
        monthname="March";
        } else {if (curmonth==3){
        monthname="April";
        } else {if (curmonth==4){
        monthname="May";
        } else {if (curmonth==5){
        monthname="June";
        } else {if (curmonth==6){
        monthname="July";
        } else {if (curmonth==7){
        monthname="August";
        } else {if (curmonth==8){
        monthname="September";
        } else {if (curmonth==9){
        monthname="October";
        } else {if (curmonth==10){
        monthname="November";
        } else {if (curmonth==11){
        monthname="December";
        }}}}}}}}}}}}

document.write("Today is " + dayname + ", " +monthname+ " "
 + curdate + ", 19" + curyear);
// End of comments -->
</script>


<script>
<!--
function print(obj) {
        document.write("&quot"+obj.text+"&quot")
        if (obj.author!=null){
        document.write("<br> -" + obj.author + "<br>")
        }
        else {
        document.write("<br>")
        }
}
```

```
function quote(text, author) {
    this.text = text;
    this.author = author;
}

numquotes=5
quote1=new quote("I really wish I was less of a thinking
 man and more a fool who's not afraid of rejection.",
"Billy Joel");
quote2=new quote("Without compassion, there can be no end to
 hate","Billy Joel");
quote3=new quote("Big Brother is Watching","George Orwell")
quote4=new quote("He who does not live somewhat for others,
 does not live fully",null)
quote5=new quote("Life can be tragic:  You're here today and
 you're here tomorrow.",null)


today=new Date()
seconds=today.getSeconds()
choice=((seconds)%(numquotes))
document.write("<p>")

if (choice==0){
    print(quote1)}
if (choice==1){
    print(quote2)}
if (choice==2){
    print(quote3)}
if (choice==3){
    print(quote4)}
if (choice==4){
    print(quote5)}
if (choice==5){
    print(quote6)}
if (choice==6){
    print(quote7)}
if (choice==7){
    print(quote8)}
//  End of Comment Body-->
</script>
```

Syntax Example

```
today=new Date()
curyear=today.getYear()
```

Comments

The JavaScript *Date* object is used to extract or create parts of date and time information. It can also be used for other functions such as calculating time zone offsets or creating random numbers.

Online Example

"Brock Williams' Home Page," by Brock Williams, email: **brock@mcn.net**

URL: **http://www.mcn.net/~brock/index.html**

Description

This page uses the *Date* object in many different areas. The colors of the page change according to the time of day, it implements a clock (described in a later example), the current date is displayed, and a random quote is displayed using the current number of seconds to derive the random number.

Step-by-Step

1. One can create a date object as follows:

```
todaysdateobject = new Date()
```

With no parameters to *Date()*, the current date and time on the machine executing the script will be assigned to the object. A specific date and time can be assign by using one of the following parameter formats.

```
new Date("month day, year hours:minutes:seconds")

new Date(year, month, day)

new Date(year, month, day, hours, minutes, seconds)

new Date(milliseconds)
```

JavaScript internally records the *Date* object by using the number of milliseconds from January 1, 1970 0:00:00.

2. Here are the methods for the *Date* object:

The *get* methods are used to retrieve the parameter from the *Date* object, whereas the *set* methods are used to assign the parameter to the *Date* object. See the following table.

Method	*Purpose*
getTime() setTime(value)	Number of milliseconds since January 1, 1970 0:00:00.
getYear() setYear(value)	Year minus 1900.
getMonth() setMonth(value)	Month in the form January=0, Febuary=1, and so on.
getDate() setDate(value)	Date of the month.
getDay() setDay(value)	Day of the week in the from Sunday=0, Monday=1, and so on.
getHours() setHours(value)	Hour of the day from 0–23.
getMinutes() setMinutes(value)	Minutes of the hour.
getSeconds() setSeconds(value)	Seconds of the minute.
getTimezoneOffset()	Minutes difference from GMT.
toGMTString()	Date string in standard format.
toLocaleString()	Date string in system specific format.
Static Methods (always referred to as Date.method)	
Date.parse("dateString")	Converts the string to milliseconds from January 1, 1970 0:00:00.
Date.UTC(year, month, day [, hrs] [, min] [, sec])	Coverts the time and date to milliseconds from January 1, 1970 0:00:00.

3. The first section of the code gets the hour from the current time. It uses the current hour in a series of *if* statements to change certain parameters of the page. For example, if it is between 10:00 A.M. and 6:00 P.M., the page will display a background with a blue sky and clouds. However, if it is between 6:00 P.M. and midnight, the page will have a nighttime background.

4. The next section of code presented is used to display the current date. The day of the week and month obtained by the corresponding methods are integers, so a series of *if-else* statements are used to get the string text of the day and month. To display the correct year, the string "19" must prefix the year value.

5. To print the random quote, the number of seconds is retrieved from the current time. The remainder of this value is divided by the number of quotes to give a random value from 0 to the number of quotes minus 1. This random number is used to display one of the quotes. As random number generators go, this is not very "random." The numbers will be in a predictable cycle. However, for this task, it works well.

Notes

There are a few improvements that could be made to this page:

- First, to account for years 2000 and beyond, it would be better to display the year as *1900 + curyear* instead of prefixing "19" to *curyear.*

- Second, the large *if-else* statements could be avoided through the use of arrays. For example, set up an array of months: *month[0] = "January", month[1] = "February"*, and so on. The text of the month could then be accessed by: *monthname = month[curmonth].*

Related Techniques

Creating Random Phrases

Flashing Color Over Frames

Grouping Variables Together

Creating a Real-Time Clock

Using the Date Object

Type: JavaScript object

Used in: Methods concerning the date and time

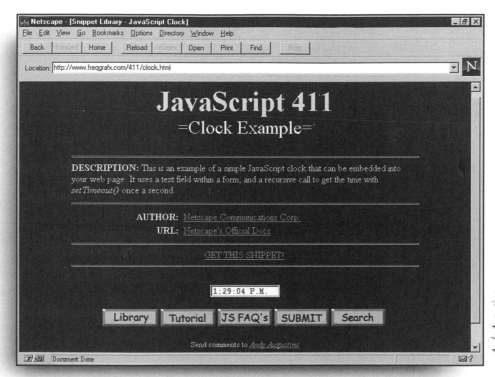

Andy Augustine

```
<SCRIPT LANGUAGE="JavaScript">
<!-- HIDE ME FROM THAT BROWSER
var timerID = null
var timerRunning = false

function stopclock(){
    // cannot directly test timerID on DEC OSF/1 in beta 4.
    if(timerRunning)
        clearTimeout(timerID)
    timerRunning = false
}
```

continues

```
function startclock(){
    // Make sure the clock is stopped
    stopclock()
    showtime()
}

function showtime(){
    var now = new Date()
    var hours = now.getHours()
    var minutes = now.getMinutes()
    var seconds = now.getSeconds()
    var timeValue = "" +
    timeValue  += ((minutes < 10) ? ":0" : ":") + minutes
    timeValue  += ((seconds < 10) ? ":0" : ":") + seconds
    timeValue  += (hours >= 12) ? " P.M." : " A.M."
    document.clock.face.value = timeValue
    timerID = setTimeout("showtime()",1000)
    timerRunning = true
}
//-->
</SCRIPT>
</HEAD>

<BODY
  onLoad="startclock()"
  link=abFFaa
  alink=ab6599
  vlink=DCFFDC
  BGCOLOR="#000000"
  TEXT="#ffffff">



<CENTER>
<FORM NAME="clock" onSubmit="0">
    <INPUT TYPE="text" NAME="face" SIZE=14 VALUE ="">
</FORM>
<P>
</CENTER>
```

Syntax Example

```
var now = new Date()
var hours = now.getHours()
```

Comments

The *Date* object is used here to extract the current time. It is edited in such a way to display the correct 12-hour time in a traditional format. Also available from the *Date* object are methods to access the day, month, year, day of the week, time zone information and other things. Any imaginable style of calendar displays can be created with these methods.

Online Example

"Snippet Library—JavaScript Clock," by Andy Augustine, email: **mohammed@freqgrafx.com**

JavaScript Code from Netscape Communications Corp.

URL: **http://www.freqgrafx.com/411/clock.html**

Description

In this page a function is created in which the *Date* object is used to obtain the current time. The time is then displayed in a text object and the function is recursively called every second to update the time.

Step-by-Step

1. To display the time in 12-hour format, first the hours, minutes, and seconds of the current date are retrieved using the corresponding *get* functions.

   Conditional operators place the parameters in the correct format. To display the correct hour when it is greater than 12, the hour minus 12 is used. Otherwise, the normal hour is used.

   As for the minutes and seconds, if there is only one digit (less than 10), a ":0" is displayed before the number. Otherwise, a ":" is displayed before the number. Similarly, a "P.M." or "A.M." is added depending on the hour value.

2. To display the time, the page uses the command:

   ```
   document.clock.face.value = timeValue
   ```

   Clock is the name of the form object, *face* is the name of the text object and *value* is the property of the text object. Thus, *document.clock.face.value* represents the contents of that text form, and assigning *timeValue* to it displays the string.

3. This clock script is implemented using three functions. In the body of the function, the *OnLoad* event handler will launch the *startclock()* function. This function simply calls the *stopclock()* and then the *showtime()* functions.

The *stopclock()* function checks to see whether the clock is already "running" by checking the Boolean variable *timerRunning* that would be set in the *showtime()* function as follows:

```
if(timerRunning)
        clearTimeout(timerID)
    timerRunning = false
```

If *timerRunning* is true the *clearTimeout* window method is executed using the *timerID* obtained from the *setTimeout* window method to stop the recursion process present in the *showtime()* function.

In the *showtime()* function the time is calculated and displayed as shown. Using the *setTimeout* window method the function is called again after 1,000 milliseconds.

Notes

There is one small bug in this code. If the time is 12:30:15 A.M., for example, the program will display 0:30:15 A.M., when it should display the actual time.

To correct this, replace the code to display the hour:

```
((hours > 12) ? hours - 12 : hours)
```

with:

```
((hours > 12) ? hours - 12 : ((hours == 0) ? 12 : hours))
```

Related Techniques

Using Time-Dependent Web Page Properties

Scrolling Text Field Banner

Creating Random Phrases

Creating Time-Dependent Documents

Using the String Object to Create Variable Documents

Type: JavaScript

Used in: Built-in JavaScript object

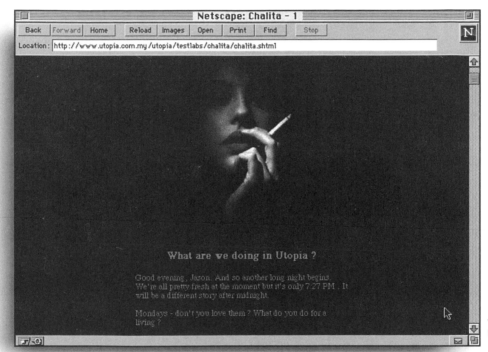

Cyclops

```
<HTML><HEAD><TITLE>Chalita - 1</TITLE>
<SCRIPT LANGUAGE = "Javascript">



function whattime() {
    var now = new Date();
    hours = now.getHours();
    var minutes = now.getMinutes();
    realtime = ((hours > 12) ? hours - 12 : hours);
```

continues

```
        realtime += ((minutes < 10) ? ":0" : ":") + minutes;
        realtime += ((hours < 12) ? " AM " : " PM ");
        if (hours < 12) {
                if (hours < 5) {

welcome += "Hi " + visitor + ", you can't sleep either ?
Medusa's typing away in silence and I'm sat here with, well,
nothing to do.  It's hot. It's dark.  It's been too long.
I could really do with a good ... ";

welcome += "<P>No. Why torment myself ?  Medusa probably
doesn't go that way.  What's a girl to do ? ";

welcome += "<P>And what about you ?  What turns you on ?
Sorry, I don't mean to embarass you.<BR>  But tell me : what
  brings  you  here at " + hours + ":" + minutes + " in the
morning ?  I don't suppose you're near us by any chance ?";
                }

                else {

                        if (hours < 9) {
...}

                        else {
...

                                }

                        }


function specialday() {
    if (numday == 2) {
            if (hours <12) {
daymsg += "Monday morning - what a drag.  A full week ahead
of you. ";
                    }
else daymsg += "Mondays - don't you love them ?  What do you
do for a living ? ";
            }


specialday();


function message1() {
    document.write (welcome);
    }
```

```
function message2() {
    document.write (daymsg);
    document.write ("</TD></TR></TABLE>");
    }

function endmsg() {
    document.write(departmsg);
    document.write ("</TD></TR></TABLE>");
    }

</SCRIPT>
</HEAD>

<BODY>

<h3>What are we doing in Utopia ?</H3>

<SCRIPT>
if (GetCookie('chalita') != null) {
    message1();
    }
else {
    askname();
    }
message2();

</SCRIPT>
</BODY>
</HTML>
```

Syntax Example

```
if (hours < 9) {
welcome += "Up early or still haven't gone to bed yet?"}
```

Comments

This page is different every time you hit it. It knows your name, the day, date, and time, and whether you've been there before. It even knows how many days are left until Christmas!

Online Example

"Chalita," by Cyclops, email: **cyclops@utopia.com.my**

URL: **http://www.utopia.com.my/utopia/testlabs/chalita/chalita.shtml**

Description

A sultry woman's face out of the gloom...a friendly, conversational tone...she really seems interested in you...but wait! It's just a Web page!

The secret is that the text on the page is dynamic; it changes depending on what name you give, and what day and time it is. The writing style sets the tone, and the customization projects the sense of a person behind the words (of course if it were really dynamic, it would have a sultry man appear if the user was a woman).

Step-by-Step

This script uses the *Date* object to determine the time and date; it uses Cookies to keep track of whether you have visited. In this section, however, the use of the string object is the focus.

After figuring out the time, Cyclops writes:

```
            if (hours < 5) {
welcome += "Hi " + visitor + ", you can't sleep either ?
Medusa's typing away in silence and I'm sat here with, well,
nothing to do.  It's hot. It's dark.  It's been too long.
I could really do with a good ... ";

welcome += "<P>No. Why torment myself ?  Medusa probably
doesn't go that way.  What's a girl to do ? ";

welcome += "<P>And what about you ?  What turns you on ?
Sorry, I don't mean to embarass you.<BR>  But tell me : what
  brings  you  here at " + hours + ":" + minutes + " in the
morning ?  I don't suppose you're near us by any chance ?";
                        }
```

welcome is a string variable. Recall that the += operator adds the value to the variable, or in the case of strings, concatenates the given value with the string (in other words, it sticks the words on the end).

The first three expressions add sentences to *welcome*. It should be possible to combine these into one long expression, but there is a bug in Netscape 2.0 that crops up if a single string literal is too long ("literal," meaning a specific string given by text within quotes).

The final expression adds text to *departmsg*. Notice that your name, called visitor, is liberally sprinkled in the text, as well as the hours and minutes.

These and other strings continue to grow throughout the script, until it is time to show them on the page, which is done from a script embedded directly in the body:

```
if (GetCookie('chalita') != null) {
        message1();
        }
else {
        askname();
        }
message2();
```

If you have a Cookie called chalita, you get message1; otherwise, it asks you your name. You would have a Cookie if you had visited the site before.

Message1 is a simple function:

```
function message1() {
        document.write (welcome);
        }
```

It writes the string *welcome*, that we spent so long creating. And so it goes, until the page is full.

Notes

The *document.open* or *document.close* methods are not used because the same page will not be redrawn within the script.

Related Techniques

Displaying a Calendar Month

Using Time-Dependent Web Page Properties

Displaying a Calendar Month

Using JavaScript *for* Loops

Type: JavaScript statement

Used in: The JavaScript *for* statement

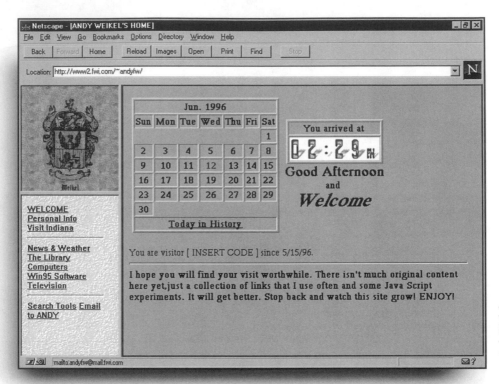

```
function montharr(m0, m1, m2, m3, m4, m5, m6, m7, m8, m9, m10, m11)
{
    this[0] = m0;
    this[1] = m1;
    this[2] = m2;
    this[3] = m3;
    this[4] = m4;
    this[5] = m5;
    this[6] = m6;
    this[7] = m7;
    this[8] = m8;
    this[9] = m9;
```

```
      this[10] = m10;
      this[11] = m11;
}
function calendar()
{
   var monthNames = "JanFebMarAprMayJunJulAugSepOctNovDec";
   var today = new Date();
   var thisDay;
   var monthDays = new montharr(31, 28, 31, 30, 31, 30, 31, 31, 30,
      31, 30, 31);

   year = today.getYear() + 1900;
   thisDay = today.getDate();

   // do the classic leap year calculation
   if (((year % 4 == 0) && (year % 100 != 0)) || (year % 400 == 0))
      monthDays[1] = 29;

   // figure out how many days this month will have...
   nDays = monthDays[today.getMonth()];

   // and go back to the first day of the month...
   firstDay = today;
   firstDay.setDate(1);
   // and figure out which day of the week it hits...
   startDay = firstDay.getDay();

   document.write("<TABLE BORDER=2 align=LEFT>");
   document.write("<TR><TH COLSPAN=7>");
   document.write(monthNames.substring(today.getMonth() * 3,
      (today.getMonth() + 1) * 3));
   document.write(". ");
   document.write(year);
 document.write("<TR><TH>Sun<TH>Mon<TH>Tue<TH>Wed<TH>Thu
      <TH>Fri<TH>Sat");
document.write("<TR>");
   column = 0;
   for (i=0; i<startDay; i++)
   {
      document.write("<TD>");
      column++;
   }
   for (i=1; i<=nDays; i++)
   {
      document.write("<TD><center><b>");
      if (i == thisDay)
         document.write("<FONT COLOR=\"#FF0000\">")
      document.write(i);
```

continues

369

```
     if (i == thisDay)
       document.write("</b></center></FONT>")
     column++;
     if (column == 7)
     {
         document.write("</center><TR>"); // start a new row
         column = 0;
     }
  }
  document.write("<TR><td COLSPAN=7><b><CENTER>
 <A HREF=http://www.unison.com/wantinfo/today/>
Today in History</A></CENTER>");
document.write("</TABLE></CENTER>");

}
```

Syntax Example

```
for (i ; i<N ; i++) {
```

Comments

The *for* statement is one of the easiest ways to make controlled looping structures in JavaScript. Loops can be used in various ways. They can be used to initialize or search through array. This page uses them for the repetitive structure of the calendar to shorten the JavaScript code. Usually, any repetitive task can be made easier using *for* loops.

Online Example

"ANDY WEIKEL'S HOME," by Andy Weikel, email: **andyfw@mail.fwi.com**

URL: **http://www2.fwi.com/~andyfw/**

Description

This page creates a calendar of the current month, highlighting the current day.

Step-by-Step

An example of a *for* statement is

```
for ( i=0 ; i<10 ; i+=2 ) {
statements
}
```

This *for* statement will start at *i=0*, and increment *i* by 2 each loop until *i<10*. The loop will be executed a total of five times.

In the *calendar()* function, arrays and various calculations with the *Date* object are used to find what the current month is, the number of days in that month, and the day of the week in which the first day of the month is.

With this information, the *document.write* method is used to display a table on the page.

```
document.write("<TABLE BORDER=2 align=LEFT>");
   document.write("<TR><TH COLSPAN=7>");
```

First the title of the month is displayed along with the days of the week.

```
    document.write(monthNames.substring(today.getMonth() * 3,
      (today.getMonth() + 1) * 3));
   document.write(". ");
   document.write(year);
  document.write("<TR><TH>Sun<TH>Mon<TH>Tue<TH>Wed<TH>Thu
        <TH>Fri<TH>Sat");
document.write("<TR>");
```

Then a *for* loop is used to display blank spaces in the table until the first day of the month is reached.

```
    column = 0;
    for (i=0; i<startDay; i++)
    {
       document.write("<TD>");
       column++;
    }
```

Then another *for* loop is used to display the rest of the days.

```
    for (i=1; i<=nDays; i++)
    {
       document.write("<TD><center><b>");
```

If statements are used within the *for* loop to make the current day a different color and to start a new row if the end of a column is reached.

```
    if (i == thisDay)
       document.write("<FONT COLOR=\"#FF0000\">")
    document.write(i);
    if (i == thisDay)
      document.write("</b></center></FONT>")
    column++;
    if (column == 7)
    {
       document.write("</center><TR>"); // start a new row
       column = 0;
    }
}
```

At the end of the table a link is placed that links the user to a "Today in History" site.

Related Techniques

Using Time-Dependent Web Page Properties

Recording Last Visit Information

Using JavaScript Cookies

Type: JavaScript property

Used in: Document object

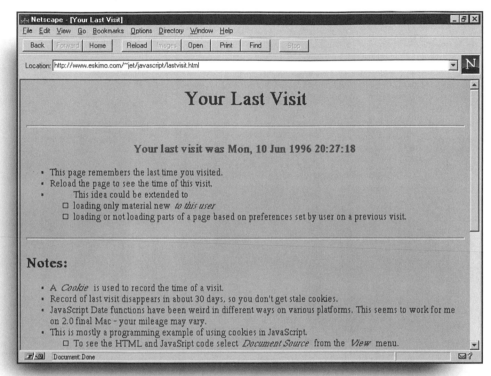

James Thiele

```
<HEAD>
<SCRIPT LANGUAGE="JavaScript">
<!-- to hide script contents from old browsers
//
//  Cookie Functions
//  Written by:  Bill Dortch, hIdaho Design
//  The following functions are released to the public domain.
//
//
// "Internal" function to encode cookie value.  This permits cookies to
// contain whitespace, comma and semicolon characters.
//
```

continues

```
function encode (str) {
  var dest = "";
  var len = str.length;
  var index = 0;
  var code = null;
  for (var i = 0; i < len; i++) {
    var ch = str.charAt(i);
    if (ch == " ") code = "%20";
    else if (ch == "%") code = "%25";
    else if (ch == ",") code = "%2C";
    else if (ch == ";") code = "%3B";
    else if (ch == "\b") code = "%08";
    else if (ch == "\t") code = "%09";
    else if (ch == "\n") code = "%0A";
    else if (ch == "\f") code = "%0C";
    else if (ch == "\r") code = "%0D";
    if (code != null) {
      dest += str.substring(index,i) + code;
      index = i + 1;
      code = null;
    }
  }
  if (index < len)
    dest += str.substring(index, len);
  return dest;
}

//
// "Internal" function to decode cookie values.
//
function decode (str) {
  var dest = "";
  var len = str.length;
  var index = 0;
  var code = null;
  var i = 0;
  while (i < len) {
    i = str.indexOf ("%", i);
    if (i == -1)
      break;
    if (index < i)
      dest += str.substring(index, i);
    code = str.substring (i+1,i+3);
    i += 3;
    index = i;
    if (code == "20") dest += " ";
    else if (code == "25") dest += "%";
    else if (code == "2C") dest += ",";
    else if (code == "3B") dest += ";";
    else if (code == "08") dest += "\b";
```

```
    else if (code == "09") dest += "\t";
    else if (code == "0A") dest += "\n";
    else if (code == "0C") dest += "\f";
    else if (code == "0D") dest += "\r";
    else {
      i -= 2;
      index -= 3;
    }
  }
  if (index < len)
    dest += str.substring(index, len);
  return dest;
}


//
// "Internal" function to return the decoded value of a cookie
//
function getCookieVal (offset) {
  var endstr = document.cookie.indexOf (";", offset);
  if (endstr == -1)
    endstr = document.cookie.length;
  return decode(document.cookie.substring(offset, endstr));
}


//
//  Function to return the value of the cookie specified by "name".
//    name - String object containing the cookie name.
//
function GetCookie (name) {
  var arg = name + "=";
  var alen = arg.length;
  var clen = document.cookie.length;
  var i = 0;
  while (i < clen) {
    var j = i + alen;
    if (document.cookie.substring(i, j) == arg)
      return getCookieVal (j);
    i = document.cookie.indexOf(" ", i) + 2;
    // i = document.cookie.indexOf(" ", i) + 1;
    if (i == 0) break;
  }
  return null;
}


//
//  Function to create or update a cookie.
//    name - String object object containing the cookie name
//    value - String object containing the cookie value.  May contain
```

continues

```
//      any valid sting characters, including whitespace, commas and quotes.
//   expires - Date object containing the expiration data of the cookie,
//      or null to expire the cookie at the end of the current session.
//
function SetCookie (name, value, expires) {
  document.cookie = name + "=" + encode(value) +
((expires == null) ? "" : ("; expires=" + expires.toGMTString()));
}

//  Function to delete a cookie. (Sets expiration date to current date/time)
//   name - String object containing the cookie name
//
function DeleteCookie (name) {
  var exp = new Date();
  var cval = GetCookie (name);
  document.cookie = name + "=" + cval + "; expires=" + exp.toGMTString();
}
////////////////////////////////////////////////////////////////////////////
function setLastVisitCookie()
{
var nowDate = new Date()
var expdate = new Date()

    expdate.setTime (expdate.getTime() + 30*(24 * 60 * 60 * 1000)
    // 30 days from now
   SetCookie ("Last_Visit", nowDate.toGMTString(), expdate)
}

// -- > <! -- end hiding contents from old browsers  -->
</SCRIPT>

<TITLE>Your Last Visit
</TITLE>
</HEAD>

<BODY onLoad="setLastVisitCookie()">

<CENTER>
<H1>Your Last Visit</H1>
<HR>
<SCRIPT LANGUAGE="JavaScript">
<!-- to hide script contents from old browsers

var lastVisit = GetCookie("Last_Visit")
var htmlOut = ""

    if (lastVisit == null) {
    htmlOut += "No record of you visiting in last 30 days."
    } else {
    htmlOut += "Your last visit was " + lastVisit.substring(0,25)
    } // if
```

```
    document.write("<H3>")
    document.write(htmlOut.bold().fontcolor("red"))
    document.write("</H3>")

// --> <!-- end hiding contents from old browsers  -->
</SCRIPT>
</CENTER>
```

Syntax Example

```
SetCookie("BirthYear", "1970" , expiredate)
```

Comments

Due to security reasons there is no way to read or write to a generic file on the user's machine. The only way to save or retrieve information is through a "cookie" file maintained by the browser. A cookie is simply a string variable with an expiration date attached to it. A possible use for cookies might be to remember the users addresses so they don't always need to enter it in a form. Another use might be to remember the user's top score in a JavaScript game.

Online Example

"Your Last Visit," by James Thiele, email: **jet@eskimo.com**

Cookie functions, by Bill Dortch, email: **feedback@hidaho.com**

URL: **http://www.eskimo.com/~jet/javascript/lastvisit.html**

Description

This page uses cookies to remember the last time the user visited the page or to detect whether the user has visited the page at all in the last 30 days. A message is displayed on-screen showing the time and date of the users' last visit, or a message showing that they have not visited within the last six months.

Step-by-Step

1. Using Bill Dortch's functions makes cookies easy to use. To create a cookie, use the function:

```
SetCookie(name, value, expires)
```

name is the cookie name used to access the cookie later.

value is the string that the cookie should store. This is whatever data you wish to store for subsequent visits by the user.

expires is a *Date* object to specify when the cookie should be automatically deleted.

2. To recall a cookie use the function:

```
GetCookie(name)
```

name is the name of the cookie when it was created.

This function will return the string value of the cookie.

3. To delete a cookie use the function:

```
DeleteCookie(name)
```

name is the name of the cookie when it was created.

4. Using the *onLoad* event handler the *setLastVisitCookie()* function is called. In this function, the *SetCookie()* function creates a cookie called *"Last Visit,"* stored with the current date and expires 30 days from the current date.

Within the page, the *GetCookie()* function is used to check the *"Last Visit"* cookie. If the cookie value is null a statement is displayed indicating there was no visit in the last 30 days, otherwise a statement is displayed using the string from the cookie.

Notes

A cookie can be read only by the Web site that created it.

Related Techniques

User Customized Links in a Frame

Using Time-Dependent Web Page Properties

Saving Form Values for Future Visits

Using JavaScript Cookies

Type: Property

Used in: Document object

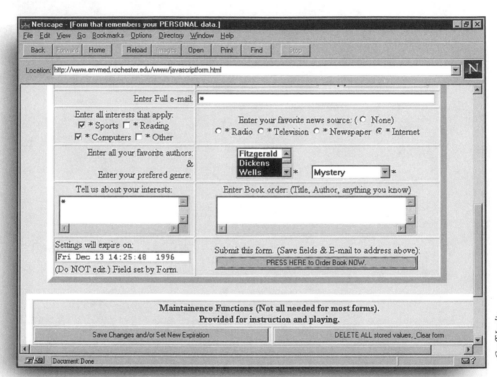

Geoff Inglis

```
<script language="javascript">
<!-- begin script

//3-Mar-1996 Copyright (C) 1996 by Geoff Inglis. You may
//use these routines in your pages (commercial or noncommercial)
//if you include these three lines. You may not Re-sell this code.

TheCookieName = 'BigCookieinthesky';
numDays = 183; //Days 'till Cookie expires(eg. 183 days = 6 months)

function WriteOneBigCookie () {
   var expire = new Date ();
   expire.setTime (expire.getTime() + (numDays * 24 * 3600000));
```

```
    //6 months from now!
//                                  (dd) (hr) (ms in hr)
   var WholeCookie = expire ;

//Text entry
   WholeCookie = WholeCookie + '`' +
checknull(document.TestForm.Entry1.value);
   WholeCookie = WholeCookie + '`' +
checknull(document.TestForm.Entry2.value);
   WholeCookie = WholeCookie + '`' +
checknull(document.TestForm.Entry2b.value);
   WholeCookie = WholeCookie + '`' +
checknull(document.TestForm.Entry2c.value);
   WholeCookie = WholeCookie + '`' +
checknull(document.TestForm.Emailadd.value);

//CheckBoxes
   WholeCookie = WholeCookie + '`' + document.TestForm.Entry4.checked;
   WholeCookie = WholeCookie + '`' + document.TestForm.Entry5.checked;
   WholeCookie = WholeCookie + '`' + document.TestForm.Entry6.checked;
   WholeCookie = WholeCookie + '`' + document.TestForm.Entry7.checked;

//Radio button
   WholeCookie = WholeCookie + '`' + setChkIndx(document.TestForm.Entry8);

//Select Form (One entry)
   WholeCookie = WholeCookie + '`' + document.TestForm.Entry9.selectedIndex;

//Select Form (Multiple entries)
   WholeCookie = WholeCookie + '`' + findChkIndx_MS(document.TestForm.Entry10);

//Textarea
   WholeCookie = WholeCookie + '`' + checknull(document.TestForm.Entry11.value);

//Put cookie in the Oven Bake 'till done.
  document.cookie = TheCookieName +"=" + escape (WholeCookie) +
                    "; expires=" + expire.toGMTString() ;
}

//**Edit this function for each corresponding function above.
//  They are numbered in the order they are placed in the Cookie
//  starting with zero which is ALWAYS the expriation date.

function UpdateForm () {

//Get the Cookievalue then use a Cookie Cutter (parseCookie) to slice it up.
TheCookieValue =  GetCookie(TheCookieName);
```

continues

```
//FORM action
  document.TestForm.action = 'mailto:inglis@axsnet.com,' +
parseCookie(TheCookieValue,5);

//TEXT input Form
  document.TestForm.ExpDate.value  = parseCookie(TheCookieValue,0);

  document.TestForm.Entry1.value   = parseCookie(TheCookieValue,1);
  document.TestForm.Entry2.value   = parseCookie(TheCookieValue,2);
  document.TestForm.Entry2b.value  = parseCookie(TheCookieValue,3);
  document.TestForm.Entry2c.value  = parseCookie(TheCookieValue,4);
  document.TestForm.Emailadd.value = parseCookie(TheCookieValue,5);

//CheckBoxes
  document.TestForm.Entry4.checked = (parseCookie(TheCookieValue,6)=='true')?
true:false ;
  document.TestForm.Entry5.checked = (parseCookie(TheCookieValue,7)=='true')?
true:false ;
  document.TestForm.Entry6.checked = (parseCookie(TheCookieValue,8)=='true')?
true:false ;
  document.TestForm.Entry7.checked = (parseCookie(TheCookieValue,9)=='true')?
true:false ;

//RadioButton
  if (parseCookie(TheCookieValue,10) != "*" )
        document.TestForm.Entry8[parseCookie(TheCookieValue,10)].checked = true;

//Select Form (One entry)
  if (parseCookie(TheCookieValue,11) != "*" )
        document.TestForm.Entry9.selectedIndex = parseCookie(TheCookieValue,11);

//Select Form (Multiple Entries)
     setChkIndx_MS(document.TestForm.Entry10,parseCookie(TheCookieValue,12));

//Textarea
  document.TestForm.Entry11.value = parseCookie(TheCookieValue,13);
}

//If user enters nothing then put back the *.
function checknull(theEntry) { //In case the user left it blank!
 if (theEntry == "") return "*";
 return theEntry;
}

//Get and return the index of THE checked radio button
 function setChkIndx(theName) {
   for (var i=0; i < theName.length; i++ ) {
   if (theName[i].checked == true) return i;
   }
 return "*"; // One item is always supposed to be checked but...
 }
```

```
//Find and return list of indexes of *all* the selected MULTIPLE selects. YUCK.
//Return list of indexes, seperated by ",".
 function findChkIndx_MS(theName) {
 var indxlist = "";
   for (var i=0; i < theName.options.length; i++ ) {
   if (theName.options[i].selected == true) indxlist = indxlist + "," + i;
   }
 return (indxlist == "")?indxlist = "*":indxlist;
 }


//Use the list to SET all stored MULTIPLE selects.
// Most efficient storage for a very long list, but messy.
// Requires clearing all before loading to get only those checked.
 function setChkIndx_MS(formObj,theList) {
   for (var i=0; i < formObj.options.length; i++) {
   formObj.options[i].selected = false;} //clear all.
   var ilen = 0;
   while ( ilen < theList.length-1 ) {
    var indxstart = theList.indexOf(',',ilen);
    if (indxstart == -1) return;

    ilen = theList.indexOf(',',indxstart+1);
    if (ilen == -1) ilen = theList.length;

    //make sure its an integer before using as subscript
    var indx = parseInt(theList.substring(indxstart+1,ilen) ,10);
    formObj.options[indx].selected = true;
   }
 }


//Get the cookie from a list of possible cookies. Honest!
function GetCookie (CookieName) {
  var cname = CookieName + "=";
  var i = 0;
  while (i < document.cookie.length) {
    var j = i + cname.length;
    if (document.cookie.substring(i, j) == cname){
      var leng = document.cookie.indexOf (";", j);
      if (leng == -1) leng = document.cookie.length;
      return unescape(document.cookie.substring(j, leng));
    }
    i = document.cookie.indexOf(" ", i) + 1;
    if (i == 0) break; //thats -1 plus 1, duh.
  }
  return "*";
}


//Set the Cookie with expire date in the past - 2 days to get it for sure.
function DelEatCookie (name) {
  var expire = new Date();
```

continues

383

```
    expire.setTime (expire.getTime() - 2 * 86400001);  //-2 days ago. Stale Cookie
    document.cookie = name + "=*; expires=" + expire.toGMTString();
}

//Parse Big  Cookie. A CookieCutter if you will.
function parseCookie(cookieValue, citem) {
    var indx = 0, citemlen =0;
    if ( cookieValue == null ) return "*"//Data has expired or never entered.
    if ( cookieValue == "*"  ) return "*"//Data has expired or never entered.
    for(var i=0; i < citem; i++) {
        indx = ( citem==0 )?0:cookieValue.indexOf("`", indx + 1)+1;}
        citemlen=(cookieValue.indexOf("`",indx)>0)
          ?cookieValue.indexOf("`", indx+1):cookieValue.length;
    return cookieValue.substring(indx, citemlen);
}

// end script -->
</script>



<TD align="center">
Submit this form. (Save fields & E-mail to address above):<BR>
<input type="submit"
value=" PRESS HERE to Order Book NOW. "
    onClick="
    document.TestForm.action = 'mailto:test@envmed.rochester.edu,' +
 document.TestForm.Emailadd.value;
    WriteOneBigCookie();
    UpdateForm();
```

Syntax Example

```
document.cookie= "cookie1=" datastring + "expires=" + expdate
```

Comments

Normally, form data is blank when a page is revisited. Through the use of cookies this page will remember form data that was previously entered.

Online Example

"Form that remembers your PERSONAL data," by Geoff Inglis, email:
inglis@axsnet.com

URL: **ttp://www.envmed.rochester.edu/www/javascriptform.html**

Description

This page uses cookies to remember what the user has entered in a form if entered within the last six months.

Step-by-Step

1. The submit button object in the form has an *onClick* event handler that executes three statements:

```
document.TestForm.action = 'mailto:test@envmed.rochester.edu,'
+ document.TestForm.Emailadd.value;
WriteOneBigCookie();
UpdateForm();
```

The first statement assigns a URL to the *action* property of the form. The property sends the form data to that URL. Normally that URL is a CGI script, but in this case the *mailto:* protocol is used to send the form data via email.

2. Then, the *WriteOneBigCookie()* function used to store the form data in a cookie. First, the current date is obtained and six months of milliseconds is added to it to determine the expiration date of the cookie. This expiration date is stored in a string object called *WholeCookie*. Then the value of every object in the form (if not blank) is appended to this string delimited by "`" characters. At the end of the function, the name of the cookie, the *WholeCookie* string, and the expiration date are assigned to *document.cookie*.

The *UpdateForm()* function is the same function used when the document is loaded. The function *GetCookie()* is called to retrieve the cookie from the user's machine. Then the *ParseCookie()* function is used several times to extract each value from the string obtained from the cookie. Each value is then stored in the form values on the page to display them.

Related Techniques

Recording Last Visit Information

User Customized Links in a Frame

Responding to User Form Data

Recording Optional Information

Using JavaScript Functions (Argument Property)

Type: JavaScript structure

Used in: Cookies

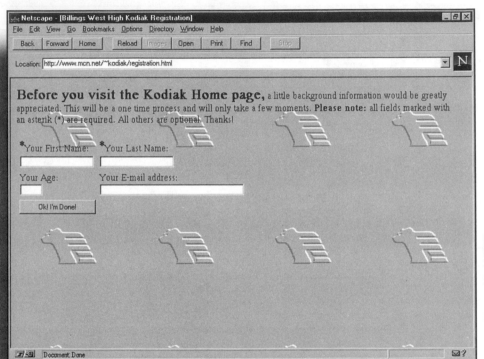

Kevin Hein and Brock Williams

```
<script>
function savecookie(obj) {
var passed=true
var first=obj.fname.value
var last=obj.lname.value
if (first.length<=1) {
    alert("First Name is a required element.  Please enter
 your first name.")
passed=false
}
if (last.length<=1) {
    alert("Last Name is a required element.  Please enter your
 last name.")
passed=false
}
```

```
today=new Date()
time=today.getTime()
expdate=new Date(time +120*24*60*60*1000)
cookie=escape(first)+"#&#"+escape(last)
cookie+=((obj.age.value==null) ? "#age#":("#age#"+obj.age.value))
cookie+=((obj.mail.value==null) ? "#mail#":("#mail#"+obj.mail.value))
if (passed==true) {
SetCookie("bwhskodiak",cookie,expdate,"/~kodiak",".mcn.net");
location.href="http://www.mcn.net/~kodiak/index.html"
}
}


function SetCookie(name, value) {
var argv = SetCookie.arguments;
var argc = SetCookie.arguments.length;
var expires = (argc > 2) ? argv[2] : null;
var path = (argc > 3) ? argv[3] : null;
var domain = (argc > 4) ? argv[4] : null;
var secure = (argc > 5) ? argv[5] : false;
document.cookie = name + "=" + escape (value) +
    ((expires==null) ? "" : ("; expires="
+ expires.toGMTString())) +
    ((path==null) ? "" : ("; path=" + path)) +
    ((domain==null) ? "" : ("; domain=" + domain)) +
    ((secure==true) ? "; secure" : "");

}
</script>


<form name="info" method="post">
<table>
<tr><td><font size=+2>*</font>Your First Name: <br>
<input type=text name="fname" size=15></td>
<td>
<font size=+2>*</font>Your Last Name: <br>
<input type=text name="lname" size=15></td>
</tr>
<tr>
<td>Your Age: <br>
<input type=text name="age" size=4></td>
<td>Your E-mail address: <br>
<input type=text name="mail" size=30></td>
</tr>
<tr>
<td><input type="button" name="done" value="Ok! I'm Done!"
onClick="savecookie(this.form)"></td>
</tr>
</table>
</form>
```

Syntax Example

```
arg1 = SetDate.arguments[1]
```

Comments

Occasionally, it is useful for a function to take an optional number of parameters. You might have a function that you would like to use a number of different ways. The ability to use the *arguments* property of the function allows you to be more flexible in the design of the function.

Online Example

"Billings West High Kodiak Registration," by Kevin Hein, email: **kevinh@mcn.net** and Brock Williams, email: **brock@mcn.net**

URL: **http://www.mcn.net/~kodiak/registration.html**

Description

This page contains a form with some elements that it considers optional. The first and last name are required, but the age and email data are optional. It saves all this data in a cookie for later use. It uses the data to personalize the Web pages by using your information.

Step-by-Step

1. In the form on this page are four text objects named *fname, lname, age,* and *mail.* A button will call the *savecookie()* function and submit this form when the button is clicked. This function will check to see if the first two required text objects are given.

2. The *fname* and *lname* text object values are added to a string. Using a conditional operator, the age and mail text object value are added to that string, if they are not null.

3. Then the *SetCookie()* function is called.

The *SetCookie()* function is passed five parameters. Note that only two parameters are in the *SetCookie()* declaration. *SetCookie.arguments.length* is used to find how many parameters were actually passed to the function. *SetCookie.arguments[i]* is an array of all the parameters passed to the function. Conditional operators are used to save the parameters, and then they are all saved to document.cookie.

Related Techniques

Recording Last Visit Information

Responding to User Form Data

Playing Sound with JavaScript

Using the Window.location Object to Load a File

Type: JavaScript

Used in: Object, property of the window object

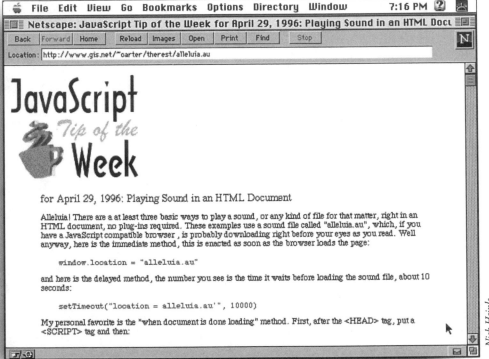

```
<HTML>

<HEAD>

<TITLE>JavaScript Tip of the Week for April 29, 1996:
Playing Sound in an HTML Document</TITLE>
<SCRIPT LANGUAGE = "JavaScript">
```

```
function PlaySound(){
        window.location = "alleluia.au"
}
</SCRIPT></HEAD>

<BODY onLoad = "PlaySound()">
</BODY></HTML>
```

Syntax Example

```
window.location = "alleluia.au"
```

Comments

Although this technique consists only of a single statement, it is powerful and flexible enough for a closer look.

Online Example

"Playing Sound in an HTML Document," by Nick Heinle, email: **carter@gis.net**

URL: **http://www.gis.net/~carter/therest/960429.html**

Description

This technique demonstrates three different opportunities to play a sound using JavaScript: when the page loads, at a set duration after the page loads, or when a particular action is taken.

Step-by-Step

The key to playing a sound is this statement:

```
window.location = "alleluia.au"
```

Whenever the browser encounters this statement, it tries to set the location of the current window to the URL *"alleluia.au."* If that URL were an HTML file, that file would appear. In this case, it is a sound file; therefore, the browser refers to what it's supposed to do with that type of file. Most browsers will download it, launch a simple sound player, and play the sound, while other browsers will play the sound with a plug-in.

If this statement is in a function:

```
function PlaySound(){
        window.location = "alleluia.au"
}
```

then calling the function will play the sound. This is most impressively done in the *<BODY>* tag:

```
<BODY onLoad = "PlaySound()">
```

The *onLoad* event occurs when the page is finished loading; that's when you'll get your alleluia.

Notes

This technique works with other MIME types, such as Shockwave movies, Acrobat files, and QuickTime movies.

Related Techniques

Working with Multiple Windows

Displaying Repeating Information on a Page

Document Object (Write Method)

Type: JavaScript object

Used in: Window object

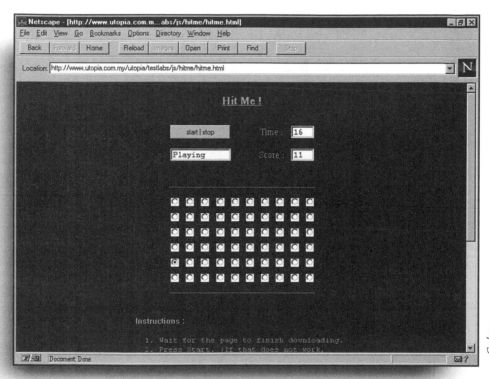

```
<!-- This game was created by Chas Sweeting, Medusa, and Cyclops -->
<!-- on May 4 th 1996.  In memory of 3 crazy summers in Seoul.   -->

numrows = 6   // the number of rows = y coordinate
numcols = 10  // the number of cols = x coordinate

function layout(){
var holeid = 0;
```

continues

```
document.write("<FORM NAME = \"dmz\"><CENTER><TABLE CELLSPACING = 2 >
<TR><TD COLSPAN = "+numcols+"><HR SIZE = 1></TD></TR>");
for (var j = 0; j < numrows; j+=1){
 document.write("<TR>");
 for (var i = 0; i < numcols; i+=1){
document.write("<TD ALIGN = \"center\" VALIGN = \"center\">");
  document.write("<INPUT TYPE = \"radio\"
  onClick = \"hithead(" + holeid + ")\"></TD>");
  holeid += 1;
  }
 document.write("</TR>");
}
document.write("<TR><TD COLSPAN = "+numcols+">
<HR SIZE = 1></TD></TR></TABLE></CENTER></FORM>");
}
```

Syntax Example

```
for ( j=1 ; j<=20 ; j++ )
 document.write('<img src="pattern.gif">')
```

Comments

To display repeating objects in a page, you could simply use x number of statements to display the object. An easier and quicker method is to use a *for* loop and *document.write* methods in JavaScript. The code is shorter and faster to download.

Online Example

By Cyclops, email: **cyclops@utopia.com.my**

URL: **http://www.utopia.com.my/utopia/testlabs/js/hitme/hitme.html**

Description

This page implements a game using an array of radio buttons. Instead of using 60 statements to draw the array, JavaScript accomplishes the task using only a few lines of code.

Step-by-Step

The *layout()* function is used in this page to create the array of radio buttons. HTML code is written to the page using the *document.write* method. First, the code to establish the form and the table for the radio buttons is written.

To create the radio buttons, two nested *for* loops are used. The outer *for* statement loops refer to the number of rows desired; the inner *for* statement loops refer to the number of columns desired. Within the inner loops are statements that align and create the radio buttons. By executing these statements 60 times, the combination of these loops will present the desired display of radio buttons.

Related Techniques

Implementing a Game Using Form Objects

Creating Animated Radio Buttons

Displaying a Scrolling Text Field Banner

Using Recursion

Type: JavaScript process

Used in: Time-controlled loops

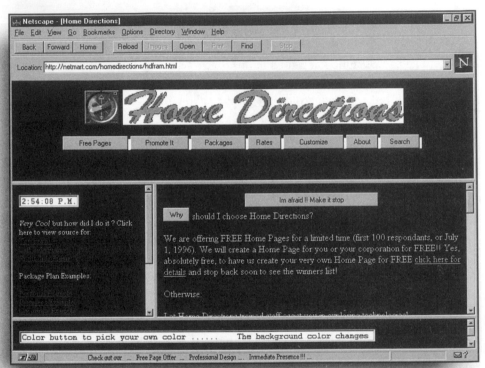

```
<HTML><HEAD>
<TITLE>Scrolling Link</TITLE>
<script language="JavaScript">
<!--
//
//  Home Page Creation Script
//  (C) Copyright 1996 by Kevin Gorsline(gorsline@ix.netcom.com)
//  For more examples go to Home Directions Web site at
//             http://homedirections.com
//
```

```
// You may freely use this script.
// If you do, please leave this section in site and drop me a note.
//
var wait=105, timer1;
//
// Substitute msg1 and 2 with your message
//
var msg1="   The background color changes in each frame every
 hour until noon ... ";
var msg2="  After that we fade to BLACK... Use the Custom Color
 button to pick your own color ......";
var msg=msg1+msg2;
//
// create and write the ScrollBanner
//
function ScrollBanner() {
        msg = msg.substring (1, msg.length) + msg.substring (0,1);
   document.ScrollBanner.message.value=msg;
   timer1=setTimeout("ScrollBanner()", wait);
}
//
// Call the pause function to stop this ScrollBanner
//
function pause() {
   clearTimeout(timer1);
   timer1=setTimeout("ScrollBanner(500)",15000);
}
// -->
</script>
</HEAD>
<BODY  onLoad="ScrollBanner()">
<script language="JavaScript">
<!--
document.write('<form name="ScrollBanner"><input type="text"
 name="message" value="Thanks for stopping in to Home Directions,
scrolling will commense in a minute      "
size="75" pause()><br></form>');
// -->
</script>
</BODY>
</HTML>
```

Syntax Example

```
function DummyLoop(){
timerid = setTimeout("DummyLoop()",10000)
}
```

Comments

Recursion occurs when a function calls itself. It is commonly used in JavaScript in combination with the *setTimeout* method to create a time-controlled loop. The function will call itself after the number of milliseconds specified in the *setTimeout* method.

Online Example

"Home Directions," by Home Directions, email: **gorsline@ix.netcom.com**

URL: **http://netmart.com/homedirections/hdfram.html**

Description

This page creates a ticker-tape style scrolling message in a text field. The text you want to display will slowly move along the form. This is a good way to attract the user's attention to your page. Here you may list what is new about your Web page.

Step-by-Step

Within the page there is a text object called *"message";* this is where the scrolling message will be displayed. It does not matter what the initial value of the text object is because it is quickly replaced by the scrolling message. The *onLoad* event handler starts the banner by executing the *ScrollBanner()* function. The message to be displayed is stored in the variable *msg*. The *substring* method is used to save all the characters past the first one and to put the first character at the end. *msg* is then displayed to the text object. Using the *setTimeout* method, *ScrollBanner()* is called after *wait* number of milliseconds. Using this recursive technique, the process will continue indefinitely, creating the scrolling effect.

Notes

Some recursive scripts like this one have no end. If the JavaScript runs for a long time it may cause an out of memory error. The amount of time until the browser crashes is dependent on many variables. The computer's configuration, the number of functions, the time between functions will all contribute to the time. For most applications, you should be safe if you switch pages within 10 minutes or so.

Related Techniques

Flashing Color Over Frames

Automating a Web Page Tour

Creating Time and Date Updates and a Status Line Scroller

Creating a Real-Time Clock

Implementing a Client-Side Search

Using Arrays

Type: JavaScript arrays

Used in: Browser documents

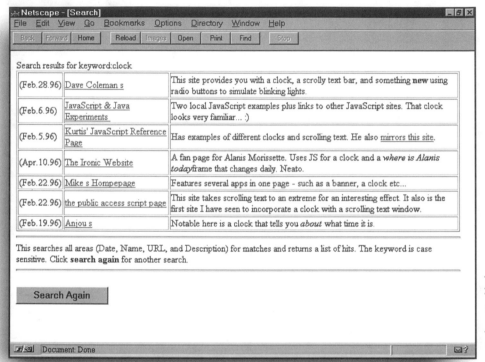

Andrew Wooldridge

```
// * JavaScript Index Search Engine        *
// *  Copyright Andrew Wooldridge          *

    var key = "";

// Functions for links object creation and manipulation

    function makeEntry (){
            this.Date = "";
            this.Name="";
            this.URL = "";
```

```
                this.Desc = "";
                this.Category = "";
                return this;
        }

    function makeArray(n) {
                this.length = n;
                for (var k = 1; k <= n; k++) {
                            this[k] = "";
                }
                return this;
        }

        function makeLinks(size) {
                            this.length = size;
                            for (var r=1; r<= size; r++) {
                                    this[r] = new makeEntry();
                                    this[r].Date = datesArray[r];
                                    this[r].Name = namesArray[r];
                                    this[r].URL = urlsArray[r];
                                    this[r].Desc = descArray[r];
                                    }
                                    return this;
                    }

// implementing object libraries
// data from home page

var linksize=0
// number of entries, is used for index for many arrays

datesArray = new makeArray(linksize);
namesArray = new makeArray(linksize);
urlsArray = new makeArray(linksize);
descArray = new makeArray(linksize);
//--------data----------

var arraycount=0

arraycount += 1
datesArray[arraycount] = "(Apr.10.96)"
urlsArray[arraycount] = "http://www.bytes.com/"
namesArray[arraycount] = "Books and Bytes"
descArray[arraycount] =
    "Has lots of technical and computer books -
    look for JS books here soon."

arraycount += 1
datesArray[arraycount] = "(Mar.24.96)"
urlsArray[arraycount] = "http://www.winternet.com/~sjwalter/javascript/"
```

continues

```
namesArray[arraycount] = "The Complete  Idiot s Guide to JavaScript"
descArray[arraycount] = "A new book out by QUE Publishing.
   I think this is the first book out on JavaScript specifically.."


      .
      .
      .


linksize = arraycount;

// ----end data ------

function showAll(linkobj) {
        for (var s=1; s<= linkobj.length; s++) {
                                    showLink(linkobj,s);
                }
            }

function showLink (links, index) {
    document.write("<tr><td>" + links[index].Date +"</td>");
    document.write("<td><a href=" + links[index].URL +">" +
    links[index].Name + "</a></td>");
    document.write("<td>" + links[index].Desc + "</td></tr>");
    }

function searchLinks(links, keyword){
    document.write("Search results for keyword:" +keyword +"<br>");

    document.write("<table border>");
    for (var q=1; q<=links.length; q++) {
                if (links[q].URL.indexOf(keyword) != -1){
                        showLink(links,q);
                        continue;
                }
                if (links[q].Desc.indexOf(keyword) != -1) {
                            showLink(links,q);
                        continue;
                }
                if (links[q].Date.indexOf(keyword) != -1) {
                            showLink(links,q);
                        continue;
                }
                if (links[q].Name.indexOf(keyword) != -1) {
                            showLink(links,q);
                            continue;
                }
            }
    document.write("</table>");
    }
```

```
// final stuff
// the main program ---

jsi = new makeLinks(linksize);
document.write("<title>Search</title><body bgcolor=white>");
searchLinks(jsi, prompt("(Warning! dont use very common keywords like
    'www' It will crash your browser!) \rSearch everywhere for :","nothing"));
document.write("<hr>");
document.write("This searches all areas (Date, Name, URL, and Description)
    for matches ");
document.write("and returns a list of hits.  The keyword is case sensitive. ");
document.write("Click <b>search again</b> for another search. <hr>");
document.write("<form><input type=button onClick='history.go(0)' value='Search
Again'></form>");

// show all the links
//document.write("<table border>");
//showAll(jsi);
//document.write("</table>");
</script>
```

Syntax Example

```
if (links[q].Desc.indexOf(keyword) != -1) {
        showLink(links,q);
```

Comments

A client-side search may be more efficient than a server-side search. The searching will take less time because no data needs to be sent between the client and server during the search. Because all of the data must be initially sent to the user in the JavaScript, a client-side search may only be feasible with a moderate amount of data. Also, if you do not have access to any kind of server programs, client-side searches may be your only option.

Online Example

"Search," by Andrew Wooldridge, email: **andreww@c2.org**

URL: **http://www.c2.org/~andreww/javascript/search**

Description

This page has an index of various JavaScript related URLs along with dates, names, and descriptions of the URLs stored in the script. The user can enter a keyword in a dialog box to search the index. The script will then return the information of all instances of the keyword to the page.

Step-by-Step

1. All of the information in this page is referenced using a custom object called *makeLinks*. An instance of this object is created using the command:

```
jsi = new makeLinks(linksize);
```

The data can then be accessed from the object *jsi*. Contained in this object are arrays of strings for each part of the different links. This is done by the following *for* loop in the custom object's function.

```
for (var r=1; r<= size; r++) {
        this[r].Date = datesArray[r];
        this[r].Name = namesArray[r];
        this[r].URL = urlsArray[r];
        this[r].Desc = descArray[r];
        }
```

This assigns all arrays to the object. For example, the name of the fifth link in the list can now be accessed by the command *jsi.this[5].Name*.

2. With the custom object prepared to access all the information, it can now be searched. A *prompt* method is used to display a dialog box on the page where the user can enter a keyword to be searched. The *jsi* object along with this keyword are passed as parameters to the *searchLinks()* function. The *jsi* object is renamed *links* in this function. A *for* loop is used in this function to check each value in *links*. The *indexOf* method is used in an *if* statement to see if the keyword is part of any of these value. If so, the *showLink()* function is used to display all the information for that link.

3. To do another search a button displayed to do so. An *onClick* event handler executes the statement *history.go(0)*. This statement tells the browser to go to the current page in the history list. This is similar to pressing reload on your browser. The prompt will be redisplayed and the user can start another search.

Notes

The *continue* command is used in each of these *if* statements in the *searchLinks()* function to jump to the next loop in the *for* loop. For example, say the word "coffee" is contained in both the description and name properties of a link. After "coffee" was found in the description and the link was displayed, you do not want the JavaScript to find "coffee" in the name and display the link again. Thus, the *continue* command is needed.

Related Techniques

Grouping Variables Together

Creating Random Phrases

Storing Information Using a Custom Object

Creating a Status Line Display for Selected Links

Using the OnMouseOver Event Handler

Type: JavaScript event handler

Used in: Link objects

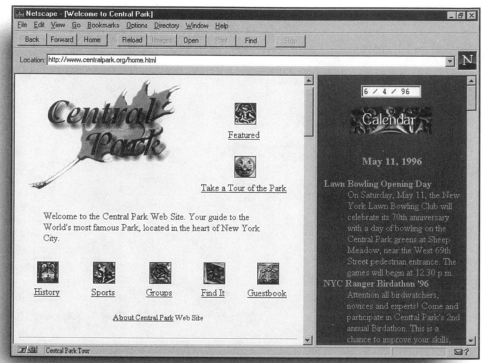

Jay Fayloga & Liana Fayloga

```
<TABLE BORDER=0 WIDTH=100% CELLPADDING=10><TR>

<TD VALIGN="top">
<img src="images/home.gif" alt="Welcome to Central Park"
border=0 height=192 width=260>
</TD>
```

```
<TD VALIGN="bottom" ALIGN="center">
<A HREF="featured/index.html" TARGET="_top"
 onMouseOver="self.status='Featured This Month'; return true">
<img src="images/icons/icon05DONE.jpg" alt="Featured" border=1
 height=35 width=35 hspace=0 vspace=8><BR>
Featured</a>
<P>
<A HREF="tour/index.html" TARGET="_top"
 onMouseOver="self.status='Central Park Tour'; return true">
<img src="images/icons/icon01DONE.jpg" alt="Tour" border=1
 height=35 width=35 hspace=0 vspace=8><BR>
Take a Tour of the Park</a>
</TD>

</TR></TABLE>
```

Syntax Example

```
<A HREF='' onMouseOver='alert("Hi!")'> link </A>
```

Comments

OnMouseOver is an event handler that executes JavaScript when the mouse moves over a link. The default condition when you move the mouse over a link is to display the URL of the link to the status bar. You can use this event handler to change what is displayed in the status bar or execute any other JavaScript function. You can display text and pictures about that link in another frame, for example.

Online Example

"Welcome to Central Park," by Jay Fayloga, email: **fayloga@centralpark.org** and Liana Fayloga, email: **liana@centralpark.org**

URL: **http://www.centralpark.org/home.html**

Description

This page has a number of links with pictures and text. Instead of displaying the URL to the link in the status bar, the *OnMouseOver* event handler is used to display text describing the link in the status bar.

Step-by-Step

In the linking tags, the *onMouseOver* event handlers contain a command such as,

```
self.status='Central Park Tour'; return true
```

In this case, *self* refers to the window object and *status* refers to the property that represents the status bar. Assigning the string *'Central Park Tour'* to this property will cause this string to be displayed on the status bar. This event handler requires the *return true* statement (or any expression that gives a *return true*) to execute the statement. Note that certain functions such as *alert()* or *confirm()* will make the link "unlinkable." This means that moving the mouse to the link will always execute the function and the URL can't be accessed.

Related Techniques

Grouping Variables Together

Displaying MouseOver Information to a Form

Storing Information Using a Custom Object

Using the Custom Object

Type: JavaScript object

Todd Grupe

```
function makeArray(num) {
   for (var i=0; i<num; i++) {
      this[i+1] = ""
   }
}

function strToArray(phr) {
   lngth = phr.length;
   for (var i=0; i<lngth; i++) {
```

continues

```
      this[i+1] = phr.charAt(i);
   }
   return this;
}

function enterArr() {
   for (var i=0; i<39; i++) {
      this[i] = " "
   }
}

function
 makeObject(alphabet,code,quote,enteredArray,solveArray,doneAlready){
   this.alphabet = alphabet;
   this.code = code;
   this.quote = quote;
   this.enteredArray = enteredArray;
   this.solveArray = solveArray;
   this.doneAlready = doneAlready;
}

var numOfCodes = 12;
var numOfQuotes = 100;
var alphabet = "ABCDEFGHIJKLMNOPQRSTUVWXYZ.?!,;:-\"\'* ";
var code = codes[random(numOfCodes)]
var ch = random(numOfQuotes)
var quote = quotes[ch]
var enteredArray = new enterArr()
var solveArray = new strToArray(quote)
var doneAlready = new makeArray(numOfQuotes)
var crypto = new
 makeObject(alphabet,code,quote,enteredArray,solveArray,doneAlready)
crypto.doneAlready[ch] = "1";
```

Syntax Example

```
var payroll = new Database;
```

Comments

In addition to the built-in objects given by JavaScript, you can create your own objects. This is a convenient way to organize data in a collective format. Functions you assign to the object become methods of the object, whereas variables and arrays assigned to the object become properties of the object. The methods and properties of the custom object can be accessed in the same way as the built-in objects.

Online Example

"CypherSpace," by Todd Grupe, email: **tgrupe@netvoyage.net**

URL: **http://www.netvoyage.net/~tgrupe/crypto.htm**

Description

This page implements a cryptogram game completely controlled by JavaScript. A cryptogram is a puzzle in which each letter in a phrase is replaced by a different letter. The author of this page creates a custom object with properties that contain all the information about the cryptogram and the user's status in solving that cryptogram.

Step-by-Step

1. The *makeObject* function shows how a typical custom object is defined.

```
function
 makeObject(alphabet,code,quote,enteredArray,solveArray,doneAlready){
    this.alphabet = alphabet;
    this.code = code;
    this.quote = quote;
    this.enteredArray = enteredArray;
    this.solveArray = solveArray;
    this.doneAlready = doneAlready;
}
```

The six properties in this object are created using a command of the form:

```
this.variable = variable
```

This makes the variable into a property of the object. A method is created in the same way, but instead of using a variable, you use the name of a function in your JavaScript.

2. An object of the type of *makeObject* is created using the *new* command:

```
var crypto = new
 makeObject(alphabet,code,quote,enteredArray,solveArray,doneAlready)
```

The default values of the properties of this object are defined by the values of *alphabet, code*, and so on. This object is now referred to as *crypto*. Other objects could be created the same way using the *new* command with a different object name.

3. Here is how these properties are used in the JavaScript:

alphabet is a string that stays constant within the script. It is used to reference a standard order of characters and punctuation.

code is a string similar to a form of alphabet with the characters mixed up. It is randomly picked from an array of strings called *codes*. This string is used to describe the encryption of the cryptogram.

quote is a string that contains the current non-encrypted quote in the game.

enteredArray is an array that initialized to 40 empty characters. Each value in the array is used to store the user's choice to what he thinks the letters in the cryptogram actually are. For example, if the user thinks that D represents W, the *crypto.eneteredArray[4]* would equal W.

solveArray is an array with the same data as *quote*. Each element in the array is a single character in *quote*.

doneAlready is an array that indicates whether a quote has been used, by storing a "1" in the array if that number quote has been used.

Related Techniques

Grouping Variables Together

Creating a Multiple Choice Test

Streaming Text into Documents

Using the document.open and document.close Methods

Type: Methods of the document object

Used in: JavaScript statements

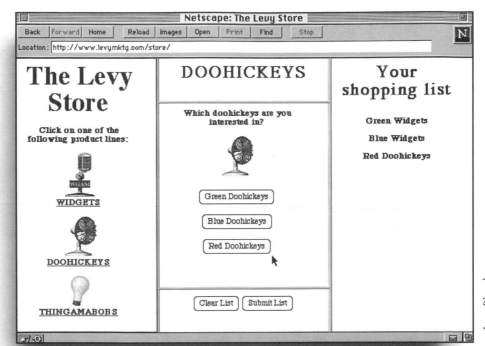

Jason Bloomberg

```
index.html:

<html><head><title>The Levy Store</title>
<script language="JavaScript">
var righttext="<html><head></head><body bgcolor='ffffff'><center><b>
<font size=+3>Your shopping list</font><p>";

var newlist = true;
```

continues

```
function loadright(thetext)
    {
    newWin=top.open('', 'right');
    newWin.location.href='right.html';
    if (newlist)
            {
            newWin.document.write(righttext);
            newlist = false;
            }
  newWin.document.write(thetext + "<p>");
    }

function clear()
    {
    newWin=top.open('', 'right');
    newWin.document.close();
    newWin.document.clear();
    newWin.document.write(righttext);
    newlist = false;
    }
</script>
</head>

<frameset cols="200,*,200">
    <frame src="left.html" name="left" noresize>
    <frame src="middle.html"  name="middle" noresize scrolling="no">
    <frame src="right.html"  name="right" noresize>
</frameset>
</html>

dtext.html:

<html><head><title>Levy Store</title></head>
<body bgcolor="ffffff">
<b>Which doohickeys are you interested in?
<img src="fan.gif" width=52 height=58>
<form>
<input type="button" value="Green Doohickeys" onClick="top.loadright('Green
    Doohickeys')">
</form>
</b></body></html>
```

Syntax Example

```
newWin.document.close();
newWin.document.open();
```

Comments

It is a common belief among HTML coders that once the browser displays a page, the only way to change that page is to reload it. JavaScript makes it easy to change the value of form elements, like the text in text fields, but what about the regular text on the page?

Although you cannot remove text from a page without reloading the page, it is possible to add more text to a page without reloading it. The key to this trick is the *document.open* and *document.close* methods.

Online Example

"The Levy Store," by Jason Bloomberg, email: **jbloomberg@lhouse.com**

URL: **http://www.levymktg.com/store**

Description

I developed this example of data streaming to illustrate one approach to a "shopping basket" site. The user can choose any of three product lines in the left frame, and then choose any of three members of the selected line in the center frame. Whenever the user selects a product, it appears in the rightmost frame.

The user can select different product lines and continue to add products to the "shopping list." When they are done, they either click "clear list" or "submit list" to start over.

Step-by-Step

Every time you click a product button, text must appear on the shopping list:

```
<input type="button" value="Green Doohickeys"

onClick="top.loadright('Green Doohickeys')">
```

which executes the function loadright. The function *loadright*, in turn, executes the following statement:

```
newWin.document.write(thetext + "<p>");
```

Where the variable *thetext* contains the text to be added to the rightmost frame.

415

The magic comes in clearing and reinitializing the shopping list. When the user clears the list, the function *clear* is executed:

```
newWin=top.open('', 'right');

newWin.document.close();

newWin.document.clear();

newWin.document.write(righttext);
```

First, I define the window *newWin* as the one in the frame called "right." Next, I close the document in that frame. Then I clear the document using the *document.clear* method. finally, I write the text that I want to appear at the top of the document into the frame "right."

Notes

Note that I only use *document.open* method when I first initialize the shopping list, even though I repeatedly use the *document.close* method. JavaScript is not particular about opening documents before you close them. However, if you fail to close them, then new information sent to that document will appear at the end of the old information in the document, instead of replacing the document's contents.

Related Techniques

Creating Special Text Effects

Encrypting Text in a Page

Using Checkboxes Creatively

Using the Checkbox Object

Type: JavaScript

Used in: Object, property of the form object

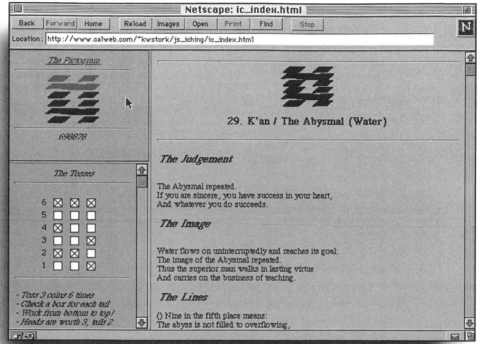

Kent Stork

```
<html>
<head>
<script language="JavaScript">
<!-- Java Script
function show_click(form) {
var l5, l4, l3, l2, l1, l0 ;

l5 = 9-(form.cb50.checked+form.cb51.checked+
form.cb52.checked)  ;
l4 = 9-(form.cb40.checked+form.cb41.checked+
form.cb42.checked)  ;
```

continues

```
l3 = 9-(form.cb30.checked+form.cb31.checked+
form.cb32.checked)  ;

function put_clicks ( form ) {
for ( var i = 5 ; i >= 0 ; i -- ) {
    document.writeln ( "<tr><td>" + (i+1) + " </td><td>" ) ;
    for ( var j = 0 ; j < 3 ; j ++ )
        document.writeln (
"<input type='checkbox' name='cb"+i+j+"'
onClick='show_click(form)'>"
        ) ;
    document.writeln ( "</td>" ) ;
}
}
// -- -->
</script>
</head>

<body bgcolor = "90b090">
<center>
<i>The Tosses<hr>
<form method="post">
<table border="0">
<script> put_clicks ( document.form ) ; </script>
</table>
<hr></center>
<p>
</form>
</body>
</html>
```

Syntax Example

```
<input type='checkbox' name='cb"+i+j+"'
onClick='show_click(form)'>
```

Comments

Because the *onClick* event handler works with checkboxes, they can be used as buttons that have the added feature of appearing checked or unchecked.

Online Example

"The Meditation Practice of the I-Ching, or Chinese Book Of Changes," by Kent Stork, email: **kwstork@calweb.com**

URL: **http://www.calweb.com/~kwstork/js_iching/ic_index.html**

Description

The I-Ching can tell your fortune based on the results of tossing three coins six times. After you enter the results of the coin tosses in the checkboxes in the lower-left frame, an ancient Chinese pictogram automatically appears in the upper-left. Click the completed pictogram, and your fortune appears on the right.

Step-by-Step

The text of the lower-left page, the one with the checkboxes, is included because the other two frames do little more than respond to your choices of checkboxes.

1. Instead of creating 18 repetitive checkbox declarations in HTML, in this instance, a JavaScript is directly in the body of the document:

```
<script> put_clicks ( document.form ) ; </script>
```

It is important to remember that JavaScripts can go just about anywhere; if you want to use one to create HTML within a page, place the script where the HTML goes.

2. The *put_clicks* function causes a table to be created, with 18 checkboxes defined as follows:

```
document.writeln ("<input type='checkbox'
name='cb"+i+j+"'onClick='show_click(form)'>") ;
```

You must look carefully to see that the *document.writeln* method writes four strings to the page: the first is *"<input type='checkbox' name='cb"*; the second is i; the third is j; and the fourth is *"onClick='show_click(form)'>"*. The variables i and j range from 5 to 0 and 0 to 2, respectively, creating 18 checkboxes in all, with names like cb03 and cb41.

3. After these checkboxes are part of the page, clicking one executes the *show_click* function. (The parameter "form" is passed to this function so that *show_click* knows which form the particular checkbox is in.)

The *show_click* function uses the checked property of each checkbox to calculate numbers it will use to create the pictograms:

```
l5 = 9-(form.cb50.checked+form.cb51.checked+form.cb52.checked)  ;
```

The expression *form.cb50.checked* is boolean, meaning it is either true or false, depending on whether checkbox cb50 is checked. You should wonder, then, how three of these booleans can be added together, subtract the result from 9, and set that value to the variable l5? (That's l5 as in L5, not fifteen—numbers can't be variables!)

The secret is in the loose typing of JavaScript variables. As the browser reads this statement from left to right, it sees the L5 = 9 - ..., and at that point, it knows L5 will be a number because the 9 is a number. What follows must then be forced to be a number. JavaScript requires that "true" be evaluated as 1, and "false" be evaluated as 0. Therefore, the statement L5 = 9 - (true + false + true) will assign the value 7 to L5 because L5 = 9 - (1 + 0 + 1).

4. The script then uses the proper formulas to calculate the correct pictograms and writes the pictogram to your cookie; the next time you come to the I-Ching, it will remember your last pictogram. (A nice touch don't you think?)

Notes

This example uses *document.writeln*, instead of the more common *document.write* to write HTML to the page. The only difference is that the *writeln* places a return character at the end, which is nothing more than whitespace as far as HTML is concerned (that is, it doesn't appear anyway). Therefore, when writing HTML to the page, *write* and *writeln* are equivalent (except in a *<PRE>* tag, where return characters appear).

Loose variable typing is one of the strengths of JavaScript, and one of the most confusing aspects. It is also one of the most important differences between JavaScript and Java, which features strong typing.

Related Techniques

Streaming Text into Documents

Using a Text Grid

User-Customized Links in a Frame

Navigating Tricks and Pitfalls Using Scrolling Lists

Using the selectedIndex Property

Type: JavaScript

Used in: Property of select object or options array

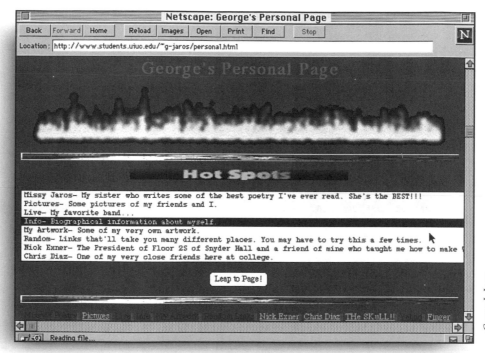

George J. Jaros

```
<html>
<head>
<TITLE>George's Personal Page</TITLE>
<SCRIPT LANGUAGE="JavaScript">
function leapto(form) {
    var myindex=form.dest.selectedIndex
    window.open(form.dest.options[myindex].value,"_top","");
}
</SCRIPT>
</head>
<Body>
```

continues

```
<CENTER><FORM NAME="myform"><SELECT NAME="dest" SIZE=8>
<OPTION VALUE="http://www.students.uiuc.edu/~g-jaros/
missy.html">Missy
Jaros- My sister who writes some of the best poetry
I've ever read. She's the BEST!!!
<OPTION VALUE="http://www.students.uiuc.edu/~g-jaros/pictures.html">Pictures-
Some pictures of my friends and I.
<OPTION VALUE="http://www.students.uiuc.edu/~g-jaros/
live.html">Live- My favorite band...
<OPTION VALUE="http://www.students.uiuc.edu/~g-jaros/
info.html">Info- Biographical information about myself.
<OPTION VALUE="http://www.students.uiuc.edu/~g-jaros/
myart.html">My Artwork- Some of my very own artwork.
</SELECT>
<P>
<INPUT TYPE="BUTTON" VALUE="Leap to Page!" onClick="leapto(this.form)">
</FORM></CENTER>

</html>
```

Syntax Example

```
var myindex=form.dest.selectedIndex
window.open(form.dest.options[myindex].value,"_top","");
```

Comments

The goal was to have a scrolling list of long descriptions of Web pages to link from. Unfortunately, it runs into the dreaded Netscape 2.0 image size bug.

Online Example

"George's Personal Page," by George J. Jaros, email: **g-jaros@students.uiuc.edu**

URL: **http://www.students.uiuc.edu/~g-jaros/personal.html**

Description

This personal page has a very interesting feature: a scrolling text box full of Web page descriptions. Below the box is a "Leap to page!" button that takes you to the selected page.

When you first encounter this page in Netscape 2.0, the button simply does not work. You must leave the page and return before the JavaScript will work. This bug only occurs when a page has images that do not have their width and height specified.

Step-by-Step

1. First, a standard scrolling option list is set up:

```
<FORM NAME="myform"><SELECT NAME="dest" SIZE=8>
<OPTION VALUE="http://www.students.uiuc.edu/~g-jaros/
info.html">Info- Biographical information about myself.
<OPTION VALUE="http://www.students.uiuc.edu/~g-jaros/
myart.html">My Artwork- Some of my very own artwork.

...

</SELECT>
<P>
<INPUT TYPE="BUTTON" VALUE="Leap to Page!" onClick=
"leapto(this.form)"></FORM>
```

2. The values of the *<OPTION>* tags are simply the URLs to which you want to link. Next, when you click the "Leap to Page!" button, the *leapto* function is executed:

```
function leapto(form) {
   var myindex=form.dest.selectedIndex
   window.open(form.dest.options[myindex].value,"_top","");
}
```

Leapto assigns the value *selectedIndex* of the option list to the variable *myindex*, and then passes this value to the *window.open* method. *selectedIndex* represents the number of the selected option, where the first option is 0.

The *selectedIndex* is actually a property of either the *<SELECT>* object (as in the first statement), or the *<OPTIONS>* array (as in the second statement). *form.dest.options* is an array that corresponds to the option list, so the value of one of its elements is the value of that option (which in this case, is the destination URL).

Notes

Note that a target of *"_top"* is specified for the *window.open* method; otherwise, a new window would be created. This attribute is followed by an empty string(""), which is unnecessary. This indicates a desire to not change the window settings.

Also note that the variable *myindex* did not have to be used; the function could have been expressed as a single expression:

```
window.open(form.dest.options
[form.dest.selectedIndex].value,"_top");
```

Related Techniques

Using Scrolling Option Lists

Loading a Page via a Selection List

Controlling Interaction Among Open Windows

Using the Opener Object

Type: JavaScript

Used in: Object; property of the window object

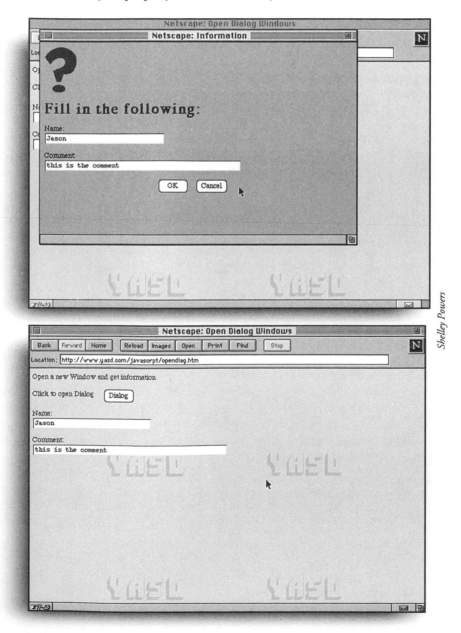

Shelley Powers

File: opendiag.htm

```
<HTML>
<HEAD><TITLE> Open Dialog Windows </TITLE>
<SCRIPT LANGUAGE="JavaScript">
<!-- hide script from old browsers


function OpenDialog(iType, sMessage) {

    newWindow=window.open("diag.htm","",
            "toolbar=no,directories=no,width=500,height=300")
    if (newWindow != null && newWindow.opener == null)
            newWindow.opener=window
    }

// end hiding from old browsers -->
</SCRIPT>
</HEAD>

<BODY>
<H1> Open a new Window and get information</H1>

<FORM NAME="CallDiag">
<INPUT TYPE="button" NAME="OpenWin" VALUE="Dialog"
    onClick="OpenDialog()">

Name:<br><INPUT type="text" size=30 Name="Name">
<p>
Comment:<br><INPUT type="text" size=50 Name="Comment">
</FORM>
</BODY>
</HTML>
```

File: diag.htm

```
<HTML>
<HEAD><TITLE> Information</TITLE>
<SCRIPT LANGUAGE="JavaScript">
<!-- hide script from old browsers


function SetInformation() {
    opener.document.CallDiag.Name.value=
            document.DiagForm.Name.value
    opener.document.CallDiag.Comment.value=
            document.DiagForm.Comment.value

    window.close()
    }
// end hiding from old browsers -->
```

```
</SCRIPT>
</HEAD>

<BODY>

<H1>Fill in the following:</H1>

<FORM NAME="DiagForm">

Name:<br><INPUT type="text" size=30 Name="Name">
Comment:<br><INPUT type="text" size=50 Name="Comment">

<INPUT type="button" Value="  OK  "
    onClick="SetInformation()">

<INPUT type="button" Value="Cancel" onClick="window.close()">
</CENTER>
</FORM>
</BODY></HTML>
```

Syntax Example

```
if (newWindow != null && newWindow.opener == null)
newWindow.opener=window;

opener.document.CallDiag.Name.value = document.DiagForm.Name.value;
```

Comments

A floating tool palette is one of the best uses of multiple windows. It has been difficult, however, for the tool palette to refer to the window that created it. Now Netscape 3.0 has an easy solution to this problem.

Online Example

"Open Dialog Windows," by Shelley Powers of YASD, email: **shelleyp@yasd.com**

URL: **http://www.yasd.com/javascrpt/opendiag.htm**

Description

This example simply demonstrates the *opener* property. The first window has two text boxes and a button called "Dialog." Click the dialog button and another window is created.

This window prompts you to enter information into two text fields, and then click the OK button. Clicking OK closes the second window; you see that the values you typed into that window have now been transferred to the first window.

Step-by-Step

Clicking the Dialog button opens a new window with the *window.open* method. In this script, however, are the following two lines:

```
if (newWindow != null && newWindow.opener == null)
      newWindow.opener=window
```

First, there are two checks: that the window *newWindow* really exists, and that it has not been assigned an opener yet. Next, the *opener* property of the *new* window is assigned the value window, which refers to the *old* window.

If you look in the script in the new window, you see:

```
opener.document.CallDiag.Name.value =
document.DiagForm.Name.value
```

This statement takes the value of one of the text fields in the new window and assigns it to the value of the corresponding text field in the old window, which it refers to as opener.

Notes

As this is being written, Netscape 3.0 is still in beta, so it is not clear just how this property will work.

Related Techniques

Working with Multiple Windows

Working with Multiple Windows

Using the Document Object in a Second Window

Type: JavaScript

Used in: Object, property of the window object

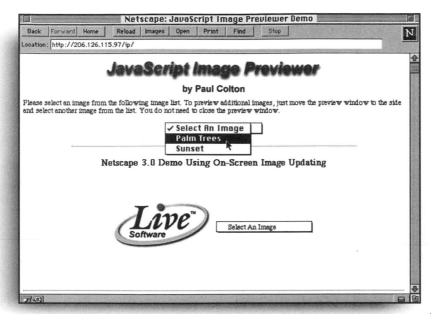

Paul Colton

```
<HTML>
<HEAD>

<SCRIPT>
    // JavaScript Image Preview Demo
    // by Paul Colton

    function display_image(form) {

selectionname =
form.imagename.options[form.imagename.selectedIndex].text;
selection =
form.imagename.options[form.imagename.selectedIndex].value;
myWindow = window.open("", "Preview","toolbar=0,location=0,
directories=0,status=0,menubar=0,scrollbars=0,resizable=0,
copyhistory=0,width=200,height=255");

myWindow.document.open();
myWindow.document.write("<HTML><HEAD>");
...
myWindow.document.write("</BODY></HTML>");
myWindow.document.close();
    }

</SCRIPT>

<TITLE>JavaScript Image Previewer Demo</TITLE>

</HEAD>
<BODY BGCOLOR=FFFFFF TEXT=000000>
<FORM>
<select NAME="imagename" onChange="display_image(this.form)">
<option value="image0.gif">Select An Image
<option value="image1.gif">Palm Trees
<option value="image2.gif">Sunset
</select>
</FORM>

</BODY>
</HTML>
```

Syntax Example

```
myWindow.document.open();

myWindow.document.write("<HTML><HEAD>");
```

Comments

It has always been possible to open several browser windows at once, and to navigate in each one separately. With the advent of JavaScript you can now open and close new windows with the characteristics you desire. These windows can be used for floating palettes, special toolbars, and many other uses.

Online Example

"JavaScript Image Preview Demo," by Paul Colton, email: **contact@livesoftware.com**

URL: **http://jrc.livesoftware.com/ip**

Description

Here is a simple example of creating a new window. Choose an image—either palm trees or a sunset—from a popup menu. The selected image appears in a new window, which also has a "Close" button that closes that window.

Step-by-Step

1. The first step is to interpret your choices in the option list.

```
<select NAME="imagename" onChange="display_image(this.form)">
<option value="image0.gif">Select An Image
<option value="image1.gif">Palm Trees
<option value="image2.gif">Sunset
</select>
```

2. Whenever the option changes, the function *display_image* is called. No button is required because the *onChange* event handler is used.

```
function display_image(form) {
 myWindow = window.open("", "Preview",
➧"toolbar=0,location=0,directories=0,status=0,menubar=0,
scrollbars=0,resizable=0,copyhistory=0,width=200,
height=255");
```

3. The first statement in *display_image* creates a window by opening one (because windows are objects, naturally!). The *window.open* method accepts many attributes: the first attribute is the URL (which is left blank because an entirely new window will be created, and it doesn't need to load a file).

431

The window's name is the second attribute (Note: if this name is already the name of an existing frame, that frame will be affected, and a new window won't be created).

The third attribute is actually 10 attributes in one. In one fell swoop the toolbar, the location, the directories buttons (at the top of the window), the status bar (at the bottom of the window), the menubar (except on Macs), the scrollbars, the size box, and the history are all turned off! And if that weren't enough, the size of the new window is specified in pixels. The desired result is a bare window.

```
myWindow.document.open();
myWindow.document.write("<HTML><HEAD> ...</BODY></HTML>");
myWindow.document.close();
}
```

4. The next three statements go together. The *document.open* method on the new window (not to be confused with the *window.open* method!) readies the new window for HTML. The *write* method is used to dump all the desired HTML into the new window. Next, the *document.close* method must be called; otherwise, the HTML may not actually appear on-screen.

Notes

The *window.open* method has a bug in it in Netscape 2.0. The URLs do not always load into the new window. To avoid this problem, do not load a file into the new window.

In most cases, text written to a window with *document.write* will appear as soon as the *write* method is executed; therefore, it is possible to have a page that continues growing as you take action. You should call *document.close* when you are finished.

Related Techniques

Controlling Interaction Among Open Windows

Removing a Browser Window

Removing a Browser Window

Window Object (Close Method)

Type: JavaScript object

Used in: Browser windows

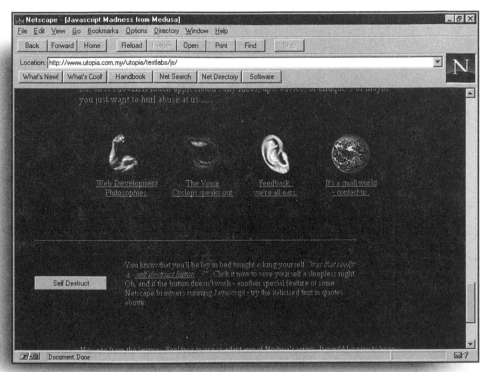

Cyclops

```
function bomb1() {
    alert('Initialising Core Dump.')
    alert('Installing Boot Sector Virus.')
    alert('Memory Dump Completed. CPU Digested.');
    alert('And Curiosity Kills Another Cat');
    window.close()
}
```

continues

```
<INPUT TYPE="button" Value="Self Destruct" onClick="bomb1()">
</TD>
<TD>
<FONT SIZE = "2">
You know that you'll be lay in bed tonight asking
yourself <EM>"was that really a <A HREF = "javascript:bomb1()">
self destruct button</A> ?"</EM>.
Click it now to save yourself a sleepless night.
Oh, and if the button doesn't work - another special feature of some
Netscape browsers running JavaScript - try the italicised text
in quotes above.
</FONT></TD>
```

Syntax Example

```
RemoteWin.close()
```

Comments

Sometimes when you click a link, you want the current page and the next page to both be available on-screen. This is when you use the window open method to create a new browser window. There is no theoretical limit to how many browser windows you can have open. However, with many windows open it may be confusing or annoying. Thus, use the window close method to close these extra windows (perhaps through *onClick* event handlers on buttons in the windows).

Online Example

"Javascript Madness from Medusa," by Cyclops, email: **cyclops@utopia.com.my**

URL: **http://www.utopia.com.my/utopia/testlabs/js/**

Description

This page jokingly uses a "self-destruct button" to close the current window. This really isn't a useful technique as it is used here. However if this section of JavaScript was present in a spawned window, it would be a useful way for you to close that window.

Step-by-Step

1. On this page is a button object labeled "Self Destruct." An *onClick* event handler within the button object executes the *bomb1()* function. There is also a link in the text that will execute the *bomb1()* function.

   This function uses several alert messages to fool the user into thinking something bad is going to happen.

2. The *window.close()* command is executed. This command closes the current window, and if that happens to be the default browser window, the browser closes as well.

Related Techniques

Creating a Remote in a Separate Window

Part III

VBScript
Techniques

Creating User-Defined Subs and Functions in VBScript

Using the *Sub() ... End Sub* and *Function() ... End Function* Statements

Type: VBScript procedure

Used in: Microsoft Internet Explorer 3.0 VBScript enhanced pages

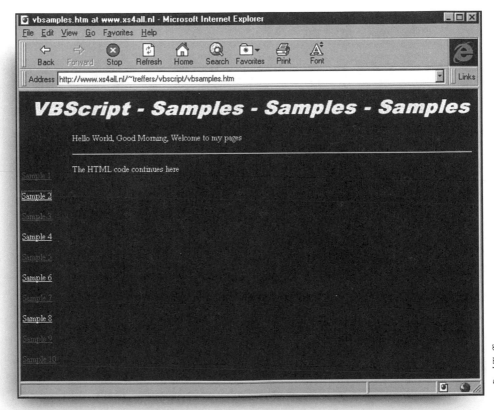

Paul Treffers

```
<HTML>
<HEAD>
<TITLE>Paul's VB Pages</TITLE>
</HEAD>
<SCRIPT LANGUAGE="VBScript">
```

continues

```
    Dim strTimeOfDay
    Dim strConstructed


    strTimeOfDay = RetrieveDay()
    strConstructed = ConstructWelcome(strTimeOfDay)
    Call WriteToHTML(strConstructed)


    Function RetrieveDay()
            'Function to Retrieve
            Dim strHours
            numHours = Hour(Now)
            If Hours < 12 then
                strReturnValue = "Good Morning"
            Else
                If Hours < 17 then
                    strReturnValue = "Good Afternoon"
                Else
                    strReturnValue = "Good Evening"
                End if
            End if
            RetrieveDay = strReturnValue
    End Function


    Function ConstructWelcome(strTimeDay)
            'Function to Construct
            Dim strLeftPart
            Dim strRightPart
            strLeftPart = "Hello World, "
            strRightPart = ", Welcome to my pages"
            ConstructWelcome = strLeftPart & strTimeDay & strRightPart
    End Function


    Sub WriteToHTML(strWriteString)
            'Sub to Display
            Document.Write StrWriteString
    End Sub


</SCRIPT>


<HR>
The HTML code continues here
</HTML>
```

Syntax Example

```
Sub Subname(Parm1,Parm2...) ... End Sub
```

Subname is the name of the subroutine. The *Parm1, Parm2...*parameters are optional. *End Sub* marks the end of the subroutine.

```
Function Functionname(Parm1,Parm2...) ... End Function
```

Subname is the name of the (user-defined) function. The *Parm1, Parm2...*parameters are optional. *End Function* marks the end of the function.

Comments

Subs and functions enable you to write user-defined subs and functions. Subs are also used to create event-handlers like the *OnClick* event-handler. Parameters are optional and usually passed by reference. There is a subtle difference between subs and functions in that functions are able to return a value, whereas subs are not. Use subs and functions in VBScript for repetitive tasks or complex pieces of VBScript code. Subs and functions can also easily be copied to other VBScripts to cut development time.

Online Example

"Paul Treffers VB Pages," by Paul Treffers, email: **treffers@xs4all.nl**

URL: **http://www.xs4all.nl/~treffers/vbscript/vbsamples.htm** (Sample2)

Description

This example is an optimized version of "*How to use VBScript to place text into a HTML document.*" This VBScript is broken into three elements: Retrieve, Construct, and Display. This approach makes the VBScript more readable and the source is easier to maintain.

Step-by-Step

1. To specify the type of script that is being executed, you must place the *<SCRIPT>* tag in the HTML source. The *<LANGUAGE>* keyword specifies the type of script. In this case it's VBScript:

```
<SCRIPT LANGUAGE="VBScript">
```

439

2. The variables *strTimeOfDay* and *StrConstructed* are declared here for further use.

```
Dim strTimeOfDay
Dim strConstructed
```

3. The user-defined function *RetrieveDay()* is called here. The return value of *RetrieveDay()* is stored in the variable *strTimeOfDay:*

```
strTimeOfDay = RetrieveDay()
```

4. The *ConstructWelcome* function is called here. The return value of *RetrieveDay()*, stored in *strTimeOfDay*, is passed as a parameter.

```
strConstructed = ConstructWelcome(strTimeOfDay)
```

5. This is the last call of the main routine. The subroutine *WriteToHTML* is called. The parameter *strConstructed* is the result of the *ConstructWelcome* function. The VBScript ends after the call is completed.

```
Call WriteToHTML(strConstructed)
```

6. The function *RetrieveDay* constructs a string depending on the outcome of the *Hour()* function call. The *RetrieveDay* function returns three kinds of strings: "*Good Morning,*" "*Good Afternoon,*" and "*Good Evening.*"

```
Function RetrieveDay()
        'Function to Retrieve
        Dim strHours
        numHours = Hour(Now)
        If Hours < 12 then
            strReturnValue = "Good Morning"
        Else
           If Hours < 17 then
             strReturnValue = "Good Afternoon"
           Else
             strReturnValue = "Good Evening"
           End if
        End if
```

7. The return value *strReturnValue* is placed in the reserved variable *RetrieveDay*. Each user-defined function has a reserved variable that carries the same name as the function. This variable holds the outcome of the function and is returned to the caller.

```
RetrieveDay = strReturnValue
```

8. The *End Function* statement marks the end of the function.

```
End Function
```

9. The *ConstructWelcome* function constructs the "Welcome" string. The parameter *strTimeDay* parameter is placed between "Hello World" and "Welcome to my pages" Note the *&* operator. It concatinates strings.

```
Function ConstructWelcome(strTimeDay)
        'Function to Construct
        Dim strLeftPart
        Dim strRightPart
        strLeftPart = "Hello World, "
        strRightPart = ", Welcome to my pages"
        ConstructWelcome = strLeftPart & strTimeDay & strRightPart
End Function
```

10. The *WriteToHTML* subroutine places the result of the previous function calls into the HTML document.

```
Sub WriteToHTML(strWriteString)
'Sub to Display
Document.Write StrWriteString
End Sub
```

11. The *</SCRIPT>* marks the end of the VBScript.

```
</SCRIPT>
```

Related Techniques

Creating Client-Side Imagemaps in VBScript

Using Microsoft Internet Explorer Object Model to Retrieve System Information

Using the Internet Explorer Object Model to Retrieve System Information

Using Internet Explorer's Object Model

Type: Internet Explorer objects

Used in: Microsoft Internet Explorer 3.0 VBScript enhanced pages

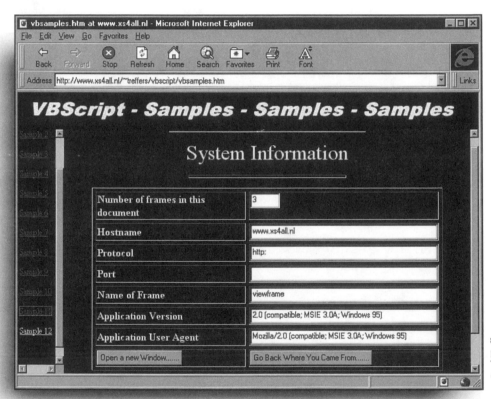

Paul Treffers

```
<SCRIPT LANGUAGE="VBScript">
Sub window_onLoad()
    Document.SYSINFO.Hostname.value = window.location.hostname
    Document.SYSINFO.ApplicationUserAgent.value = window.navigator.userAgent
    Document.SYSINFO.ApplicationVersion.value = window.navigator.appVersion
    Document.SYSINFO.Name.value = window.name
    Document.SYSINFO.Port.value = window.location.port
    Document.SYSINFO.Protocol.value = window.location.protocol
    Document.SYSINFO.WindowFramesCount.value = window.top.window.frames.Length
  end sub
```

```
  Sub GoBack_OnClick()
      Window.History.Back
  End Sub
  Sub OpenNew_OnClick()
        window.open "http://www.xs4all.nl/~treffers/vbscript/index.html",_
        "myWindow", "toolbar=no, location=no"
    End Sub
</SCRIPT>
<HTML>
<HEAD>
<TITLE>System Information</TITLE>
   <X-SAS-WINDOW TOP=28 BOTTOM=435 LEFT=8 RIGHT=700>
</HEAD>
<BODY TEXT="#FFFF00" BGCOLOR="#000080">
    <FORM ACTION="" METHOD="POST" NAME="SYSINFO">
<P ALIGN=CENTER><FONT SIZE=7><HR WIDTH="50%">System Information<HR
SIZE="5" WIDTH="40%"></FONT><TABLE BORDER=1 CELLSPACING=5
CELLPADDING=1 WIDTH="90%">
    <TR>
       <TD>
          <P><B><FONT SIZE=5>Number of frames in this
          document</FONT></B>
       </TD><TD>
          <P>
          <INPUT TYPE=text SIZE=5 NAME="WindowFramesCount">
</TD></TR>
    <TR>
       <TD>
          <P><B><FONT SIZE=5>Hostname </FONT></B>
       </TD><TD>
          <P>
          <INPUT TYPE=text SIZE=53 NAME="Hostname">
</TD></TR>
    <TR>
       <TD>
          <P><B><FONT SIZE=5>Protocol</FONT></B>
       </TD><TD>
          <P>
          <INPUT TYPE=text SIZE=53 NAME="Protocol">
</TD></TR>
    <TR>
       <TD>
          <P><B><FONT SIZE=5>Port</FONT></B>
       </TD><TD>
          <P>
          <INPUT TYPE=text SIZE=53 NAME="Port">
</TD></TR>
    <TR>
       <TD>
```

continues

443

Using the Internet Explorer Object Model to Retrieve System Information

```
            <P><B><FONT SIZE=5>Name of Frame</FONT></B>
        </TD><TD>
          <P>
          <INPUT TYPE=text SIZE=53 NAME="Name">
</TD></TR>
   <TR>
     <TD>
          <P><B><FONT SIZE=5>Application Version</FONT></B>
        </TD><TD>
          <P>
          <INPUT TYPE=text SIZE=53 NAME="ApplicationVersion">
</TD></TR>
   <TR>
     <TD>
          <P><B><FONT SIZE=5>Application User Agent</FONT></B>
        </TD><TD>
          <P>
          <INPUT TYPE=text SIZE=53 NAME="ApplicationUserAgent">
</TD></TR>
   <TR>
     <TD>
          <P>
          <INPUT TYPE=BUTTON
            VALUE="Open a new Window......." NAME="OpenNew"> 
</TD><TD>
          <P>
          <INPUT TYPE=BUTTON
            VALUE="Go Back Where You Came From......." NAME="GoBack">
</TD></TR>
</TABLE></P>

<P> </P>

<P> </P>
     </FORM>
</BODY>
</HTML>
```

Syntax Example

The property *HostName* of the *Location* object returns the *host* part of a URL:

```
Window.Location.Hostname
```

The property *UserAgent* of the *Navigator* object returns information about the WWW browser:

```
Window.Navigator.UserAgent
```

The property *App Version* of the *Navigator* object returns version information about the WWW browser:

```
Window.Navigator.AppVersion
```

The property *Name* of the *Window* object returns the name of the view window name in the WWW browser:

```
Window.Name
```

The property *Port* of the *Navigator* object returns information about the WWW browser:

```
Window.Location.Port
```

The property *Protocol* of the *Location* object returns information that is being used by the WWW browser:

```
Window.Location.Protocol
```

This property returns the number of frames in a WWW browser screen:

```
Window.Top.Window.Frames.Length
```

The *History* object enables you to browse through the history list of the WWW browser. You can specify the number of steps back or forward with the *n* parameter. The *g* parameter must be used to display a specific document in the history list:

```
Window.History.Back n
```

```
Window.History.Forward n
```

```
Window.History.Go g
```

The *Window.Open* methods opens a new WWW browser window. You must specify a URL as one of the arguments:

```
Window.Open "http://www.xs4all.nl/~treffers/vbscript/index.html"
    , "myWindow", "toolbar=no, location=no"
```

Comments

The *Object Model* of the *Microsoft Internet Explorer* is very important in VBScripting. All of the objects in this model can perform very useful methods and the properties let you retrieve or set all kinds of settings. A detailed overview of *Microsoft's Internet Explorer Object* model is available in the *ActiveX SDK* or at Microsoft's Internet site.

Online Example

"Paul Treffers VB Pages," by Paul Treffers, email: **treffers@xs4all.nl**

URL: **http://www.xs4all.nl/~treffers/vbscript/vbsamples.htm**

Description

This example is a mix of properties that retrieve system information, a method that opens a new Internet Explorer Window, and a method displays the previous HTML document in the history list of the *Internet Explorer*. The retrieved system information is displayed in HTML form. This form also contains two buttons, one for opening a new instance of the WWW browser and the other button retrieves the previous document from the WWW browsers' history list.

Step-by-Step

1. To specify the type of script that is being executed, you must place the *<SCRIPT>* tag in the HTML source. The *<LANGUAGE >* keyword specifies the type of script. In this case it's VBScript:

```
<SCRIPT LANGUAGE="VBScript">
```

2. The *Window Object OnLoad* event is used here to retrieve all the information that is needed to fill the form in the HTML document.

```
Sub window_onLoad()
```

3. The following code retrieves the information from the object model and places this information in the HTML form elements.

```
Document.SYSINFO.Hostname.value = window.location.hostname
Document.SYSINFO.ApplicationUserAgent.value =
window.navigator.userAgent
Document.SYSINFO.ApplicationVersion.value =
window.navigator.appVersion
```

446

```
Document.SYSINFO.Name.value = window.name
Document.SYSINFO.Port.value = window.location.port
Document.SYSINFO.Protocol.value = window.location.protocol
Document.SYSINFO.WindowFramesCount.value = _
        window.top.window.frames.Length
end sub
```

4. The last two subs in this VBScript handle the *OnClick* events that can be raised by the buttons in the HTML form. The *GoBack_OnClick* event handler instructs the WWW browser to retrieve the previous document in the history list. The second event handler, *OpenNew_Click()* opens a new WWW browser window to display a HTML document.

```
Sub GoBack_OnClick()
   Window.History.Back
End Sub
Sub OpenNew_OnClick()
        window.open "http://www.xs4all.nl/~treffers/vbscript/
index.html",_
        "myWindow", "toolbar=no, location=no"
End Sub
```

5. The *</SCRIPT>* tag marks the end of the VBScript in the HTML document:

```
</SCRIPT>
```

Notes

The *Window.Open* method is not fully inplemented within the beta version of the Microsoft Internet Explorer.

Related Techniques

Controlling Frames in VBScript

Creating Surprise Links Using a Randomizer

Using the VBScript's *RND()* Function

Type: Built-in functions

Used in: Microsoft Internet Explorer 3.0 enhanced pages

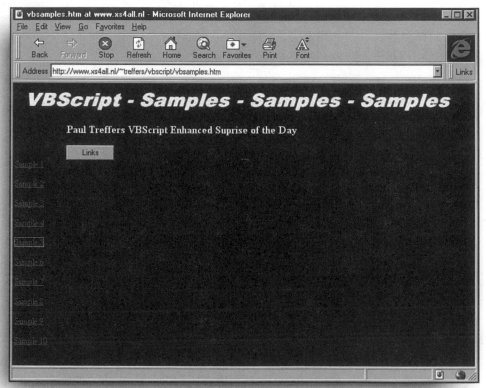

Paul Treffers

```
<HTML>

<HEAD>
<TITLE>Surprise Surprise !!!!!</TITLE>
<H2>Paul Treffers VBScript Enhanced Surprise of the Day</H2>
</HEAD>
```

```
<FORM NAME="SurpriseForm">
<INPUT NAME="Submit" TYPE="BUTTON" VALUE="Links">
</FORM>


<SCRIPT LANGUAGE="VBScript">
<!--
Dim
Dim intNrURL
'Define your url array size here
intNrURL = 6
Dim strURLArray(6)
       strURLArray(1)= "http://www.xs4all.nl/~treffers/"
       strURLArray(2)= "http://www.xs4all.nl/~treffers/as400.htm"
       strURLArray(3)= "http://www.dsl.nl/"
       strURLArray(4)= "http://www.xs4all.nl/~treffers/funny.htm"
       strURLArray(5)= "http://www.xs4all.nl/~treffers/vislog.htm"
       strURLArray(6)= "http://www.xs4all.nl/~treffers/log.htm"


Sub Submit_OnClick()
     intIndex = RollTheDice()
     Call ShowSurprise intIndex
End sub


Sub ShowSurprise(ByVal x)
     Parent.Navigate strURLArray(x)
End sub


Function RollTheDice()
     RollTheDice = Int((intNrURL * Rnd) + 1)
End Function


</SCRIPT>

</BODY>
</HTML>
```

Syntax Example

```
Dim strURLArray(10)
```

The *Dim* statement declares a variable or array. An array always needs to be declared before it's used. An array is a collection of variables in one structure. The number of elements in an array needs to be declared as well.

The *(10)* in the Syntax example defines an array with 11 elements (the index 0 points also to an element). The number of elements in an array is also called *the dimension*.

Each element in an array has a unique index number. This pointer (index) must be used to retrieve the contents of an element.

The *Rnd()* function returns a random number:

```
iValue = Rnd()
```

The *parent.navigate* method (which follows) instructs the Microsoft Internet Explorer to retrieve and display the HTML pages of a URL. (*strURL* is the string that contains the URL):

```
Parent.navigate strURL
```

Comments

This example is very simple but effective. It's possible to define a huge list of URLs. If you want to extend the example with more URLs, don't forget to adjust the dimension of the *strURLArray* array by changing the value of *intNrURL*.

Online Example

"Paul Treffers VBScript Pages," by Paul Treffers, email: **treffers@xs4all.nl**

URL: **http://www.xs4all.nl/~treffers/vbscript/vbsamples.html** (Sample 3)

Description

This VBScript has two important elements:

- An array that stores a list of URLs.

- A random number generator function called *RND()*. The *RND()* function returns an integer value that retrieves a string value from the *strURLArray* by index number. This example uses the integer variable *intNrURL* to store array's dimension (number of URLs).

Step-by-Step

1. This sample uses a form button to surprise the viewer. The form button calls the *SupriseMe_Click* event handler. The event handler calls the function to retrieve a random number and calls a subroutine to display the surprise link, as shown:

```
<HTML>


<HEAD>
<TITLE>Surprise Surprise !!!!!</TITLE>
<H2>Paul Treffers VBScript Enhanced Surprise of the Day</H2>
</HEAD>



<FORM NAME="SurpriseForm">
<INPUT NAME="SurpriseMe" TYPE="BUTTON" VALUE="Links">
</FORM>
```

2. To specify the type of script that is being executed, you must place the *<SCRIPT>* tag in the HTML source. The *<LANGUAGE>* keyword specifies the type of script. In this case it's VBScript:

```
<SCRIPT LANGUAGE="VBScript">
```

3. To be able to use an array, you must declare it.

```
Dim intNrURL
intNrURL = 6
Dim strURLArray(6)
```

4. The *strURLArray* array is filled with URLs here:

```
strURLArray(1)= "http://www.xs4all.nl/~treffers/"
strURLArray(2)= "http://www.xs4all.nl/~treffers/as400.htm"
strURLArray(3)= "http://www.dsl.nl/"
strURLArray(4)= "http://www.xs4all.nl/~treffers/funny.htm"
strURLArray(5)= "http://www.xs4all.nl/~treffers/vislog.htm"
strURLArray(6)= "http://www.xs4all.nl/~treffers/log.htm"
```

5. The form buttons need an event handler that is executed whenever the form button is clicked (a mouse click is an event and needs to be handled by VBScript code). This event handler calls the *RollTheDice()* function, which returns a random number that is passed as parameter to the *ShowSurprise* subroutine. This subroutine instructs the WWW browser to retrieve and display the WWW pages of the URL.

```
Sub Submit_OnClick()
   Dim intIndex
   intIndex = RollTheDice()
   Call ShowSurprise intIndex
End sub
```

6. The *ShowSurprise* subroutine passes one parameter. This parameter (called, mysteriously, *x*) holds the random number. This number is used to retrieve the correct URL from the *strURLArray* array. The *Parent.navigate* method instructs the Internet Explorer WWW browser to display the WWW page.

```
Sub ShowSurprise(ByVal x)
     Parent.navigate strURLArray(x)
End sub
```

7. The function *RollTheDice* is declared here. This function uses the *rnd()* function to retrieve a random number. This random number is between 1 and 6 (or *intNrURL*):

```
Function RollTheDice()
     RollTheDice = Int((intNrURL * Rnd) + 1)
End Function
```

8. The *</SCRIPT>* tag marks the end of the script.

```
</SCRIPT>
```

Related Techniques

Creating Popup Menus

Creating Interactive Form Button Event Clicks

Creating Client-Side Imagemaps in VBScript

Using the *MouseMove()* and *OnClick()* Events

Type: VBScript events

Used in: Microsoft Internet Explorer 3.0 VBScript enhanced pages

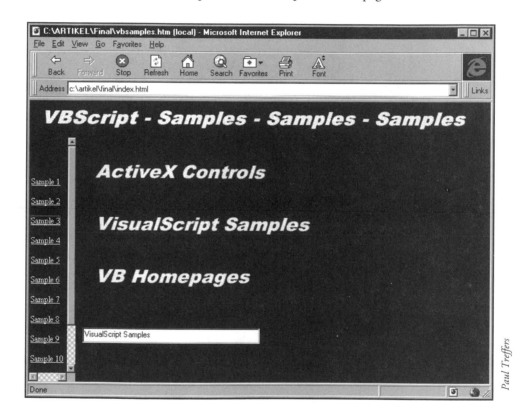

Paul Treffers

```
<HTML>
<HEAD>
<TITLE>VBScript sample:  Mouse tracking</TITLE>
</HEAD>
<BODY TEXT="#FFFF00" BGCOLOR="#000040" LINK="#FFFFFF"
VLINK="#FF0000">
<A id="Image" href=""> <IMG SRC="vbSCRIPT.jpg" ALT="Clickable Map Image"
```

continues

```
    BORDER=0></A>
<BR><BR>
<INPUT TYPE="text" NAME="MessageLink" SIZE=50>
</FONT>

<SCRIPT LANGUAGE="VBScript">
  Dim mX, mY
  Sub Image_MouseMove(s, b, x, y)
    mX = x
    mY = y
    If InPlace(x,y,18,15,357,75) Then
     Call LinkMessage("Active Controls")
    ElseIf InPlace(x,y,8,86,357,160) then
     Call LinkMessage("VisualScript Samples")
    ElseIf InPlace(x,y,8,171,357,240) then
     Call LinkMessage("VB Homepage")
    Else
      Call LinkMessage("VBScripting Pages")
    End If
  End Sub

  Sub Image_OnClick()
   If InPlace(mX,mY,18,15,357,75) Then
     location.href = "http://www.microsoft.com/activex/controls/"
   ElseIf InPlace(mX,mY,8,86,357,160) then
     location.href = "http://www.microsoft.com/vbscript/"
   ElseIf InPlace(mX,mY,8,171,357,240) then
     location.href = "http://www.xs4all.nl/index.html"
   End If
  End Sub

  Function InPlace(xpos, ypos, Rect_x1, Rect_y1, Rect_x2, Rect_y2)
   Inplace =  xpos > Rect_x1 And xpos < Rect_x2 And ypos >
      Rect_y1 And ypos < Rect_y2
  End Function

  Sub LinkMessage(Text)
   MessageLink.Value = Text
  End Sub
</SCRIPT>
</BODY>
</HTML>
```

Syntax Example

The following event is raised when a mouse click occurs:

```
Sub Link_OnClick()
```

This event is raised when a mouse is moved:

```
Sub Link_MouseMove(s, b, x, y)
```

The *Sub_Image_MouseMove* event has four values that you can use:

s   Shift State

b   Button Pressed

x   X Position

y   Y Position

Comments

The document contains an anchor named "Image", which raises the *MouseMove* and *OnClick* events as the mouse moves or a section is clicked. These events must be declared in your VBScript by declaring two subs: *Sub Image_MouseMove()* and *Sub Image_OnClick()*. The Image section in the *Sub* relates to the "Image" anchor in the HTML Document.

Online Example

"Paul Treffers VB Pages," by Paul Treffers, email: **treffers@xs4all.nl**

URL: **http://www.xs4all.nl/~treffers/vbscript/index.html**

Description

This VBScript replaces a server-side imagemap handler. The existing imagemap file was converted to VBScript to create a client-side imagemap handler. This "client-side imagemap" approach has several advantages over traditional imagemaps, including:

- Less band-width overhead

- Easier to test off-line because there is no call to a server-side imagemap handler

- More interactive

This script gives the users more information about the link they are about to click.

Step-by-Step

1. To specify the type of script that is being executed, you must place the *<SCRIPT>* tag in the HTML source. The *<LANGUAGE >*keyword specifies the type of script. In this case it's VBScript:

```
<SCRIPT LANGUAGE="VBScript">
```

2. The *mX* and *mY* variables are declared to store the current x,y mouse position. These variables are used in the *OnClick* event.

```
Dim mX, mY
```

3. The *Sub MouseMove* is declared here. Only the *x* and *y* parameters are used here. These parameters are stored in the variables *mX* and *mY* for later use.

```
Sub Image_MouseMove(s, b, x, y)
  mX = x
  mY = y
```

4. The *Inplace* function determines whether the mousepointer position *x* is between (*7* and *169*) and the *y* mousepointer position is between (*108* and *134*). If the *x,y* position is correct, the *Inplace* function returns a *True* and the subroutine *LinkMessage* is called. If the *x,y* position is not correct, the *Inplace* function returns *False* and nothing happens. The *LinkMessage* subroutine displays a link description in the *messagelink* label.

```
If InPlace(x,y,18,15,357,75) Then
   Call LinkMessage("Active Controls")
  ElseIf InPlace(x,y,8,86,357,160) then
   Call LinkMessage("VisualScript Samples")
  ElseIf InPlace(x,y,8,171,357,240) then
   Call LinkMessage("VB Homepage")
  Else
```

5. If the VBScript reaches this point, the mousepointer *x,y* is not in a region where a link description is to be displayed. But the *LinkMessage* subroutine is called to display a standard description.

```
   Call LinkMessage("VBScripting Pages")
  End If
End Sub
```

6. The *Sub Image_OnClick* is declared here. The x,y mousepointer position is retrieved from the *Mx* and *My* variables.

```
Sub Image_OnClick()
  If InPlace(Mx,My,7,108,169,134) Then
```

7. The *location.href = "link"* method instructs the browser to jump to the URL "*link*".

```
    location.href = "http://www.microsoft.com/activex/controls/"
  ElseIf InPlace(mX,mY,8,86,357,160) then
    location.href = "http://www.microsoft.com/vbscript/"
  ElseIf InPlace(mX,mY,8,171,357,240) then
    location.href = "http://www.xs4all.nl/index.html"
  End If
```

8. The *End Sub* statement marks the end of the subroutine *Sub Image_Onclick()*.

```
  End Sub
```

9. The *Inplace* function determines if the mousepointer position *xpos* is between (*Rect x1* and *Rect x2*) and the *ypos* mousepointer position is between (*Rect y1* and *Rect y2*). If the *xpos,ypos* position is correct, the *Inplace* function returns a *True*. If the *xpos,ypos* position is not correct, the *Inplace* function returns a *False*.

```
Function InPlace(xpos, ypos, Rect_x1, Rect_y1, Rect_x2, Rect_y2)
  Inplace =  xpos > Rect_x1 And xpos < Rect_x2 And ypos >__
        Rect_y1 And ypos < Rect_y2
  End Function
```

10. The *Sub LinkMessage* has one parameter: *Text*. This parameter places the link description in the label *Messagelink*.

```
    Sub LinkMessage(Text)
    MessageLink.Value = Text
    End Sub
```

11. The *</SCRIPT>* tag marks the end of the script.

```
</SCRIPT>
```

Related Techniques

Creating Client-Side Imagemaps in JavaScript

Creating Popup Menus

Using the Internet Explorer Menu ActiveX Control

Type: ActiveX control

Used in: Microsoft Internet Explorer 3.0 enhanced pages

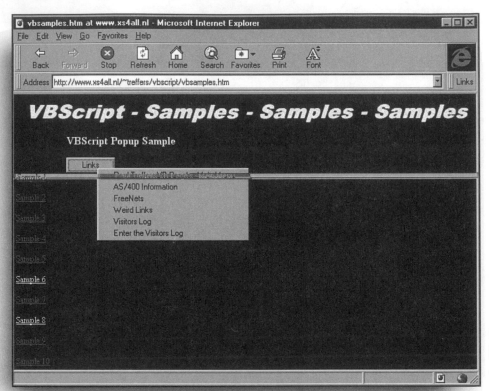

Paul Treffers

```
<HTML>

<HEAD>
<TITLE>New Page</TITLE>
<H2>Paul Treffers VB Script Enhanced Pages</H2>
</HEAD>
```

```
<FORM NAME="ValidForm">
<INPUT NAME="Submit" TYPE="BUTTON" VALUE="Links">
</FORM>


<OBJECT ID="Iepop1" WIDTH=1 HEIGHT=1
 CLASSID="CLSID:7823A620-9DD9-11CF-A662-00AA00C066D2"
 CODEBASE="http://www.microsoft.com/ie/download/activex/
                    iemenu.ocx#Version=4,70,0,1082">
    <PARAM NAME="enable" VALUE="1">
    <PARAM NAME="ScreenX" VALUE="400">
    <PARAM NAME="ScreenY" VALUE="400">
    <PARAM NAME="Menuitem[0]" VALUE="Paul Treffers VB Page's - Main Menu">
    <PARAM NAME="Menuitem[1]" VALUE="AS/400 Information">
    <PARAM NAME="Menuitem[2]" VALUE="FreeNets">
    <PARAM NAME="Menuitem[3]" VALUE="Weird Links">
    <PARAM NAME="Menuitem[4]" VALUE="Visitors Log">
    <PARAM NAME="Menuitem[5]" VALUE="Enter the Visitors Log">
</OBJECT>


<SCRIPT LANGUAGE="VBScript">
  Dim strURLArray(10)
      strURLArray(1)= "http://www.xs4all.nl/~treffers/"
      strURLArray(2)= "http://www.xs4all.nl/~treffers/as400.htm"
      strURLArray(3)= "http://www.dsl.nl/"
      strURLArray(4)= "http://www.xs4all.nl/~treffers/funny.htm"
      strURLArray(5)= "http://www.xs4all.nl/~treffers/vislog.htm"
      strURLArray(6)= "http://www.xs4all.nl/~treffers/log.htm"


Sub Iepop1_Click(ByVal x)
     Parent.navigate strURLArray(x)
End sub


Sub SubMit_OnClick
    call Iepop1.PopUp()
End Sub

</SCRIPT>

</BODY>
</HTML>
```

Syntax Example

What follows is the declaration of the *Internet Explorer Popup menu ActiveX* control:

```
<OBJECT ID="Iepop1" WIDTH=1 HEIGHT=1
CLASSID="CLSID:7823A620-9DD9-11CF-A662-00AA00C066D2"
CODEBASE="http://www.microsoft.com/ie/download/activex/iemenu.ocx#
Version= 4,70,0,1082">
    <PARAM NAME="enable" VALUE="1">
    <PARAM NAME="ScreenX" VALUE="400">
    <PARAM NAME="ScreenY" VALUE="400">
    <PARAM NAME="Menuitem[0]" VALUE="Paul Treffers VB Page's ">
    <PARAM NAME="Menuitem[1]" VALUE="AS/400 Information">
    <PARAM NAME="Menuitem[2]" VALUE="FreeNets">
    <PARAM NAME="Menuitem[3]" VALUE="Weird Links">
    <PARAM NAME="Menuitem[4]" VALUE="Visitors Log">
    <PARAM NAME="Menuitem[5]" VALUE="Enter the Visitors Log">
</OBJECT>
```

The following event is raised when a popup menu item is clicked:

```
Sub Iepop1_Click(ByVal x)
    .....
End sub
```

Comments

This technical sample uses the *iemenu.ocx* control. This control is automatically downloaded when needed.

Online Example

"Paul Treffers VBScript Pages," by Paul Treffers, email: **treffers@xs4all.nl**

URL: **http://www.xs4all.nl/~treffers/vbscript/vbsamples.htm**

Description

This VBScript uses an *ActiveX* control to display a popup menu. This popup menu is raised by a form button that instructs the *ActiveX* control to display the popup menu. The popup menu structure consists of two properties: the *caption* of the menu item and the *index* of the menu item. This *index* value is very important. It is passed to the *Click* event and starts at 0 (the first menu item).

When a menu item is clicked, the *ActiveX* control raises an event called *Sub Iepop1_Click(ByVal x)*. The popup menu *Index* is used to display the correct WWW page. All of the URLs of the WWW pages are stored in an array called *strURLArray*. This array's base is 0 (first menu) item. The *x* parameter is used to retrieve the corresponding URL from the *strURLArray*.

The pages are retrieved by using the *Parent.navigate* method. This code is very easy to maintain and the popup menu is very easy to extend with other menu items.

Last but not least, the popup menu is raised by the following statement:

```
call Iepop1.PopUp()
```

Step-by-Step

1. This sample uses a form button to raise the popup menu. The form button calls a subroutine that contains a method that raises the popup menu:

```
<HTML>


<HEAD>
<TITLE>New Page</TITLE>
<H2>Paul Treffers VB Script Enhanced Pages</H2>
</HEAD>


<FORM NAME="ValidForm">
<INPUT NAME="Submit" TYPE="BUTTON" VALUE="Links">
</FORM>
```

2. To specify the type of ActiveX control that is being executed, you must place the control declaration in the HTML source by using the *<OBJECT>* tag. The declaration consists of two sections. The OLE registration:

```
<OBJECT ID="Iepop1" WIDTH=1 HEIGHT=1
CLASSID="CLSID:7823A620-9DD9-11CF-A662-00AA00C066D2"
CODEBASE="http://www.microsoft.com/ie/download/activex/iemenu.ocx#
Version= 4,70,0,1082">
```

And the property settings of the *ActiveX* control:

```
    <PARAM NAME="enable" VALUE="1">
    <PARAM NAME="ScreenX" VALUE="400">
    <PARAM NAME="ScreenY" VALUE="400">
    <PARAM NAME="Menuitem[0]" VALUE="Paul Treffers VB Page's ">
    <PARAM NAME="Menuitem[1]" VALUE="AS/400 Information">
    <PARAM NAME="Menuitem[2]" VALUE="FreeNets">
    <PARAM NAME="Menuitem[3]" VALUE="Weird Links">
    <PARAM NAME="Menuitem[4]" VALUE="Visitors Log">
    <PARAM NAME="Menuitem[5]" VALUE="Enter the Visitors Log">
</OBJECT>
```

The *PARAM NAME="menuitem[0]" Value="...."* statement defines a menu item. This sample has six menu items. The *menuitem[..]* defines the menu item index.

3. To specify the type of script that is being executed, you must place the *<SCRIPT>* tag in the HTML source. The *<LANGUAGE>* keyword specifies the type of script. In this case it's VBScript:

```
<SCRIPT LANGUAGE="VBScript">
```

4. To be able to use an array you must declare it:

```
Dim strURLArray(10)
```

5. The *strURLArray* array is filled here:

```
 strURLArray(1)= "http://www.xs4all.nl/~treffers/"
strURLArray(2)= "http://www.xs4all.nl/~treffers/as400.htm"
strURLArray(3)= "http://www.dsl.nl/"
strURLArray(4)= "http://www.xs4all.nl/~treffers/funny.htm"
strURLArray(5)= "http://www.xs4all.nl/~treffers/vislog.htm"
strURLArray(6)= "http://www.xs4all.nl/~treffers/log.htm"
```

6. The *iemenu.ocx ActiveX* control raises a *Click* event. This event needs to be declared in VBScript:

```
Sub Iepop1_Click(ByVal x)
```

7. The *Iepop1_Click event* passes one parameter. This parameter (called mysteriously *x*) holds the menu index that is clicked by the user. The menu item index is used to retrieve the correct URL from the *strURLArray* array. The

Parent.navigate method instructs the Internet Explorer WWW browser to display the WWW page.

```
 Parent.navigate strURLArray(x)
End sub
```

8. The Sub *Submit_OnClick* is declared here. This subroutine is called by the form button *Submit* and raises the popup menu (see Step 1).

```
Sub SubMit_OnClick
    call Iepop1.PopUp()
End Sub
```

9. The *</SCRIPT>* tag marks the end of the script.

```
</SCRIPT>
```

Notes

The declaration of the *ActiveX* control is quite complex. I strongly recommend Microsoft ActiveX Control Pad to get acquainted with ActiveX controls. This very useful program assists you with defining and configuring ActiveX controls. You can download the Microsoft ActiveX Control Pad at **http://www.microsoft.com/workshop/author/cpad/**

Related Techniques

Creating Client-Side Imagemaps in VBScript

Creating a Tab Strip

Using the Internet Explorer Tab ActiveX Control

Type: ActiveX control

Used in: Microsoft Internet Explorer 3.0 enhanced pages

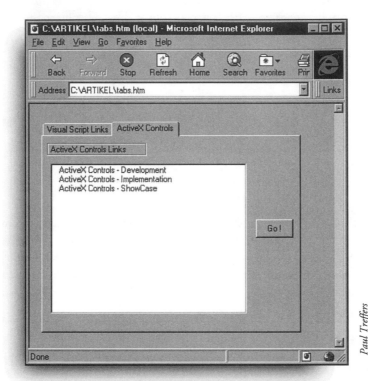

Paul Treffers

```
<HTML>

<TITLE>New Page</TITLE>
<H2>Paul Treffers VB Script Enhanced Pages</H2>
</HEAD>

<OBJECT CLASSID="CLSID:812AE312-8B8E-11CF-93C8-00AA00C08FDF"
ID="Layout3_alx" STYLE="LEFT:0;TOP:0">
<PARAM NAME="ALXPATH" REF VALUE="Layout3.alx">
 </OBJECT>
</HTML>
```

```
<SCRIPT LANGUAGE="VBScript">
<!--
Sub Layout3_OnLoad()
call FillVBScript()
End Sub


Sub FillVBScript()
  MessageText.Caption = " VBScript Controls Links"
  ListBox1.Clear
  ListBox1.Additem "VBScript - Development"
  ListBox1.Additem "VBScript - Implementation"
  ListBox1.Additem "VBScript - ShowCase"
End Sub


Sub FillActiveXControls()
  MessageText.Caption = " ActiveX Controls Links"
  ListBox1.Clear
  ListBox1.Additem "ActiveX Controls - Development"
  ListBox1.Additem "ActiveX Controls - Implementation"
  ListBox1.Additem "ActiveX Controls - ShowCase"
End Sub


Sub TabStrip1_Click(Index)
   Select Case TabStrip1.Value
     Case 0
        Call FillVBScript
     Case 1
        Call FillActiveXControls
   End Select
End sub


Sub CommandButton1_Click()
     Alert "About to go to: " & ListBox1.List(ListBox1.ListIndex)
End Sub


</SCRIPT>


<DIV ID="Layout3" STYLE="LAYOUT:FIXED;WIDTH:311pt;HEIGHT:233pt;">
    <OBJECT ID="TabStrip1"
     CLASSID="CLSID:EAE50EB0-4A62-11CE-BED6-00AA00611080"
STYLE="TOP:7pt;LEFT:5pt;WIDTH:274pt;HEIGHT:223pt;TABINDEX:0;ZINDEX:0;">
```

continues

```
        <PARAM NAME="ListIndex" VALUE="0">
        <PARAM NAME="Size" VALUE="9666;7867">
        <PARAM NAME="Items" VALUE="Visual Script Links;ActiveX Controls;">
        <PARAM NAME="TipStrings" VALUE="VBScript Links
                                   to ActiveX Controls;">
        <PARAM NAME="Names" VALUE="Tab1;Tab2;">
        <PARAM NAME="NewVersion" VALUE="-1">
        <PARAM NAME="TabsAllocated" VALUE="2">
        <PARAM NAME="Tags" VALUE=";;">
        <PARAM NAME="TabData" VALUE="2">
        <PARAM NAME="Accelerator" VALUE=";;">
        <PARAM NAME="FontCharSet" VALUE="0">
        <PARAM NAME="FontPitchAndFamily" VALUE="2">
        <PARAM NAME="FontWeight" VALUE="0">
        <PARAM NAME="TabState" VALUE="3;3">
    </OBJECT>
    <OBJECT ID="MessageText"
     CLASSID="CLSID:978C9E23-D4B0-11CE-BF2D-00AA003F40D0"
STYLE="TOP:29pt;LEFT:11pt;WIDTH:106pt;HEIGHT:14pt;ZINDEX:1;">
        <PARAM NAME="Caption" VALUE=" Visual Script Links">
        <PARAM NAME="Size" VALUE="3739;494">
        <PARAM NAME="SpecialEffect" VALUE="3">
        <PARAM NAME="FontCharSet" VALUE="0">
        <PARAM NAME="FontPitchAndFamily" VALUE="2">
        <PARAM NAME="FontWeight" VALUE="0">
    </OBJECT>
    <OBJECT ID="CommandButton1"
     CLASSID="CLSID:D7053240-CE69-11CD-A777-00DD01143C57"
STYLE="TOP:110pt;LEFT:231pt;WIDTH:40pt;HEIGHT:20pt;TABINDEX:3;ZINDEX:2;">
        <PARAM NAME="Caption" VALUE="Go !">
        <PARAM NAME="Size" VALUE="1411;706">
        <PARAM NAME="FontCharSet" VALUE="0">
        <PARAM NAME="FontPitchAndFamily" VALUE="2">
        <PARAM NAME="ParagraphAlign" VALUE="3">
        <PARAM NAME="FontWeight" VALUE="0">
    </OBJECT>
    <OBJECT ID="ListBox1"
     CLASSID="CLSID:8BD21D20-EC42-11CE-9E0D-00AA006002F3"
STYLE="TOP:51pt;LEFT:15pt;WIDTH:206pt;HEIGHT:165pt;TABINDEX:1;ZINDEX:3;">
        <PARAM NAME="ScrollBars" VALUE="3">
        <PARAM NAME="DisplayStyle" VALUE="2">
        <PARAM NAME="Size" VALUE="7267;5821">
        <PARAM NAME="MatchEntry" VALUE="0">
        <PARAM NAME="FontCharSet" VALUE="0">
        <PARAM NAME="FontPitchAndFamily" VALUE="2">
        <PARAM NAME="FontWeight" VALUE="0">
    </OBJECT>
</DIV>
```

Syntax Example

This is the declaration of the *HTML Layout* control:

```
<OBJECT CLASSID="CLSID:812AE312-8B8E-11CF-93C8-00AA00C08FDF"
ID="Layout3_alx" STYLE="LEFT:0;TOP:0">
<PARAM NAME="ALXPATH" REF VALUE="Layout3.alx">
 </OBJECT>
```

The *alert* statement shows a *Msgbox* with *strMessage* as the message (the *strMessage* is a string value):

```
Alert strMessage
```

Comments

This technical sample uses the *HTML Layout* control. This control uses an *.ALX* file that contains the complete *VBScript/ActiveX* controls definition and event-handler source code. The *.ALX* file is generated by using Microsoft's Control Pad.

Online Example

"Paul Treffers VBScript Pages," by Paul Treffers, email: **treffers@xs4all.nl**

URL: **http://www.xs4all.nl/~treffers/vbscript/popupsample.index.html**

Description

This example uses an *HTML Layout* file to display and control a tab interface. This approach has many advantages. The most important advantage is to create a file with the *Control Pad.* This *Control Pad* enables you to design a form collection of controls (standard *Windows 95* controls like Tab controls, push buttons, and labels). You can also attach event handlers to those controls.

The *Control Pad* generates an *.ALX* file that you can insert into your HTML document. The source file of the *.ALX* file looks very similar to a normal *VBScript/ActiveX Control* source, but the Web browsers handle this *HTML Control* file as one separate object.

The Tab control contains two Tab pages: *Visual Script Links* and *ActiveX Controls*. Each tab in a tab strip has its own unique *Index* value. The *Index* value starts at 0 for the first tab from the left. This tab strip has two tabs, therefore the *Index* values are 0 and 1.

The *Tab Strip* sample shows a tab interface with one listbox and one push button. The listbox is filled with links to *ActiveX-* and *VBScript*-related WWW pages. There is one major event handler called *Sub TabStrip1_Click(Index)*. This *TabStrip_Click* event is raised whenever a tab of the tab strip is clicked, and passes one parameter called *Index*. The parameters contain the value of the current active tab.

Step-by-Step

1. This sample uses an HTML Control file (.ALX) to display the tab strip. The declaration looks a lot like the declaration of an ActiveX control because *ActiveX* controls and *HTML Control* files are OLE based.

```
<HTML>


<TITLE>New Page</TITLE>
<H2>Paul Treffers VB Script Enhanced Pages</H2>
</HEAD>


<OBJECT CLASSID="CLSID:812AE312-8B8E-11CF-93C8-00AA00C08FDF"
ID="Layout3_alx" STYLE="LEFT:0;TOP:0">
<PARAM NAME="ALXPATH" REF VALUE="Layout3.alx">
 </OBJECT>
</HTML>
```

2. The *.ALX* source file is explained here. Remember: This is a generated file with the *Microsoft Control Pad*. You don't need to insert this code into an HTML document. All of the declarations and code are present in the *Layout3.alx* file. The HTML Layout file does contain some source code that you must program yourself. Every VBScript needs to be declared by using the *<SCRIPT>* tag:

```
<SCRIPT LANGUAGE="VBScript">
<!--
```

3. The *HTML Control Layout* has two events that you can use. The *Onload* and *Unload* event. *OnLoad* event calls a subroutine that fills the listbox with links. This subroutine is called *FillVBScript*.

```
Sub Layout3_OnLoad()
   call FillVBScript()
End Sub
```

4. The *HTML Control Layout* consists of four controls: a *Tab Strip*, a *Label*, a *Listbox*, and a *Push Button*. The *Label* and *Listbox* controls are dynamic because they are being changed by *VBScript* source. The *Tab Strip* and *Push Button* are static, but the static controls are able to perform an action. The Sub *FillVBScript* changes the caption of the Label control called *MessageText*.

It also clears the Listbox *Listbox1* and fills the Listbox with three new links about VBScript programming. The *FillActiveXControls* sub is very similar. Only the *MessageText* caption and Listbox entries are different.

```
Sub FillVBScript()
  MessageText.Caption = " VBScript Links"
  ListBox1.Clear
  ListBox1.Additem "VBScript - Development"
  ListBox1.Additem "VBScript - Implementation"
  ListBox1.Additem "VBScript - ShowCase"
End Sub


Sub FillActiveXControls()
  MessageText.Caption = " ActiveX Controls Links"
  ListBox1.Clear
  ListBox1.Additem "ActiveX Controls - Development"
  ListBox1.Additem "ActiveX Controls - Implementation"
  ListBox1.Additem "ActiveX Controls - ShowCase"
End Sub
```

5. The Subroutine *TabStrip1_Click* is an event handler. This event is raised when a Tab in a Tab Strip is being clicked. This event handler passes one parameter called *Index*. This parameter contains the Index value of the current active Tab in the Tab Strip. The *Select Case...Case...End Case* structure determines which subroutine needs to be called to fill the Listbox and Label controls.

```
Sub TabStrip1_Click(Index)
   Select Case TabStrip1.Value
   Case 0
     Call FillVBScript
   Case 1
      Call FillActiveXControls
   End Select
End sub
```

6. The Subroutine *CommandButton1_Click* is the event handler for the *Push Button*. This example shows only the link selection of the Listbox in a message box:

```
Sub CommandButton1_Click()
   Alert "About to go to: " & ListBox1.List(ListBox1.ListIndex)
End Sub


</SCRIPT>
```

7. The following section is the declaration of the *HTML Layout Control* elements
(tab strip, label, listbox, and push button controls). The .ALX control file is
declared here:

```
<DIV ID="Layout3" STYLE="LAYOUT:FIXED;WIDTH:311pt;HEIGHT:233pt;">
```

8. The following section is the declaration of the Tab Strip control. It starts with the
OLE registration and some dimension information:

```
<OBJECT ID="TabStrip1"
     CLASSID="CLSID:EAE50EB0-4A62-11CE-BED6-00AA00611080"
STYLE="TOP:7pt;LEFT:5pt;WIDTH:274pt;HEIGHT:223pt;TABINDEX:0;ZINDEX:0;">
```

9. The properties of the control are defined here:

```
<PARAM NAME="ListIndex" VALUE="0">
     <PARAM NAME="Size" VALUE="9666;7867">
     <PARAM NAME="Items" VALUE="Visual Script Links;ActiveX Controls;">
     <PARAM NAME="TipStrings" VALUE="VBScript Links;Links
                                 to ActiveX Controls;">
     <PARAM NAME="Names" VALUE="Tab1;Tab2;">
     <PARAM NAME="NewVersion" VALUE="-1">
     <PARAM NAME="TabsAllocated" VALUE="2">
     <PARAM NAME="Tags" VALUE=";;">
     <PARAM NAME="TabData" VALUE="2">
     <PARAM NAME="Accelerator" VALUE=";;">
     <PARAM NAME="FontCharSet" VALUE="0">
     <PARAM NAME="FontPitchAndFamily" VALUE="2">
     <PARAM NAME="FontWeight" VALUE="0">
     <PARAM NAME="TabState" VALUE="3;3">
```

10. The declaration of the control ends with the *</OBJECT>* tag.

```
</OBJECT>
```

11. The following section is the declaration of the Label control:

```
<OBJECT ID="MessageText"
   CLASSID="CLSID:978C9E23-D4B0-11CE-BF2D-00AA003F40D0"
STYLE="TOP:29pt;LEFT:11pt;WIDTH:106pt;HEIGHT:14pt;ZINDEX:1;">
     <PARAM NAME="Caption" VALUE=" Visual Script Links">
```

```
        <PARAM NAME="Size" VALUE="3739;494">
        <PARAM NAME="SpecialEffect" VALUE="3">
        <PARAM NAME="FontCharSet" VALUE="0">
        <PARAM NAME="FontPitchAndFamily" VALUE="2">
        <PARAM NAME="FontWeight" VALUE="0">
    </OBJECT>
```

12. The following section is the declaration of the Push Button control:

```
<OBJECT ID="CommandButton1"
  CLASSID="CLSID:D7053240-CE69-11CD-A777-00DD01143C57"
STYLE="TOP:110pt;LEFT:231pt;WIDTH:40pt;HEIGHT:20pt;TABINDEX:3;ZINDEX:2;">
        <PARAM NAME="Caption" VALUE="Go !">
        <PARAM NAME="Size" VALUE="1411;706">
        <PARAM NAME="FontCharSet" VALUE="0">
        <PARAM NAME="FontPitchAndFamily" VALUE="2">
        <PARAM NAME="ParagraphAlign" VALUE="3">
        <PARAM NAME="FontWeight" VALUE="0">
    </OBJECT>
```

13. The following section is the declaration of the Listbox control:

```
<OBJECT ID="ListBox1"
  CLASSID="CLSID:8BD21D20-EC42-11CE-9E0D-00AA006002F3"
STYLE="TOP:51pt;LEFT:15pt;WIDTH:206pt;HEIGHT:165pt;TABINDEX:1;ZINDEX:3;">
        <PARAM NAME="ScrollBars" VALUE="3">
        <PARAM NAME="DisplayStyle" VALUE="2">
        <PARAM NAME="Size" VALUE="7267;5821">
        <PARAM NAME="MatchEntry" VALUE="0">
        <PARAM NAME="FontCharSet" VALUE="0">
        <PARAM NAME="FontPitchAndFamily" VALUE="2">
        <PARAM NAME="FontWeight" VALUE="0">
    </OBJECT>
</DIV>
```

Notes

The declarations of *HTML Layout Control* elements are quite complex. They contain information about the OLE registration, the look and feel of the controls, and the property settings of these controls. The *Control Pad* does all of the source code generating for you. You can download the *Control Pad* at this URL: **http://www.microsoft.com/workshop/author/cpad/**

Related Techniques

Creating Interfaces with the ActiveX Layout Control

Performing Downloads

Using the PreLoader Control

Type: ActiveX control

Used in: Microsoft Internet Explorer 3.0 VBScript enhanced pages

Paul Treffers

```
<OBJECT ID="PreLoader" WIDTH=1 HEIGHT=1 TYPE="application/x-oleobject"
 CLASSID="CLSID:16E349E0-702C-11CF-A3A9-00A0C9034920"
 CODEBASE="/workshop/activex/gallery/ms/preload/other/
        iepreld.ocx#Version=4,70,0,1115">
   <PARAM NAME="URL" VALUE="welcome.htm">
   <PARAM NAME="Enable" VALUE="0">
</OBJECT>
```

```
<OBJECT ID="timer" TYPE="application/x-oleobject"
       ALIGN=middle
 CLASSID="CLSID:59CCB4A0-727D-11CF-AC36-00AA00A47DD2"
 CODEBASE="/workshop/activex/gallery/ms/timer/other/
                  ietimer.ocx#version=4,70,0,1115">
    <PARAM NAME="Interval" VALUE="100">
    <PARAM NAME="Enabled" VALUE="True">
</OBJECT>


<SCRIPT LANGUAGE="VBScript">

Sub Timer_Timer()
    If IsObject(PreLoader) Then
            Timer.Enabled=0
            PreLoader.Enable=1
    End If
End Sub



Sub PreLoader_Complete
    Window.Location.href = PreLoader.CacheFile
End Sub



Sub PreLoader_Error
    alert "Error"
End Sub


</SCRIPT>

<HTML>
<HEAD>
<TITLE>Downloading with the Preload Control</TITLE>
 </HEAD>
<BODY BGCOLOR="#008080">
<P ALIGN=CENTER><IMG SRC="download.gif" WIDTH=455 HEIGHT=1
   ALIGN=bottom></P>
</BODY>
</HTML>
```

Syntax Example

The *PreLoader. URL* property setting is used to specify the location of the file. The *strArgument* is a string that contains the URL of the file:

```
PreLoader.URL = strDocument
```

The *PreLoader.Enable=1* method instructs the preloader control to retrieve the file:

```
PreLoader.Enable=1
```

The *PreLoader.CacheFile* property returns a string variable where the preloaded file is located in the cache of the WWW browser:

```
PreLoader.CacheFile
```

This event is raised after the preload of the file is completed:

```
Sub PreLoader_Complete
```

This event is raised when the preload of the file has failed:

```
Sub PreLoader_Error
```

Comments

The *PreLoader* control is ideal for filling the WWW browser's cache with files. This speeds up WWW site viewing because there is no need for the WWW browser to retrieve the files from the Internet.

Online Example

"Paul Treffers VB Pages," by Paul Treffers, email: **treffers@xs4all.nl**

URL: **http://www.xs4all.nl/~treffers/vbscript/vbsamples.htm**

Description

This example uses the *PreLoader* control to download a document from the WWW server. This control places the file in the cache. The *PreLoad.CacheFile* property is used to provide the *Window.Location.href* method with an HTML document. A timer control is used to start the preload of the file and raises an event called *Timer_Timer*.

In this event, the property setting *PreLoad.Enable* is set to 1 to preload the file.

Step-by-Step

1. The *PreLoader* and *Timer* control objects are declared here. The preload control is already configured with the *Preload.URL* property setting:

    ```
    <OBJECT ID="PreLoader" WIDTH=1 HEIGHT=1 TYPE="application/x-oleobject"
     CLASSID="CLSID:16E349E0-702C-11CF-A3A9-00A0C9034920"
     CODEBASE="/workshop/activex/gallery/ms/preload/other/iepreld.ocx
            #Version=4,70,0,1115">
        <PARAM NAME="URL" VALUE="welcome.htm">
        <PARAM NAME="Enable" VALUE="0">
    </OBJECT>


    <OBJECT ID="timer" TYPE="application/x-oleobject"
      ALIGN=middle
     CLASSID="CLSID:59CCB4A0-727D-11CF-AC36-00AA00A47DD2"
     CODEBASE="/workshop/activex/gallery/ms/timer/other/ietimer.ocx
            #version=4,70,0,1115">
        <PARAM NAME="Interval" VALUE="100">
        <PARAM NAME="Enabled" VALUE="True">
    </OBJECT>
    ```

2. To specify the type of script that is being executed, you must place the *<SCRIPT>* tag in the HTML source. The *<LANGUAGE>* keyword specifies the type of script. In this case it's VBScript:

    ```
    <SCRIPT LANGUAGE="VBScript">
    ```

3. The Timer event checks if the preloader control is present in the HTML document. If this condition is *True*, all of the Timer events are stopped with the *Timer.Enabled = 0* property setting. But before that, the preloader is instructed to start the preload by setting the *PreLoader.Enable* property to *1*.

```
Sub Timer_Timer()
   If IsObject(PreLoader) Then
           Timer.Enabled=0
           PreLoader.Enable=1
   End If
End Sub
```

4. The *PreLoader_Complete* event is raised when a preloaded file is placed in the cache. This sample immediately displays the preloaded file by using the *Window.Location.href* method with the *PreLoader.CacheFile* (read-only property setting is the argument of this method). The *PreLoader.CacheFile* holds the location of the filename in the cache.

```
Sub PreLoader_Complete
    Window.Location.href = PreLoader.CacheFile
End Sub


Sub PreLoader_Error
   alert "Error"
End Sub
```

5. The *</SCRIPT>* tag marks the end of the VBScript in the HTML document:

```
</SCRIPT>
```

Related Techniques

Creating Surprise Links via Popup Menus

How to Use VBScript to Place Text Into an HTML Document

Using the document.write Method

Type: VBScript method

Used in: Microsoft Internet Explorer 3.0 VBScript enhanced pages

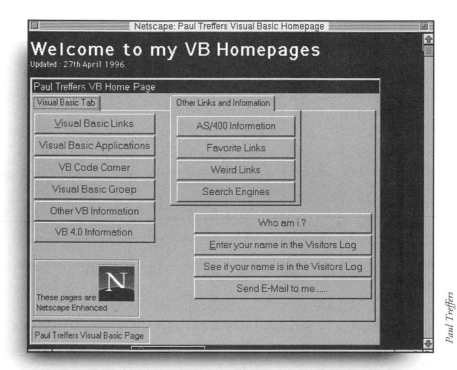

Paul Treffers

```
<HTML>
<HEAD>
<TITLE>Paul's VB Pages</TITLE>
</HEAD>
<SCRIPT LANGUAGE="VBScript">
     Dim Hours
     Hours = Hour(Now)
     If Hours < 12 then
             strTimeOfDay = "Good Morning,"
```

continues

```
        Else
                If Hours < 17 then
                        strTimeOfDay = "Good Afternoon,"
                Else
                        strTimeOfDay = "Good Evening,"
                End if
        End if
        document.write "Hello World, " &strTimeOfDay & " Welcome to my VB Pages"
</SCRIPT>
<HR>
The HTML code continues here...
</HTML>
```

Syntax Example

```
document.write strString
```

strString is the string of text you want to insert. For example:

```
document.write "Hello World"
```

```
document.write "<B>Hello World</H>"
```

Comments

The *document.write* method is a very useful feature of VBScript to write lines of static text (or even HTML tags) on an HTML page. It is best used for writing dynamic texts (such as Good Morning or Good Evening) into a page.

Online Example

"Paul Treffers VB Pages," by Paul Treffers, email: **treffers@xs4all.nl**

URL: **http://www.xs4all.nl/~treffers/vbscript/index.html** (Sample 1)

Description

I've created a "pre-loader" to welcome the visitor. I determined the actual hour by using the *hour(now)* function and used the return value of the *hour(now)* call to store a string value in a variable. This string variable is written into the HTML page to welcome the visitor.

The document.write method can also be used to place HTML tags in a document while the document is being loaded into the WWW browser.

Step-by-Step

1. To specify the type of script that is being executed, you must place the *<SCRIPT>* tag in the HTML source. The *<LANGUAGE>* keyword specifies the type of script. In this case it's VBScript:

```
<SCRIPT LANGUAGE="VBScript">
```

2. The *hour()* function returns the hour portion of a date/time internal variable. *Now* is a VBScript keyword that returns the date and time in a special format. The *Hours* and *strString* are declared by using the Dim statement. It is recommended (not required though) to declare every variable that is used in a VBScript. It makes the source more readable and is good programming style.

3. The *If...Then...Else* statement is used to evaluate whether a condition is True or False and then to store the "Good..." text into a string variable. This *If...Then...Else* statement is nested to wish the visitor a Good Morning, Afternoon, or Evening:

```
Dim Hours
Dim strString
Dim strStringAdd
Hours = Hour(Now)

If Hours < 12 then
        strTimeOfDay = "Good Morning,"
Else
        If Hours < 17 then
                strTimeOfDay = "Good Afternoon,"
        Else
                strTimeOfDay = "Good Evening,"
        End if
End if
```

479

4. To actually welcome the visitor (and give a personal touch to the HTML page), a composed string is written into the HTML page by using the *document.write* method. You can use the *&* to concatinate strings:

```
strStringAdd = " Welcome to my VB Pages"
document.write "Hello World, " & strTimeOfDay & strStringAdd
```

5. The *</SCRIPT>* tag marks the end of the VBScript in an HTML document:

```
</SCRIPT>
```

Notes

The *Document.writeLn* method is the same as the *document.write* method with the addition of a newline character at the end. Note that a newline is ignored by HTML unless it is bracketed by <PRE> tags, so in many cases *document.write* and *document.writeLn* behave exactly the same.

Related Techniques

Creating User-Defined Subs and Functions

Creating a Date/Time Triggered Marquee

Using the *Document.Write* and *Marquee* HTML Tags

Type: VBScript procedure

Used in: Microsoft Internet Explorer 3.0 VBScript enhanced pages

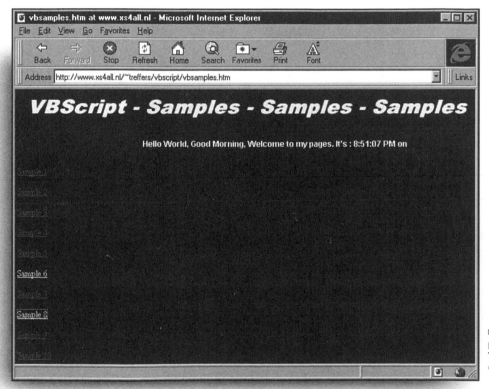

Paul Treffers

```
<HTML>

<HEAD>
<TITLE>New Page</TITLE>
</HEAD>
    <SCRIPT LANGUAGE="VBScript">
```

continues

```
<!--
 Dim strTimeOfDay
 Dim strConstructed
 strTimeOfDay = RetrieveDay()
 strConstructed = ConstructWelcome(strTimeOfDay)

 Document.Write "<FONT FACE = ARIAL SIZE = 3> "
 Document.Write "<CENTER>"
 Document.Write "<B>"
 Document.Write "<MARQUEE "
 Document.Write "ALIGN=MIDDLE "
 Document.Write "BEHAVIOR=SCROLL "
 Document.Write "DIRECTION=LEFT "
 Document.Write "SCROLLAMOUNT=10 "
 Document.Write "SCROLLDELAY=100 "
 Document.Write "WIDTH=70% "
 Document.Write ">"
 Document.Write strConstructed & ". It's : " & Time
 Document.Write " on " & Date
 Document.Write "</MARQUEE>"
 Document.Write "</B>"
 Document.Write "</CENTER>"

 Function RetrieveDay()
 'Function to Retrieve
  Dim strHours
  numHours = Hour(Now)
  If Hours < 12 then
     strReturnValue = "Good Morning"
   Else
      If Hours < 17 then
         strReturnValue = "Good Afternoon"
      Else
         strReturnValue = "Good Evening"
      End if
     End if
     RetrieveDay = strReturnValue
 End Function

 Function ConstructWelcome(strTimeDay)
      'Function to Construct
      Dim strLeftPart
      Dim strRightPart
      strLeftPart = "Hello World, "
      strRightPart = ", Welcome to my pages"
      ConstructWelcome = strLeftPart & strTimeDay & strRightPart
 End Function

</SCRIPT>
<BODY>
</BODY>
</HTML>
```

Syntax Example

```
document.write strString
```

strString is the string of text you want to insert. For example:

```
document.write "Hello World"
document.write "<B>Hello World</H>"
<MARQUEE ALIGN=MIDDLE BEHAVIOR=SCROLL DIRECTION=LEFT SCROLLAMOUNT=10
 SCROLLDELAY=100 WIDTH=70%>Marquee Message</MARQUEE>
```

This sample uses the HTML *<MARQUEE>* tag to display the Marquee message.

Comments

The *document.write* method is very flexible. You can display normal text in an HTML document window as well as construct complex HTML tags such as the *<MARQUEE>* or *<TABLE>* tags.

Online Example

"Paul Treffers VB Pages," by Paul Treffers, email: **treffers@xs4all.nl**

URL: **http://www.xs4all.nl/~treffers/vbscript/index.html**

Description

This example is an enhancement of the sample you find in the chapter. *"Subs : Not The Yellow Or Pink kind of Subs. VBScript Subroutines !".* It is enhanced with a *<MARQUEE>* tag.

Step-by-Step

1. To specify the type of script that is being executed, you must place the *<SCRIPT>* tag in the HTML source. The *<LANGUAGE>* keyword specifies the type of script. In this case it's VBScript:

```
<SCRIPT LANGUAGE="VBScript">
```

2. The variables *strTimeOfDay* and *StrConstructed* are declared here for further use:

```
<SCRIPT LANGUAGE="VBScript">
  Dim strTimeOfDay
  Dim strConstructed
```

3. The user-defined function *RetrieveDay()* is called here. The return value of *RetrieveDay()* is stored in the variable *strTimeOfDay:*

```
strTimeOfDay = RetrieveDay()
```

4. The *ConstructWelcome* function is called here. The return value of *RetrieveDay()*, stored in *strTimeOfDay*, is passed as parameter:

```
strConstructed = ConstructWelcome(strTimeOfDay)
```

5. The *document.Write* is being used to define the font size and the *<MARQUEE>* tag settings:

```
Document.Write "<FONT FACE = ARIAL SIZE = 3> "
Document.Write "<CENTER>"
Document.Write "<B>"
Document.Write "<MARQUEE "
Document.Write "ALIGN=MIDDLE "
Document.Write "BEHAVIOR=SCROLL "
Document.Write "DIRECTION=LEFT "
Document.Write "SCROLLAMOUNT=10 "
Document.Write "SCROLLDELAY=100 "
Document.Write "WIDTH=70% "
Document.Write ">"
```

6. The following statements place the variable *strConstructed* (filled earlier with the *ConstructWelcome* function call), the current time and the current date in the *<MARQUEE>* tag:

```
Document.Write strConstructed & ". It's : " & Time
Document.Write " on " & Date
```

7. The following *Document.write* statements place *"end of marquee-"*, *"end of bold-"* and *"end of center tags"*.

```
Document.Write "</MARQUEE>"
Document.Write "</B>"
Document.Write "</CENTER>"
```

8. The function *RetrieveDay* constructs a string depending on the outcome of the *Hour*() function call. The *RetrieveDay* function returns three kinds of strings: "Good Morning," "Good Afternoon," and "Good Evening"

```
Function RetrieveDay()
        'Function to Retrieve
        Dim strHours
        numHours = Hour(Now)
        If Hours < 12 then
           strReturnValue = "Good Morning"
        Else
           If Hours < 17 then
             strReturnValue = "Good Afternoon"
           Else
             strReturnValue = "Good Evening"
           End if
        End if
```

9. The return value *strReturnValue* is placed in the reserved variable *RetrieveDay*. Each user-defined function has a reserved variable that carries the same name as the function. This variable holds the outcome of the function and is returned to the caller:

```
RetrieveDay = strReturnValue
```

10. The *End Function* statement marks the end of the function:

```
End Function
```

11. The *ConstructWelcome* function constructs the "Welcome" string. The parameter *strTimeDay* parameter is placed between "Hello World" and "Welcome to my pages" Note the *&* operator. It concatinates strings:

```
Function ConstructWelcome(strTimeDay)
        'Function to Construct
        Dim strLeftPart
        Dim strRightPart
        strLeftPart = "Hello World, "
        strRightPart = ", Welcome to my pages"
        ConstructWelcome = strLeftPart & strTimeDay & strRightPart
End Function
```

12. The *</SCRIPT>* marks the end of the VBScript:

```
</SCRIPT>
```

Notes

There is also *an ActiveX Marquee Control* available. This control is a replacement for the *<MARQUEE>* tag.

Related Techniques

Creating User-Defined Subs and Functions in VBScript

Controlling Frames in VBScript

Using the Parent.Frames(x).Location.hRef Method

Type: VBScript method

Used in: Microsoft Internet Explorer 3.0 enhanced page

Paul Treffers

```
<HTML>
<HEAD>
</HEAD>
<FRAMESET FRAMEBORDER="0" FRAMESPACING="0" rows="20%,1*">
   <FRAME MARGINWIDTH="0" MARGINHEIGHT="0" src="frame1.htm"
          NAME="TOP" NORESIZE scrolling="no">
   <FRAMESET cols="30%,1*">
      <FRAME FRAME MARGINWIDTH="2" MARGINHEIGHT="0" src="FRAME2.HTM"
             NAME="HOTSPOT" NORESIZE scrolling="no">
```

continues

```
        <FRAME FRAME MARGINWIDTH="10" MARGINHEIGHT="5" src="FRAME3.HTM"
                NAME="VIEWFRAME" NORESIZE scrolling="no">
    </FRAMESET>
</FRAMESET>
</HTML>


<HTML>
<HEAD>
<TITLE>VB Subjects</TITLE>
</HEAD>
<BODY>
<OBJECT CLASSID="CLSID:812AE312-8B8E-11CF-93C8-00AA00C08FDF"
ID="FRAME2_alx" STYLE="LEFT:0;TOP:0">
<PARAM NAME="ALXPATH" REF VALUE="FRAME2.ALX">
 </OBJECT>
</BODY>
</HTML>


<SCRIPT LANGUAGE="VBScript">
<!--
'From the ActiveX HTML Layout file FRAME2.ALX
Sub HotSpot2_Click()
     Parent.frames(2).Location.Href="frame3.htm"
End Sub

Sub HotSpot5_Click()
     Parent.frames(2).Location.Href="funny.htm"
End Sub
-->
</SCRIPT>
```

Syntax Example

```
Parent.frames(2).Location.Href="frame3.htm"
```

This is a constructed property that uses several objects. The *Parent.Frames* object call identifies the frame. The *Location.Href* property defines the URL that is to be displaced in the frame. The parameter after the "=" operator is the URL that is to displayed in the frame.

Comments

The VBScript code is retrieved from the *FRAME2.ALX* file. This *HTML Control Layout* file displays an image and it uses *Hotspot* subroutines to make areas of the image clickable. This VBScript code is not included in the HTML document itself. It does, however, contain some calls that enable you to handle frames in a document.

Online Example

"Paul Treffers VBScript Pages," by Paul Treffers, email: **treffers@xs4all.nl**

URL: **http://www.xs4all.nl/~treffers/**

Description

The Frame Object is a member of the ActiveX Object Model. This object lets you control frames in VBScript. With the frame object you can control the contents by using the *Location.hRef* method.

This sample explains the techniques used to create the ActiveX enhanced home page shown in the figure. This home page consists of three frames. The upper frame contains an image with the home page header. The left frame contains an *HTML Layout Control* with a clickable imagemap, and the right frame shows other sections of the home page.

Step-by-Step

1. The main HTML document defines the dimensions of the frames that are used on this home page. This HTML code creates three frames. The top frame is called *TOP*. The frame that contains the *HTML Control Layout* is called *HOTSPOT* and the display area frame is called *VIEWFRAME*.

```
<HTML>
<HEAD>
</HEAD>
<FRAMESET FRAMEBORDER="0" FRAMESPACING="0" rows="20%,1*">
   <FRAME MARGINWIDTH="0" MARGINHEIGHT="0" src="FRAME1.HTM"
          NAME="TOP" NORESIZE scrolling="no">
   <FRAMESET cols="30%,1*">
      <FRAME FRAME MARGINWIDTH="2" MARGINHEIGHT="0" src="FRAME2.HTM"
          NAME="HOTSPOT" NORESIZE scrolling="no">
      <FRAME FRAME MARGINWIDTH="10" MARGINHEIGHT="5" src="FRAME3.HTM"
          NAME="VIEWFRAME" NORESIZE scrolling="no">
   </FRAMESET>
</FRAMESET>
</HTML>
```

2. This HTML document (*FRAME2*.HTM) occupies the HOTSPOT frame. *FRAME2.HTM* contains a *HTML Layout Control* declararation (*FRAME2.ALX*):

```
<HTML>
<HEAD>
<TITLE>VB Subjects</TITLE>
</HEAD>
<BODY>
<OBJECT CLASSID="CLSID:812AE312-8B8E-11CF-93C8-00AA00C08FDF"
ID="FRAME2.ALX" STYLE="LEFT:0;TOP:0">
<PARAM NAME="ALXPATH" REF VALUE="FRAME2.ALX">
 </OBJECT>
</BODY>
</HTML>
```

3. The *HTML Layout Control* file contains an image and eight hotspots. The *ALX* file format is readable.

You can easily read and steal VBScript code from this file. I've done this also to clarify frame handling with VBScript. Each hotspot has its own event handler. This VBScript shows two of the eight hotspots. The *Parent Object* (or the FRAME.HTM document) has its own collection of frame objects (in this case three). Each frame object has a unique index number that starts with 0 for the first frame. In this setup, my *VIEWFRAME* frame is referenced with frame index number 2. If a hotspot is clicked, the *HotSpot_Click()* event is raised.

To instruct the WWW browser to display an HTML document in a frame, you must place the *Parent.Frames(2).Location.href = "url"* statement in the event handler code.

```
<SCRIPT LANGUAGE="VBScript">
<!--
'From the ActiveX HTML Layout file FRAME2.ALX
Sub HotSpot2_Click()
      Parent.frames(2).Location.Href="frame3.htm"
End Sub


Sub HotSpot5_Click()
   Parent.frames(2).Location.Href="funny.htm"
End Sub
-->
</SCRIPT>
```

Related Techniques

Creating Client-Side Imagemaps in VBScript

Creating Interactive Form Button Event Clicks

Using the *OnClick* Event Handlers

Type: VBScript event handler

Used in: Microsoft Internet Explorer 3.0 enhanced pages

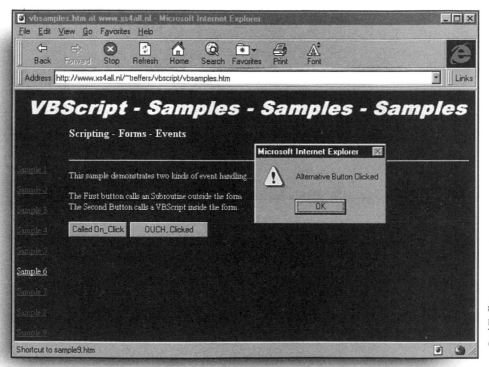

Paul Treffers

```
<HTML>
<HEAD>
<TITLE>New Page</TITLE>

<SCRIPT LANGUAGE="VBScript">
  Sub Button0_OnClick()
   Alert "Alternative Button Clicked"
  end sub
```

continues

```
</SCRIPT>

</HEAD>

<BODY>
<H2>Scripting - Forms - Events</H2>
<HR>
This sample demonstrates two kinds of event handling...<br>
<br>
The First button calls an Subroutine outside the form<br>
The Second Button calls a VBScript inside the form<br>
<FORM NAME="Form1">
   <input type="button" name="Button0" value="Called On_Click">
   <input type="button" name="Button1" value=".........InLine Script
             .......">
   <SCRIPT for="Button1" EVENT="onClick" LANGUAGE="VBScript">
      alert "I've been pressed"
      document.Form1.Button1.value="OUCH, Clicked"
         </SCRIPT>
</FORM>
</BODY>
</HTML>
</HEAD>
```

Syntax Example

This is a standard approach to handle the *OnClick* event:

```
<SCRIPT LANGUAGE="VBScript">
  Sub Button0_OnClick()
   Alert "Alternative Button Clicked"
  end sub
</SCRIPT>
<input type="button" name="Button0" value="Called On_Click">
```

This is the alternative form to handle *OnClick* events in forms:

```
<SCRIPT for="FormElement" EVENT="OnClick" LANGUAGE="VBScript">
   'Script comes here
</SCRIPT>
```

The VBScript code is included in the form itself. The *Form Element* is a form element like a push button, checkbox or radio button. The *EVENT* tag defines the event that needs to be handled. In this case it's *OnClick*.

Comments

The *OnClick* events are used often in forms. They execute a validation routine in order to submit the values in a form. The *<SCRIPT for...>* can also create event handlers for forms elements. In some cases, it can make your HTML easier to read and to maintain. By using the *<SCRIPT for..>* you immediately see what happens when a button is clicked.

Online Example

"Paul Treffers VBScript Pages," by Paul Treffers, email: **treffers@xs4all.nl**

URL: **http://www.xs4all.nl/~treffers/vbscript/vbsamples.htm** (Sample 6)

Description

This example consists of two buttons and two VBScript routines in one HTML document. The first button shows a conventional approach to form element event handling. The second button uses an *in-form script* to handle the *OnClick* event in a form. In-form means that a VBScript is included in the HTML form declaration, not in the *<SCRIPT...>* section of the HTML document.

Step-by-Step

1. The HTML document starts here with the *<HTML>* and *<TITLE>* document:

```
<HTML>
<HEAD>
<TITLE>New Page</TITLE>
```

2. This VBScript routine contains the event-handler for the first form:

```
<SCRIPT LANGUAGE="VBScript">
  Sub Button0_OnClick()
   Alert "Alternative Button Clicked"
  end sub
</SCRIPT>

</HEAD>

<BODY>
<H2>Scripting - Forms - Events</H2>
<HR>
```

```
This sample demonstrates two kinds of event handling...<br>
<br>
The First button calls an Subroutine outside the form<br>
The Second Button calls a VBScript inside the form<br>
```

3. The HTML is declared here. This form contains two buttons called *Button0* and *Button1*. The form is called *Form1*:

```
<FORM NAME="Form1">
    <input type="button" name="Button0" value="Called On_Click">
    <input type="button" name="Button1" value=".........InLine
➥Script....">
```

4. The alternative event handler for a form object is declared here. The *for* statement points to the form element *Button1*. The event type is *OnClick* and the language type is *VBScript*.

```
<SCRIPT for="Button1" EVENT="onClick" LANGUAGE="VBScript">
```

5. The following VBScript code shows a message box and it changes the button caption on the fly:

```
alert "I've been pressed"
    document.Form1.Button1.value="OUCH, Clicked"
```

6. The *</SCRIPT>* marks the end of the *in-form* script:

```
    </SCRIPT>
```

```
</FORM>
</BODY>
</HTML>
</HEAD>
```

Related Techniques

Creating Surprise Links Using a Randomizer

Index

I

J-K-L

M